Galloping Guns

Galloping Guns
The Experiences of an Officer
of the Bengal Horse Artillery
During the Second Maratha War
1804-1805

James Young

Galloping Guns: the Experiences of an Officer of the Bengal Horse Artillery During the Second Maratha War 1804-1805
by James Young

Published by Leonaur Ltd

Text in this form and material original to this edition
copyright © 2008 Leonaur Ltd

ISBN: 978-1-84677-462-1 (hardcover)
ISBN: 978-1-84677-461-4 (softcover)

http://www.leonaur.com

Publisher's Notes

The opinions expressed in this book are those of the author and are not necessarily those of the publisher.

Contents

The Second Maratha War	7
August 1804	15
September 1804	17
October 1804	50
November 1804	78
December 1804	107
January 1805	136
February 1805	176
March 1805	206
April 1805	236
May 1805	252
June 1805	258

INTRODUCTION
The Second Maratha War

The overthrow of the power of Mysore in 1800 left the East India Company, supreme in the south and east of the Peninsula, face to face with the extensive domain of the Mahratta Confederacy, extending over the whole of Central and Northern India, from the Himalayas south and beyond the Kistna, and from Cuttack on the shores of the Bay of Bengal westwards to Gujerat. A fierce and war-like people, whose roving horsemen had spread the terror of their name far beyond their own boundaries, they bade fair to be worthy foemen even for the victors of Buxar and Porto Novo, while their possession of Delhi and its impotent puppet ruler, who still personified for the mass of the Indian people the legendary empire of the Moguls, seemed to give them a prescriptive legal right to inherit the power which they in fact exercised in his name.

Fortunately for the British, neither to Shah Alam nor to any supreme chief even of their own race did the Mahrattas owe any but nominal allegiance; they were in fact no more than a loose confederacy of independent chieftains, incapable of long pursuing any coherent policy, divided by mutual jealousies and inherited rivalries, formidable when united in arms, but seldom so united for long. Blind to their own true interests, they had, as we have already seen, neglected to take advantage of England's difficulties and perils during her long struggle with Mysore, and so lost their best chance of crushing at birth the growing power of the intruders; and when they were themselves in turn assailed by the conquerors of Hyder and Tippoo, they refused to sink their mutual, differences even before the prime necessity of opposing a united front to the common enemy.

In fact, while Lord Wellesley and his Generals were methodically completing the overthrow of Tippoo, the Mahrattas were wasting their energies in a fierce internecine strife. The death in 1793 of Mahadaji Sindia removed from the scene the one statesman who had fully realised the extent of the British menace, and consistently striven to unite the whole confederacy to meet it; his successor, the incapable Daulat Rao, fell out with two of his brother chieftains, Baji Rao, the Peshwa who aimed at the recovery of the supremacy which had always been exercised by his house, in theory at least, over all the Mahratta dominions, and Jeswant Rao Holkar, who played now and throughout his life simply for his own hand.

Fighting broke out and continued with many vicissitudes of fortune until in 1802 fortune turned decisively against the Peshwa, who in desperation sought refuge in Bombay territory and implored British aid in the recovery of his dominions. This he obtained, and was triumphantly escorted back to his capital of Poona, under the terms of the Treaty of Bassein—a signal diplomatic triumph for the British, who by it accentuated the split in the Mahratta camp, and secured without fighting, not only an entry into the Peshwa's territory, but a right to interfere in the internal affairs of the confederacy. Now, at length, the warring chiefs realised to the full the danger which so nearly menaced them.

Daulat Rao Sindia, the ruler of the whole vast belt of land from the northern frontier of Hyderabad on the Godavery northward to Delhi and the Himalayan foothills, began to make ready his army for war against the British, and summoned to his aid Ragoji Bhonsla of Berar, whose territories extended from Nagpore on the west to Cuttack on the Bay of Bengal. The forces which those two chiefs could put into the field amounted in all to close on 100,000 men, among whom, in addition to the famous cavalry, there were a number of battalions and batteries armed and trained on European lines and led by French soldiers of fortune. Jeswant Rao Holkar, however, in an evil hour for his race and himself, resolved to pursue his traditional policy of selfish isolation and refused for the present to declare against the British.

During the period of long-drawn-out and insincere negotiations which extended from May to August 1803, the British armies were mustered for the war that the Governor-General saw to be inevitable. The plan of campaign consisted of a double attack on Sindia in the north and the south, combined with subsidiary operations against Bundelcund, Cuttack and Gujerat on the left flank of each of these main offensives. Of the northern operations, including those against Bundelcund and Cuttack, Lord Lake, the Commander-in-Chief, was in personal charge, with a force of 21,000 men, of whom 6000 were allotted to the former attack and 5000 to the latter theatre, leaving 10,000 for the main army. Arthur Wellesley, the Governor-General's brother, whose later career in Europe we have recently followed to its apotheosis at Waterloo, was in command in the south, having general control of the operations of his own army of 11,000 men, the Hyderabad contingent of 9000 under Stevenson, which was to co-operate with him in the main offensive, and Murray's 4000, whose mission it was to occupy Gujerat—and who, it may here be said, to save further reference to this force, succeeded in doing so with little difficulty.

In August 1803, Arthur Wellesley, realising that nothing was to be hoped for from further conversations with Sindia and the Bhonsla, exercised the discretionary power given him and moved forward from his area of concentration east of Poona against the strongly fortified little place of Ahmednagar, which he at once stormed out of hand and made his advanced base. Stevenson had meanwhile crossed the Hyderabad frontier, and the two armies effected their junction at Aurungabad. The enemy, who, to the strength of some 50,000 men, had been assembling north of the Ajunta hills, now in their turn took the offensive in the direction of Hyderabad territory, but being headed off by Wellesley, fell back slowly northwards, and were overtaken and brought to battle at Assaye. The British General, though his forces were so split up that he could only bring some 6000 men on to the field, boldly assailed the hostile left, and after fierce fighting drove them from their ground with heavy loss, practically all Sindia's infantry being destroyed; the remnant fled in disorder beyond the Tapti, followed by Stevenson, who had taken no part in the battle.

While the latter was besieging and taking the fortress of Asirgarh, Wellesley, who was refitting his army and collecting supplies at Aurungabad for a renewed offensive, was once more called on to deal with incursions by the Mahratta cavalry, who endeavoured to sweep round his left and rear to harry the country south of the Godavery. Before long, however, he was ready to resume his advance, which was directed against the Bhonsla's capital of Nagpore; Ragoji, attempting to oppose his progress, was swept aside at Argaum, and the capture by storm of the hill fortress of Gawilgarh left his territory at the mercy of the British. But before Wellesley could crown his brilliant campaign by the occupation of his opponent's capital, the latter, his spirit broken by the evil news from the north, sued humbly for terms.

Lake's campaign had been even more rapid and decisive than that of his famous lieutenant. Assembling his army of 10,000 men at Cawnpore, he set out up the Ganges and the Kali at the end of July, invested Aligarh, reputed to be one of the strongest fortresses in India, broke his way in through a series of strongly defended gates and practically annihilated the garrison. Thence he pursued his way towards Delhi, outside which city he came upon Sindia's main army, close on 20,000 men, entrenched for battle, whereas he himself had less than 5000 available. Drawing the enemy from their positions by a feigned retirement of his cavalry, he drove them from the-field by one deadly volley and a bayonet charge, and pushing on entered Shah Alam's capital city, to be hailed as a deliverer by the aged and blinded Emperor. Crossing to the west bank of the Jumna, he then marched south to Agra, where he came on part of the beaten Mahratta army standing to fight on the glacis of the place.

Having attacked and driven them off to the west, he delayed a few days to get possession of the fort, and then set off once more on the trail of his adversaries, who had now been reduced by losses and desertion to a residue of some 14,000 men only.

A march of portentous length and rapidity brought the British up with their foes at Laswari, and there was fought out on November 1 the most hotly contested and desperate battle hitherto recorded in the history of our army in India. For some time the fate of the day hung by a thread, but at length the Mahratta right was turned and broken, and their host completely destroyed or dispersed. It needed only the loss of Sindia's capital of Gwalior to complete the ruin of his fortunes, and he too was not slow to follow the example of his ally and sue for peace, which was concluded in December 1803. The British gains by the treaty were great and important, including as they did the territories of Bundelcund and Cuttack, which had fallen into their hands with little resistance soon after the outbreak of war, and all Sindia's and the Bhonsla's lands east of the Jumna and south of the Tapti.

But the task of the British, though well begun, was little more than half done as yet. Scarcely four months had passed before Jeswant Rao Holkar, resolved to try his fortune where his rivals had failed, threw down the gage in his turn, and in April 1804 Lake and his troops took the field once more against this new enemy. Holkar had learnt at least one lesson from the Mahratta defeats of the previous year, and resolved to rely for his own part no longer on artillery and infantry, who could too easily be brought to battle and beaten, but on the mobility of his masses of horsemen. Driven by Lake's advance from his first position near Jaipur, he withdrew southwards across the Chambal, leaving the fortified town of Rampura to be invested and taken by his enemies.

The hot weather being now well come, the British General deemed it impracticable to keep all his forces in the field and withdrew his main body to Agra, entrusting the observation and pursuit of Holkar to a force of 4000 men under Monson, with whom Murray from Gujerat in the south was to co-operate by an advance on Indore. The latter, however, whose military incapacity we have already learnt to know at Tarragona, failed to perform his part in the combined scheme, thus leaving all the Mahratta army free to deal with Monson, who was compelled by the pressure of immensely superior forces to a disastrous retreat of 250 miles over flooded rivers and swampy plains; all his guns and baggage had to be abandoned, and less than half his detachment eventually escaped to Agra in the last stages of exhaustion and demoralisation.

Holkar's triumph, though great and resounding, was short-lived; for the indefatigable Lake was at once at hand to restore the situation. While half the Mahratta army swung north to recover Delhi and the remainder menaced Agra to cover their movement, the British forces were being assembled for the counter-offensive at Muttra. As soon as Lake realised the situation, he pushed from his path the enemy detachment in his immediate front and hurried northward to Delhi. The garrison of that city, under the able direction of Ochterlony, though only 2500 strong, successfully held their tenfold superior assailants at bay until the sound of Lake's guns on his rear compelled Holkar hurriedly to raise the siege and flee up the west bank of the Jumna. The British Horse followed hard after him, having dropped their infantry under Fraser to deal with the Mahratta force which had remained before Agra. The Mahratta chief, turning sharp to east and south near Meerut, made his way at full speed down the Kali, reached the Ganges valley at Farrukabad and, knowing Lake to be well in rear, halted for a breathing space. But he had underestimated the energy and driving power of his pursuer; covering seventy miles in 24 hours, the British burst into his camp at dawn and scattered its occupants to the four winds. Holkar himself with a few followers alone escaped from the massacre.

Fraser's operations had been equally successful, and the enemy force in his front encountered in a strong position, backed on the fortress of Deig, had been driven to seek refuge within its walls. Lake, returning from his chase of Holkar, ordered the place to be invested and stormed, which was accordingly done; and the army, flushed with victory, proceeded to lay siege to the capital of the Jat Rajah of Bhurtpore, a former friend of the British, who had turned against them after Monson's disaster. Here, however, its victorious career received a decided setback. The fortress was large and immensely strong; Lake's artillery was hopelessly inadequate to deal with its defences; and Holkar, with the remnant of his rallied troops, was hovering in the vicinity to harry and distract the attention of the besiegers. No less than four large-scale assaults were delivered during the course of the siege, which lasted from January to April 1815, and were beaten off with severe loss, and at length Lake was compelled to draw off his baffled troops. The blow to British prestige was more important than the immediate results of the failure, for the Rajah at once made his peace with Lake and set the latter free once more to deal with Holkar. Part of the Mahratta Horse, detached to raid Lake's line of communications during the siege, had been driven eastward into Rohilcund and there defeated and dispersed, so that the residue amounted to barely 8000 men, and their leader's efforts to induce Sindia to unite with him for a final effort against the British failed before the menace of Lake's renewed advance. He therefore retreated to Ajmeer and thence northward to the Sutlej, hoping in vain to get help from the Sikhs. Lake followed him up and drove him to seek refuge in Punjab territory, where, in December 1805, the last shots of the war were fired.

Unhappily the fruits of this decisive shattering of the Mahratta power by the overthrow in succession of all their greatest chieftains were sacrificed at the conclusion of peace in January 1806. The Directors of the East India Company, alarmed at the peril and cost of Lord Wellesley's aggressive policy, had sent out Cornwallis to replace him; and on the latter's death after a few weeks in the country Barlow was appointed Governor-General with instructions to end the war at all costs and refrain from further acquisitions of territory. Accordingly Holkar found to his astonishment all his former possessions restored to him, and, what was worse, liberty to wreak his vengeance on many of his vassals who had adhered to the British cause during the war. The Mahratta power was thus scotched indeed, but not killed; for that another and even greater war was to be necessary.

None the less, the major part of the work had been accomplished by Arthur Wellesley and Lake. Of the former, whose character and career we have already discussed, it is enough to say here that he had shown himself as much a master of Eastern as later of Western warfare. His colleague and commander in these campaigns displayed qualities at least as pre-eminent-brilliant leadership in battle, tireless and all-conquering energy in advance and pursuit, an unsurpassed power of getting the best out of his officers and men, and a complete and chivalrous loyalty to inferiors and superiors alike. Of all the galaxy of great leaders who gained their fame on Indian fields, Lake's is one of the outstanding and most attractive figures.

(This introduction has been extracted by the Leonaur editors from A Short History of the British Army to 1914 by E. W. Sheppard.)

About the Author

James Young was born in Glasgow, Scotland in 1782 and was a young man in his early twenties at the time of the events related in the book you are now reading. He joined the military service of the East India Company in 1797 as a cadet in the Artillery. In 1798 he held the rank 'Fireworker' or 2nd Lieutenant.

He travelled to India in 1802, with the rank of Captain-Lieutenant—a senior among subaltern officers. There he joined the First Troop, Horse Artillery of the Bengal Army. His service during the Second Maratha War, principally against the chief—Jaswant Rao Holkar—was the subject of his journal on which this volume is based.

Following the war he transferred to the 3rd Horse Artillery as Adjutant becoming Agent for Gun Carriages—a post he held until 1817 when he was selected by the Goveror-General of India, Warren Hastings to be his Aide-de-Camp and military secretary with the rank of Lieutenant Colonel.

Young resigned from military life in 1818. He had a chequered career in civilian life in India and experienced mixed fortunes-particularly financially—but he was appointed Sheriff of Calcutta—an office he held twice—in 1838 and 1839. He left India for Europe in 1840 and died in France in 1848.

The Leonaur Editors

CHAPTER 1

August 1804

August 24th—This day in General Orders the following corps were ordered to hold themselves in readiness to take the field at the shortest notice, *viz*, the Cawnpore and Futtyghur Artillery (including the horse artillery), H.M. 8th, 27th and 29th Dragoons, the flank companies of H.M. 22nd Foot and 76th Foot and the Pioneer Corps from Cawnpore, the European Regiment from Allahabad, the 2nd Battalion 4th Regiment from Allyghur, the 1st Battalion, 21st Regiment from Agra, the 1st Regiment Cavalry and 1st and 2nd Battalion 15th Regiment from Muttra, the 4th Cavalry from Futtyghur, the 6th Cavalry from Chandoussy, the 2nd Cavalry from Khassgunge and the 3rd Cavalry from Burrelly. We expect to take the field early in September and are rather vexed at the necessity existing for our going out, before we have been well in cantonments, particularly on account of the great expense attendant on preparing anew for the field after every one supported the war at an end and all the field equipments that had survived the tear and wear of last campaign were got rid of.

August 24th to *27th*—Gave necessary orders to my servants. Repaired my tattered tent and set about making camel trunks. I bought an indifferent she camel for 125 rupees, prices of every sort doubled since the 24th. Got from G—., six dozen Madeira, to be repaid from mine now on it's way up from Calcutta, which with four dozen purchased from S—., after deducting what I owed will make my stock for the field, only seven or eight dozen.

August 30th—A detachment of 40 artillery men, under Captain Turton ordered to proceed with ordnance and store, to reinforce the Bundelkund army under Lieutenant Colonel Martindale.

The remaining part of the timely detachment of artillery, which came up from the presidency is to reinforce the artillery with the grand army. It amounts to about 80 men, with two Subalterns, Lieutenants Swiney and Gowing. All sorts of alarming rumours are around, Brigadier Monson is said to have retreated to Khoosalghur leaving Captain Hutchinson with 14 companies of sepoys and 50 day's provisions, in Rampoora.

31st—By General Orders of this evening, we are ordered to march on the morning of the second. No pay yet in orders, everyone in the greatest distress and nothing ready.

Chapter 2
September 1804

September 1st—This day to our great surprise and relief two months pay issued. Received mine and purchased a young camel and a battery tattoo, paid debts, in short got pretty comfortable and penniless and ready to start.

The reason for the precipitate orders to march on the 31st *ultimo* has now partly transpired. Holkar it is said overtook Monson in his retreats and engaged him. Whether regularly beaten or not, certain it is that the Brigadier has suffered prodigious loss, is himself with very many others, wounded. Monson, it is further said, had marched immediately after the action, still retreating towards Agra, and expecting momentarily, a renewal of the attack from Holkar. Very like the reality of a defeat all this whatever it may be called! Colonel Blair, Commandant of Agra is said to have most properly taken upon himself to order out Lieutenant Colonel Sachville Browne from Muttra, to march instantly to the relief of Monson.

Our marching, is put off to the morning of the 3rd inst. *Tant mieux*![1] say I, for we are in a sorry state of readiness, even now, to commence such marching as we shall probably undergo, to come up with Holkar.

September 3rd—Marched this morning to Kockadoo. My strongest camel with my wine and brandy (nine dozen) was left behind, either from the weakness of the camel, or too great heaviness of the trunks, perhaps both, so notwithstanding the

---
1. So much the better.

great expense I had been put to in making up these trunks I was forced to lay them aside and make up bags for my wine. A letter from Futtyghur confirms the report spread yesterday of Monson's arrival at Agra. The general court martial on Lieutenant Colonel Fawcett which assembled at Cawnpore is to follow the army and this day, it is in order to sit tomorrow. We hope it will be ready to try another commander. The grand delinquent. The conductor of a retreat so unlike that of the 10,000 or the French under Morean.

September 4th—We have this day learned more particulars of the unfortunate catastrophe of the Honourable Brigadier Monson's detachment. It was near Biana, where we lay so long last year (from December to February) that this happened, and not at Khoosalghur. Monson's camp lay on this side of a nullah and his picquets were pushed to a very great distance beyond it. The picquets were attacked and Major Sinclair with the 2nd Battalion 2nd Regiment was despatched to reinforce them. On his arrival at the place, he saw posted 600 or 800 yards in his front Holkar's whole Infantry and guns, who were collecting, and firing on him. The gallant major, with his own hand, seized the colours of the corps, and called to his men to follow him. They drove the enemy from their guns at the point of the bayonet and the major, planted his colours on one of the guns. The commander, on the other side of the nullah although he saw his best battalion engaged with ten times their number sent them unaccountably and scandalously no kind of assistance!

What is more horrible to say the detachment even retreated and left the unfortunate 2nd to their fate. Holkar, seeing them thus abandoned by their commander reiterates his attacks, and some say opened a second line of guns on them. The unfortunate Sinclair and every officer and man, were cut to pieces! Further particulars of the retreat are unknown, only that Holkar continued the pursuit as far as Futteh-poor-Sicri, within twenty-two miles of Agra, and that officers and men came singly and in a miserable plight to take shelter in Agra. Some of Colonel Monson's staff arrived two days before himself, and knew nothing of what has become of him or the detachment. This however *is* known that the two battalions of the 12th Regiment commanded by Major Radcliffe and Captain O'Donnel, when pursued, not only conducted their retreat with the greatest steadiness and regularity, but formed a line and showed front to the enemy with as much coolness and regularity as if they had been at a review. They stood repeated charges of the the enemy's cavalry with such inticipidity, they reserved their fire with such steadiness, that every charge left many of the enemy dead literally at their feet and this corps alone, it is said made good it's retreat regularly to Agra.

The 9th and 14th it is reported fled with precipitation two whole companies of the latter deserting with their arms to Holkar. A Havildar of the 9th fell out from the ranks, and summoned the men of the corps to join him and go off to the enemy when Lieutenant Lumsdaine, Adjutant of the battalion, rode out to the front and drawing a pistol shot him dead. A piece of spirited, well-timed severity, however disagreeable no doubt to Mr. Lumsdaine which deserves the highest praise, and probably was the means of preventing the whole from being annihilated. If, anything can at all soften our sorrow at so shameful and dreadful a disaster as this, it is that the rascals of Major Frith's Irregular Horse, who went off in a body to Holkar, have most of them met with their deserts in being killed by the 12th at the head of the enemy's cavalry when Holkar compelled them to fight, probably through distrust. It is the fate, the just fate, of the treacherous, to be always objects of suspicion! But their fate, may prevent future desertions from our army and thus be of eventual use to us.

September 5th—Holkar it is said has gone in person to Jyepoor, to compel the Rajah of that country to join him, no doubt, or at least to extort money from him. A considerable part of his army, is gone, they say to Muttra. Lieutenant Colonel Brown who marched from that place, to relieve Monson, was too late for that purpose and now has returned to overtake, if possible, Holkar's people at Muttra. Letters from Agra, mention a heavy cannonade having been heard in that quarter.

Some battalions of Bapoojee Sindhia's, strange to say, attacked two companies of the new Regiment, the 21st under Captain

Nicol, who were escorting treasure. These two companies threw themselves into a village, and most gallantly repulsed the enemy in several attacks, although the enemy brought guns against them and at last compelled them to take themselves off when the 21st pursued their route. Different reports are in circulation about the conduct of the Bhartpoor Rajah, another of our lately acquired allies. By one account, his troops joined Holkar and fought against Monson, by another he took a large convoy of our camels passing Wear-Fort. within the walls, fearing they would be taken by Holkar's horse, then in full possession of the whole country, unloaded and deposited the baggage and sent the camels up among the inaccessible hills. Writing at the same time to Agra, for instructions as to what he should do with them. If he is turned foe, from friend we shall have the Forts of Wear, Dig, Comeere and Bhartpoor to take, the three last of which are said to be wonderfully strong.

We continue to march extraordinarily slowly, which is odd enough, considering the pressing necessity of the folks on the other side of the Jumna. But as we set out quite suddenly and unprovided with grain, bazaars or necessaries it may be the policy of the commander-in-chief to move slowly that their supplies may overtake him from all quarters while it will be known to Holkar that he has marched a circumstance of much consequence.

We hear today that thirteen officers were killed in the late affair. Holkar, it is said, cut off the hands of many of our sepoys, who refused to serve against us!

Captain Bradford, the Commissary of bazaars, and Pay Master to Monson's army, has brought off rupees, about two-thirds of what he had in charge; the public servants all left him, and his own private servants saved this money. Lieutenant Williams, Monson's Persian interpreter, and Lieutenant Nixon his *Aid-de-camp,* one of the finest young men in the whole army, were killed as was Monson's European troopers, in defending the brigadier, when badly wounded, and trying to cross a river.

September 6th—We hear today that the European Regiment from Allahabad is ordered to the grand army, and not to Bundelkund and that a battalion of the 1st Regiment Native Infantry is on its way up. 256 recruits of the 76th passed Allahabad on their way to join the Regiment on the 1st and the 75th Regiment left Calcutta, on their way to the field, on the 13th *ultimo*. All this is excellent news, as every European soldier, is worth his weight in silver to the Government at this most critical juncture.

Holkar is said to have occupied Biana Pass, with all his Infantry and guns and to have sent his Horse, all round.

Colonel Scott, resident at Delhi, later at Lucknow, is with the army, and is said to have expressed his will to have the command of a brigade in the grand army at which every one is rejoined as the colonel is said to be a man of talents and merit. Would to God all our commanders were! *Sapientiverbum.*[2] by the bye, if ever these the lucubration of James Young—Gentleman should fall into the hands of the curious and should any of our excellent, or hyper-excellent commanders see the above "*verbum sapienti*"!, I shall only say in the words of a quaint but clever adage, "*Qui Capit, Me facit!*"

Monson, we hear, has demanded a court of enquiry which his reputation requires as in all probability it will clear him of any imputation further than his want of head or capacity to conduct ought beyond a storming party and consequently the blame, will deservedly shift itself from his wise head, to the heads of the wiseacres who gave him the important charge, such an army!, again, "*Qui Capit*" etc. etc. The more necessary be reiterated, as from good authority, I learn that our general did not give the Honourable Brigadier this command but that it originated in another quarter!

September 7th—Passed (over a bridge of boats) the Issa Nullah, which was about middle deep. Owing to the carelessness of a rascally servant of mine, all the little drawings which I have been making, and have carefully preserved for three years, to send home, one day or other; fell of the back of my tattoo, into the river; and are all more or less damaged! I have suffered a great loss by this, not only from the honest pride, I took, in looking back to view my own improvement in drawing but from the

---

2. A word to the wise.

impossibility of sending them home, remind as they are to my friends, a pleasure I had long looked forward to, with hope!

This day Lieutenant Colonel Fawcett's defence commenced and I attended the court martial. His defence, a written one, was a very good one and if he proves, what he asserts he can, I see little or no blame, that can be attributed to him. On the contrary the infancy and obloquy attempted to be thrown upon him, by his accusers, will only be retorted on themselves with tenfold disgrace from the examination of Brigade Major Robertson and Dr Hume I think Colonel Fawcett in a fair way to prove his assertions and hope he may for his army's and his own misfortunes, seem to have been owning to the penuriousness of Government in not affording him the means of obtaining any information whatever. Also to the carelessness of Captain Smith, in encamping so far from Captain Fead's party near the fort and lastly Captain Fead's own carelessness, although warned of his danger, in being taken by surprise.

September 8th—Received a letter from Cornet T. D. Steuart, 1st Cavalry at Muttrah, dated the 3rd inst., Holkar or his horse, in large bodies were all about them and they expected daily to be attacked. The Bhartpoor Rajah refused any supplies to them, and the Rajah of Hattrass. A large fort near Sassney in the Dooab, from whence they had likewise used to draw supplies, had not only refused continuing them but had stopped articles of clothing on their way to the 15th Regiment refusing to restore them without an order from Holkar. Holkar's army push up to the very gates of Agra and he is settling the Government of the conquered provinces by putting regular armies in each district and turning out ours.

September 9th—Encamped not far from the ruins of the ancient and celebrated city of Canouge, supposed by Rennel and others, to be the ancient Palibothra of Pliny. An opinion plausibly supported but all the reasons for which opinion, seems to me to apply almost equally well to Patna, which has generally been supposed to be that city especially from it's site and the colour of it's inhabitants. Be this as it may be Canouge has once been a place of prodigious extent indeed and from the strong nature of the ground surrounding it for miles, or I should rather say from it's being filled with dust and pavements of bricks, I am inclined to think it must have been of prodigious extent centuries before the Mahommedan conquest. What buildings we now see in ruins on the plains are however of comparatively modern date, like the ruins of Delhi and Agra, and as far as I have observed, are chiefly sepulchral and all of that species of architecture, which the *Moosulmauns* (or Moors) introduced into every country where they carried their religion and their arms and the character of which seems to me the same. Whether in the Alhambra at Grenada or the Taje at Agra, the country every where covered with cultivation, even the ruins of Canouge are covered with grain wherever the plough has been able to force it's way. It put in my mind the fate of Troy, the proudest city of it's time and of Virgil's pathetic exclamations "*Troja fuit!*" and the melancholy reflections caused by seeing the plough only where once stood these superb walls.

300 horse, our magnanimous ally, Diaram's, having deserted to Holkar, 900 horse (Hindoostanee) of Lieutenant Colonel Brown's army commanded by a Mr. Skinner demanded an increase of pay. The alternative being perfectly understood by them and us, in case of our refusal to comply. much alarm was excited in Brown's camp in consequence. Colonel Brown, I conjecture, wisely complied with their demands, for we yesterday heard that they pursued the treacherous Diarammians and cut them in pieces. A memorable lesson to future deserters, but which has been outdone by our friend Holkar who from some refusal of going on a particular service which they were ordered on, and as we understand, totally cut to pieces, the deserter companies of the 14th Regiment. A havildar, of one of the regiments who went off to the enemy from Monson's detachment was fool enough to return in disguise for his family and effects. He was, however, apprehended and will, I trust, suffer the punishment he so richly merits.

We hear that 4000 recruits for sepoy corps, are ordered to be immediately raised, which are for the purpose of filling up the dreadful gaps in the unfortunate regiments of Monson's detachment, as the infantry officers seem to think and hope, for the purpose of raising three new sepoy regiments. Certain it is that the Bengal army must be shortly and that too, very shortly, reinforced by several thousands more sepoys and 1000 or 1200 Golundauze at least. The artillery lost twenty-eight Europeans with Monson's party and are really quite dwindling away to a mere nominal corps from the fatal and stupid parsimony of a blind Government in a department the most essential to their existence as a state.

It is in the art of artillery and engineering alone that the country powers, have never *yet* been able to rival us. though of late years they have been making rapid strides towards it and notwithstanding this and the positive necessity which common-sense might be supposed to dictate of keeping this branch of the art of war in a state of perfect and constant effectiveness the very opposite line of conduct is pursued. And the regiment of artillery alone in their service is about two-fifths of its nominal strength in men and nearly half deficient in commissioned officers, were I to add to this wretched account the pitiful and parsimonious mode in which the commissariat and bullock departments are conducted without men, cattle, carriages even guns entertained or ready for service until the moment when they are actually wanted and it is too late to have them disciplined or fit for use I should fill up a volume instead of a page. As to the inefficiency of the sepoy establishments it cannot be better exemplified than by taking a look at the state of defence in which we were compelled to leave our own provinces.

All last campaign, and the present one, when if an enemy had got into the Dooab or got into it now he might traverse it at leisure from one end to the other without scarce meeting with even the show of opposition. I hope in a few years, to see on the Bengal establishment 60,000 Regular Infantry and 3000 effective Artillery at least. But the policy or economy of opening their purse-strings will not, I dare say appear to the Government until some severe lesson he taught them. God grant it may not be more than a mere lesson! The story of the capture of Calcutta in 1756, should as was the custom with some of the Caliphs, when they feared to forget a humiliating but useful calamity be printed in letters of gold in the grandest room of the Grand Governor General's, grand palace that it might operate as a perpetual *memento mori*. An antidote to the dreams of Universal Government and influence and the more fatal repose of "Security!" It would perhaps be an improvement on this bright idea if one of the many *aids de camp* entertained at such an expense, whether ordinary, extraordinary, supernumerary or honorary could be spared from his severe and laborious other avocations to ring daily in the ears of "Little Greatness." The words "Black Hole" and "1756" etc. etc. *caetera* descent.

September 11th—This is the anniversary of the glorious victory gained near Delhi over the Maharattas under General Louis Bourquain by the British army under H.E. General Lake and which may be said to have decided the Scindian War by making us masters of the once Great Mogul Shah Allam of Delhi and what is the more consequence by far by rendering us Lords of the whole Dooab. Thus giving to our territories in Hindoostan the excellent natural boundary of a large river, the Jumnah. Had Perron stood faithful to his employers or had Bourquain defended the passage of the river, instead of crossing to fight us, where should we now have been. And yet it is singular that that policy which not only common sense and prudence but even nature herself pointed out to us should not have been adopted and that ambition should have led our rulers, instead of being contented with this natural boundary, the Jumnah and the strong places on the opposite side with perhaps a slip of land, sufficient to secure the navigation uninterrupted to grasp at district, after district on the Mahratta side. And when territorial possession was not to be had to attempt at establishing with every petty chieftain (the nominal possessor, perhaps, of a soil, caused by sterility and drought) that irksome and ungrateful influence which while it renders us hated even by those whose cause we espouse, involve us in the inscrutable maze of native politics and sows the fruitful germ of never ending wars.

The present campaign induced by our attempts to establish our influence with a feudatory of Jeswant Rao, Holkar (the Jynagur Rajah) is, I apprehend, an instance exactly in points, How, it will terminate, should we be able to overtake our enterprising enemy, I have no doubt but an answer will not so easily be given to the question of when?

September 12th—We just have learned that Colonel Murray has occupied Indore, and is likely to cooperate with us by cutting off the retreat of Holkar, who by all accounts, is much alarmed

September 13th—The march this morning, was the longest we have yet had. Four of our horses were completely knocked up, long before the march was over and were forced to be relieved by others. Two of them died immediately after. This mortality among our horses (we have now lost three out of seventy) is the effect of overworking and fatigue entirely. We have plenty of horses but no riders. Our little troop at it's full complement is only calculated to man two guns, two howitzers, twenty-five tumbrils.

Of our whole number at this moment by death and sickness, twenty or thereabouts are *hors de combat* and yet we have a gun and a tumbril, more than our establishment which require twelve draught horses and nine drivers. The consequence of this augmentation by inversion is real diminution of our strength. Instead of six horses per carriage, we are compelled to have only four, as we have no men to drive more. These four, having, in addition to the burden of a dragoon horse on their backs to draw between them a 6-pounder, 5½ howitzer or tumbril, are quite unable to do the work, and die. Yet with certain wise heads it is considered as "augmenting our horse artillery" to add guns and horses without giving men to work them. So that like the man who starves in the midst of plenty we have the reputation of great strength, while the real fact is, that at present every gun and every horse we received as to our weakness.

What Captain B. thinks on this subject I know not but I think even the profit which he, and he alone makes by these added guns and horses would not tempt him to receive one of them, without a proportion of men and lascars to work them. If he knew what high ideas are entertained of us and the use we shall be of by everyone in the army. All which, will I know be cruelly disappointed and our shame which ought to fall on the heads of our superiors, be redoubled, or tripled in proportion to the exaggerated ideas now entertained of us in action. Four men even, an altogether too few for the management of a gun, including the casualties incident to all troops and especially to us in the mad and absurd, though bold mode, in which our (erased) means to act with us. Running up in the face of an enemy, unprotected, unannoying, until he has got so near that the enemy could kill us with their very pistols or charge us long before we could commence our first round.

What have we to do with all this changing etc. etc. If we go within 300 yards at nearest we expose ourselves to musket shot, and is not this throwing away the principal, the grand advantage of the artillery? "He being able to annoy infantry or cavalry at a distance, when their muskets or carbines cannot come near you?" It is, I affirm and unless it is to be supposed that the enemy are to be panic-struck and never dream of resistance, when they see the redoubtable horse artillery, come galloping down on them, I do not see how they possibly could fail to kill every man or horse of us, even if we could open on them. Whatever the Maharattas may do, I would only ask if any one thinks the French regiment in their place would suffer a man of us to return alive to tell the tale? Or if one of our own sepoy corps would not, by a single well-directed volley, levelled at the horses breasts put the whole of us *hors de combat!* For, be it recollected, as an argument, stronger than any other purpose against our approaching too near that if a single horse is killed in the harness, (and who can well miss such a train) the gun is rendered altogether useless until that horse is replaced. No relief may be near, and if there is, the men must dismount and the dead or wounded horse with difficulty be disengaged from the harness.

This is no work of a moment and while we are about it, must the enemy within so short a distance, we supposed to have to gone to sleep? The more I think of this subject the more it vexes me, the more I could say on it. If, (erased) does act as he says he will, in this manner he will perhaps be able to kill numbers of the enemy, before they run in on his guns or have shot all his men and horses, but he will most undoubtedly lose all his officers and *all* his brave men and leave his guns with the enemy. In my opinion (although the most obvious reasons prevent *my* opening my lips to him on the subject till called on) it is no longer a cold question of profit and loss to be calculated by ordinary rules of debtor and contra creditor, which is of most advantage to his employers and the service, the killing numbers of the enemy and losing his men, horses, and guns or killing perhaps fewer of the enemy, yet preserving his corps from annihilation.

Although this, sets the question in as striking a point of view as any mode of putting it can do. Yet there is a sentiment superior to that, which ought to govern the heart of every brave man, entrusted with the lives of his fellow subjects. Such a man although he is never to think of danger, where his services are likely to produce victory, honour or even advantage to his country. Yet, he is to be, specially when, as in the present case, success is at best problematical careful of the lives of his men not being want only and uselessly sacrificed. Yet is our commander (erased) brave even to daring but his prejudices are strong and having imbibed a fallacy and dazzling ideas of the superiority of horse artillery over every other species of force, guns, cavalry, or infantry he will not give up the dear decoits. It is but justice to him, however, to say, that I do not believe he even heard or read any arguments on the opposite side of the question to make him inclined to think non-seriously about it.

Once only did he speak of it to me a year ago, when I merely combated it slightly upon such grounds as my reason told me, made against it but since then I have thought much and read more on the subject through the advice and assistance of my most highly esteemed friend Colonel Horsferd, whose opinion at any time gospel on professional, or literary subjects with me I am happy to say, in the present instance entirely coincide, with my own from the various authors chiefly French, which he has lent me, I can see that in their opinion and in particular in the formal opinion of the committee of Marshals and Generals of French artillery assembled by the late Louis XVI to try and decide, on the uses, merits and discipline of horse artillery.

Horse, a flying artillery was to differ from all other field artillery, only in as much as that having more horses to a price and the gunners being mounted. It could with the celerity of cavalry move from point to point during action as required. But that in every other respect whatever the rules for disciplining the men and horses and using the gun were to be precisely the same as those for ordinary field artillery. Which in fact they became. The moment the gun was unlimbered and the men dismounted to commence firing.

Is this not simple, rational and intelligible! Oh that I could get (unreadable) to think it so!

In our march this day we passed Nobygunge, about five miles before we arrived to our ground. This seems to have been a large village now gone to decay. And about two miles before we came to Nobygunge and also close to it on the Bewah side are the ruins of two large s*erais* or, as they are known in England from the different Eastern story books, translated from Arabic and Persian, caravan *serais*. Places of accommodation for travellers, inns being unknown that even, most liberally, erected by generous individuals and not un-frequently by pious and patriotic monarchs all over the East. I believe, from the style of architecture of such as I have seen and from what I have read that the *serai*, at least the large capacious square *serai*, is a Mahommedan building and was unknown to India before the Moosulmaun conquest. I fancy what are called *choultries* on the coast may be Hindoo buildings for the same purpose but as I have never seen one I cannot be able to judge.

These serais however are really absolute blessings in such a hot, parched country as Hindoostan is. They are erected at moderate stages on frequented roads and generally are of a square, of rectangular shape, with towers (frequently pavilioned) at the four angles. Without they look like forts and have two or four magnificent gateways in the sides within. The terrace of the wall, which is brick, with a parapet is vaulted out into numerous cells or small houses. The arches of which, are well turned and groined. These afford lodging for man and horse while in the *serai* or area. There are one or more wells and several immense banyan or tamarind trees affording delightful and needful shade to the wearied or, as the song says, *wayworn traveller*. These excellent and truly charitable erections are, I am sorry to say like every other building of public accommodation and utility or magnificence that I have seen in India, falling rapidly into decay. Most of them are like the two I mentioned above in absolute ruins and the few that are not in this state are rapidly verging to it, and now afford little more than the mockery of shelter and refreshment.

It is a truly melancholy thing, as a most able and accurate political writer on the statistics of India in the Asiatic annual register 1802 observes that you see in the Company's territories in Bengal (he might have added in the Dooab and Hindoostan) nothing but ruins or remains of magnificent erections of public spirit, magnificence and utility, bridges, flights of steps, ghauts, serais aqueducts etc. etc. all rapidly decaying and no new ones, anywhere, rising up in their stead. All this is literally the case and I shall take a future opportunity of considering maturely and stating the reasons such as they occur to me.

September 14th—Marched to Bowgong and encamped on a prodigious, but uncultivated plain on the Agra side of the town which is prettily situated, though I should suppose in particular direction of the wind, very unhealthily, on the verge of a lake, annually formed in a hollow by the rains. This, as usual, has been a large town, not walled, but the ruin and desolation, seen by us in passing through a single long narrow street, exceeds anything I have seen, in proportion to it's size and population, at least in Agra, Delhi and Canouge. Although absolute districts of dilapidation are still largely inhabited cities this on the contrary exhibited nothing but houses falling and fallen.

Major General Wellesley, the Governor General's brother, has left Calcutta by dawk. His destination is unknown. It seems however, most generally believed that he is going to take the command of the army from Hydrabad, which I before mentioned as having marched under the command of Colonel Wallace.

The march of this day, as from it's shortness, it was soon over was not unpleasant. But sickness prevails among both our Europeans and natives to a terrible degree owing to the heat of the day and the damp dewy nights, extremes which are not easily resisted by any constitutions. Yesterday and today the home-sick-list of our little troop has been from seven to eight. We have sent two to the general hospital. The commander-in chief himself who seems to have resisted astonishingly the climate of India, hitherto, is himself indisposed. The heat is indeed astonishing.

Colonel Brown, in going to Agra from Muttra, is said to have lost all his baggage and Muttra is burnt. At headquarters they are seemingly angry with him for this move, especially as Holkar on hearing of his moving left his camp standing and run off five *koss* so that, they say they were running from each other. But I cannot think Colonel Brown, who is certainly a good office would take so important a step without orders or sufficient cause, when the colonel has assumed the command.

September 15th—Marched this morning at 4—ten miles to Manpoory. We were gratified by the view, for about three miles before we came to it, of a most beautiful house, or villa, of Mr. Cunningham, the collector of the district. As it was the first European house, we had seen since leaving Cawnpore, we were very well disposed to think it a fine one. But independent of this, Mr. Cunningham's house, is really charming. It is long, spacious of only a ground floor and with light and elegant verandahs and porticos of the ionic order. A neat park surrounds it and the out-houses, with the exception of a sleeping bungalow, are appropriate to the style of the main building, which is altogether very like the style of the Italian villas. Captain White, who commands the Sebundies, a kind of militia, a revenue force, has also a nice house in a grove near this in the rear of the cantonments of his corps. which are very neat before these houses. The less elegant bungalow of the Judge, Mr. Riley and the altogether naked and mean one of the Surgeon, Mr. Mansell "hide the diminished heads." Altogether these comfortable, English looking places, caused in us a very pleasing sensation when contrasted with all round, for many, many, miles. It is like that of meeting a human creature or a poor convent of miserable monks in the deserts of Egypt as described by the late travellers there.

Manpoory, the chief town of the district or *Zillah Etawah,* is the town where the courts of justice are held and the magistrates reside. It has only been ours since the Autumn of 1801 when we compelled the Nabob of Oude, Saadut Ally, raised to the Musnud by our all powerful hand (on the deposition of Vizier Ally) from the abject state of misery in which younger branches of reigning families in Hindoostan usually live. To cede, as we called it modestly, the best and richest half of his dominions *viz*., his lands in the Dooab to make up and to secure in future the payment of the enormous and scandalous subsidy which we forced him to agree to pay as the price of his elevation and which we knew him, at the time we imposed it on him, to be incapable of paying regularly.

I think it is no un-candid or unjust conclusion to suppose that when the subsidy usually paid by Nabobs of Oude was so enormously increased by Saadut Ally it was the settled intention of the British Government at the time (1797) not to lose so golden an opportunity as the accession of our own creature to the Nabobship for increasing our territory and that it was the summit of political and personal caution in Sir J. Shore (Lord Teignmouth) letting this rich dominion, lapse as it were into our hands, on account of non-payment of the stipend agreed on with a show of justice, the truth of which people in general would not trouble themselves to penetrate into. Had he, at once made the cession of the Dooab districts to the Company, a stipulation in raising Saadut Ally all the world would have exclaimed against the infancy and rapidity of the transaction and what was of more consequence to the Governor General himself. The House of Commons would not, as they did in all probability have let this deposition of one prince, previously established by ourselves, but whose title after a time we found defective. The erection of a new prince in his room, the real erection of the British, on the heirs of both have passed so easily as it did, while things were the show of disinterestedness.

Manpoory consists of two parts between which the road to Agra passes, both of these are walled with mud and that on the right hand has in it a pagoda or Hindoo temple with a large brick palace like a mass of inelegant red cottages heaped on the top of one another. The left hand division seems to contain chiefly bazaars and the habitations of the lower sort of people. Manpoory is indeed a very large city and without even the appearance of desolation or ruins. On the contrary it seems absolutely filled with people many of them better dressed too than are generally met with. The walls and bastion towers of both towns, were clustered with men and children to see us pass but like all places in Hindoostan not a woman except very old ones were among the number. The colour of the inhabitants is fairer, or rather yellower than usual.

Holkar, it said, has possessed himself of Muttrah and is collecting boats to cross the river. I hope he may not attempt this, or if he does, may be too much alarmed about securing his return to act with that enterprise and energy, which in my opinion if he were to exert, he would fire and desolate the Dooab from Muttra to Hurdwar sure of being joined by the Hattrass Rajah and the other numerous refractory *Zemindars* in that immense district. If he does this, he strikes at the root of our revenues and withers our sinews for the war, which to support, we shall have to drain Bengal of men and money.

I do not fear his getting across the Ganges into Rohilkund as that river is not fordable and sufficient numbers of boats cannot be procured by him to cross. This besides, would be shutting himself in the rat-trap only more securely for us. I do not think we might catch him 'en he could recross the Jumnah, but I think too that we may fail, and he is certain of ruining our country for one year at least, however the matter may end. No! Although many intelligent people seem to wish he would cross, I declare I hope he may not.

A country, the seat of war, is sure to be laid waste and ruined. Even the march of a peaceable army in India, attended as it is with such swarms of cattle and followers is destruction to the track it pursues, is like the devastating march of a swarm of locusts or plundering Tartars, as described by themselves, when they say "that where they stop the grass grows not for a year". No! Let us, as the evil must be suffered somewhere transfer it to the enemies country, or at all events keep it from our own!

September 16th—Marched at 4 this morning ten miles to Bigrai. The morning was dark and cloudy yet hot and just at daybreak a few drops of rain fell but we had nothing deserving the name of a shower. Although the sky was covered with clouds which we could see were plentifully pouring out their contents all around us.

September 17th—We passed at sunrise, Garroul, a pretty large village, midway between Manpoory and Shakoabad , (distance eight *koss*). Diaram, the refractory *Zemindar*, a Rajah of Hattrass in the Dooab, who has been long suspected of favouring Holkar and whose horse (fighting on our side) deserted to him twice, afterwards cut up, is said to be dead so (again) it is said, is Ameer Khan. A letter which I had, today, from Cuttack, from Parker, mentions that it is believed the Linois (the French admiral) has taken Prince of Wales' Island , had landed 3000 Europeans and means to take all our Eastern Islands and is actually in Madras roads. I don't believe this exactly, although the Prince of Wales' Island part of it is exceedingly probable from the shamefully small force we keep there.

Colonel Fawcett's sentence is made known to the eternal disgrace of that inquisitious Government through whose fault alone his army was unfortunate and who wished to make him their scapegoat and even like the unfortunate Admiral B. would without remorse or scruple of conscience have sacrificed the life of this innocent man to bring themselves off. He is acquitted of all the charges and honourably acquitted of the infamous imputation of shamefully misbehaving before an enemy, whom he never saw and the very existence of whom seems to be a problem! What a Government for an unfortunate, unprotected officer to serve under! What a Government for a British subject, to be under!

September 18th—Marched to Shakoabad and encamped on the Agra side of the city. on the very field of battle, where Lieutenant Colonel Conyngham, and five companies of sepoys, with a 6 pounder had his engagement with 5000 Mahratta Horse, under Monsieur Fleury, whom General Perron, with much sagacity, detached, round our army on its advancing into the Mahratta territory, in August 1803 with a view to ravage our part of the Dooab. Our frontier town was Shakoabad and Fleury thought that five companies and gun would fall an easy prey to his detachment.

In this however he was mistaken, although their cantonments, before which and their magazine they were drawn up is surrounded at 300 yards distance by an amphitheatre of sloping even sand-hills off erring the finest ground for cavalry to charge or from it's semi-circular or, enabling them to make their fire coverage to the centre when this handful of 350 men was drawn up. Yet their steadiness, and the assistance derived from poor Captain Winbolt's gun enabled them to repulse every charge. The Maharattas retired behind cover of the hills and kept up a straggling fire on them, blockading them on all hands, while parties, sent round to the town reduced the cantonments and officer's bungalows, in the rear of the party, to ashes. Thus pressed and unable to disperse such an irregular, straggling body of horse they retired into the town and took post in a house or rather courtyard resolved to defend themselves to the last, as they did not expect terms from the enemy.

Fleury blocked them up all round with his men. They had no provisions their destruction was inevitable, when their generous enemy, Fleury in person came in represented their certain fate and the folly of losing so many lives by unavailing resistance and without food or possibility of relief and offered to let them retire with their arms (the gun expected) and what private property they could remove telling them that it was the consideration of their brave defence. But above all of :

> All European gentlemen being as it were brothers, in this savage, foreign country, which made him anxious to secure their lives, while yet he retained any influence, over his unruly and ferocious troops.

> He even sent his own chosen and confidential troop to escort them to some distance and protect them from depredation. In short he behaved with feeling, honour and generosity and such terms, from such an enemy, it had been folly to refuse. Accordingly they marched off unmolested.

The Maharattas plundered everything whatever both of the officers and inhabitants and some of them, it is said went almost as far as Manpoory, where the judge, Mr. Riley fled (as well he might) but Colonel Macan's Brigade, of European and Native Cavalry, detached after Fleury, by General Lake, some compelled them to make a hasty retreat. Fleury, soon after came in on the Governor General's manifesto with Perron and the other French officers and he was treated with the respect and attention, his conduct so well merited.

Shakoabad is a large city and was flourishing and until a week ago, populous, but the terrifying report of some of Holkar's Horse, having crossed the Jumnah caused three fourths of them to run off with their effects, to some place where they concealed themselves in a place of greater security. The desolated remains of the burnt and black cantonments and bungalows present a melancholy view.

September 19th—At Calcutta, a shabby company of Golundauze or native artillery men, is ordered to be raised for the defence of Prince of Wales' Island, for the safety of which Government seem at last to be anxious after having left it nearly defenceless, since the French War broke out. To this company of artillery, not a single officer is given yet regiment or regiments of native infantry are raised, and with them, always the due proportion of officers, yet the poor neglected artillery officers are never to receive benefit by any augmentation! This is justice.

September 20th—Marched to Firozabad, the frontier town of Sindhia's territories in the Dooab. It was built by the Emperor Firoze Shah and is the first town we have yet come to, that has anything like the remains of regular and magnificent streets and houses, although they are in sad decay. The population is still considerable and the place is yet very large. This was the headquarters of Major Frith's Regiment of Irregular Hindoostanee Horse who are infamous for their desertion in a body to Holkar when with Monson's detachment. The Major, after having in that disgraceful retreat lost all his baggage and property, is now attempting to raise a new corps of the same kind.

At Firozabad or in the neighbouring fields are many grand ruins of mausoleums and in one part of the town, there are grave several hundred Moosulmaun stones. One of the tombs is still tolerably entire, it is on the west of the town, and is that of Nawaub Himmut Khan and his son. Splendid as no doubt the life of this prince was and splendid as is his tomb, yet such is the complete oblivion caused by a few revolving ages and some changes of rulers, that his very name is forgotten.

September 21st—Marched to Etimaudpoor, celebrated for a picturesque Mahommedan building in the centre of a large tank and connected with the banks by a long bridge of pointed arches. The half state of ruin, in which this house is with the aged trees growing out of the vaults and the very windows. The bridge and a tomb of seemingly more modern date on the main land give this place, altogether a very romantic air although built in the style of the mausoleums I have seen. Yet as this building has no grave or grave stone in the centre, (which is universally the mode of construction of such as I have seen) and is peculiarly situated in a pleasant piece of water, with many stairs leading closer to it as if for convenience of bathing or sailing, I am inclined to suppose it was a pleasure house. A pavilion rather than a tomb.

We heard this day that Bappoo Sindhia (Uncle of Dowlut Rao Sindhia) has crossed the Jumnah with his brigade in Holkar's service and that 4000 Pindaris, or plundering, irregular horse, have also crossed over. Bad news this!

September 22nd—We entered at daybreak exactly, a chain of ravines, or rather valleys which are formed originally by the rains, and which border the Jumnah, all round Agra, on both sides. The chain through which lay our road are the grandest. The road, or gully is very deep indeed and so narrow, as barely to admit of a single carriage. After travelling about half a mile, from the time when we first descended into this gulf, a beautiful low valley, opened on our view with a rivulet flowing through it and bordered on all sides with the different hills, at the bottoms of which the ravines wound their circuitous way.

After traversing this valley, a second chain of ravines, more grand and longer than the first, was passed and when we reascended to the level ground we entered that suburb of Agra, which extends along the convex side of that reach of the Jumnah, on the opposite side of which Agra lies for the span of three or four miles.

Of this once extensive suburb or rather part of the once Imperial city of Ackberabad (Agra) but a few houses, or huts are now inhabited by perhaps 200 people. All the rest is vast desolation! Great part of this site is ploughed, if the simple process used here, can be so termed. But such is the fertility of the soil that luxuriant crops grow, even among the walls of former palaces. Some parts of this vast space are evidently of a date greatly more modern than others. Several buildings, being in a state, even now of high preservation, while in other parts, although there are no buildings above ground, yet if but the least part of the thing covering of earth be removed, you see nothing underneath, but strata of the oldest bricks, in regular order and the ground is undermined with vaults in many places.

Ackbar, first made this city a royal residence and gave it it's name and several succeeding Emperors following his example. It attained to a prodigious size. We are told that at one time, there were on either bank of the river, fifty-three Imperial gardens. One of these, the Rambaugh in which we lived when we halted a day at Agra, on our return from last campaign in June we again visited. We were, fully recompensed for our ride of a mile or so, in the hot sun by the agreeable shade and of this truly delightful garden which we found adorned with all the green luxuriance of the season and the pavilions and shady walks of which, were doubly endeared and unduly charming to us, from the memory of the real refreshment and pleasure, which we received from their fruit's and coolness!

When in the sultry month of June, returning from a fatiguing campaign, in the worst of weather, and in one of the hottest countries where not a blade of grass far less the nearest fruit, relieved the dizzy yellowness of a burning sandy horizon, we alighted, as it were by enchantment in a sequestered spot filled with trees and vegetation and grasses with which we "solaced our parched and wearied carcases". Allowing even for the difference of season and circumstances, it must still be, I think, we confessed, that this beautiful spot is most delightful in the hot season for besides the striking beauty of contrast, which it then possesses in full. The rains of this season, render unnecessary any irrigation from without whereas in the dry and hot season, the necessity of water, to prevent the vegetation from being burnt up, occasions a constant supply of their necessary element, to be raised from the river, on the banks of which it is situated and this water, conveyed by hundreds of channels, in all directions throughout the garden fills all the conduits and fountains, and canals with clear and bubbling streams, which really convey a kind of enchantment into the scene, and recall to mind, all the fabulous stories of the *Arabian Tales*.

The only other place of note, which we visited this day was a white marble mausoleum, (erected to the memory of Etimaud-ud-Dowlah by his daughter Nour Jehan). In the rear of our tents and surrounded by four splendid gateways of red stone (the same as that of which almost all the city is built) with a wall, conduits and pavilions (octagonal as usual) towards the river side, and in the midst of a small but neat garden. This is somewhat in the style of the celebrated Taj of Agra, in as much as it is of white marble inlayed with different coloured stones and marble, in the shapes of flowers of different kinds. But it is inferior to that celebrated building not only in general effects and size, but also in the workmanship, which is not only larger in pattern but not near so delicate in the minute execution of the leaves and flowers and buds. It is besides, of two stories, so that the effect, of inside height is totally wanting.

It is still a beautiful and light looking building, but of it, I must say, as of all the Moosulmaun or Hindoo buildings I have ever seen, not even excepting the elegant Taj, that the multiplicity of minute ornaments, within and without of inlayed flowers, and writings and of relief ornaments in a truly miniature style totally destroy anything like general grandeur or magnificence of effect. A fault never to be found with the elegant simplicity of Grecian architecture and from which, at least in so great a degree, even the Saracen, as it is usually called the Gothic style of our cathedrals of example in England, is comparatively free though originally derived from the same source. In the latter the only gorgeous, (a highly fretted part), are the screens, cornices, capitals of columns, niches or doorways but in the Indian edifices that I have seen the whole superficies of the building, always within, and commonly without, is burthened with this tasteless minute workmanship.

The 8th Light Dragoons, crossed the river this day, and encamped a mile on.

September 24th—I fell in with an old Subahdar, commander of a company of native under the European officer of thirty-three years standing in the service, who was one of a few who escaped (after sinking the Regiment colours in deep water) from the massacre of poor Major Sinclair at the Banass Nullah (and not Biana as I formerly wrote). He told me numberless anecdotes of their miserable retreat and who he said it was no business of his to blame a Sahib (European Master). Yet, if their battalion had not been supported none of Holkar's army, he said would have returned as they did and he added that during all the time he had been serving the Company, it had been supposed that seven battalions were a match for all Hindoostan, that if the *General Sahib* (Monson) had stood to them the enemy would have run like sheep. For, he said "when we were attacked at Khoosalghur and Biana we formed a square without the general's orders and beat off the enemy wherever they appeared and if a single sepoy pointed his musket at a squad of eight or ten horsemen they ran as if they were pursued by an army.

They are cowardly, mean soldiers and have no discipline, nor method, nor equipment of any sort but when the general, on his elephant, ran away at Biana for Agra we all dispersed, every man to save himself as he could". Notwithstanding all these, and hundreds of other disgraceful accounts of the manner in which this truly shameful business was conducted and notwithstanding that Lieutenant Colonel Fawcett of the Company's service in what he could not possibly help was persecuted and tried for his life, yet we hear that the Honourable Lieutenant Colonel

Monson, of His Majesty's 76th Regiment has made his peace at headquarters, was well received and joins his Regiment and will command a brigade in this army

The Honourable Brigadier's detachment are now to go with the army and have, it is reported, declared that they will not serve under Colonel Monson again. God knows how true this is, but it is little to that gentleman's credit, that everyone in the army believes it to be so.

September 25th—This morning, joined the grand army at Secundra after a pleasant march of four or five miles through the remains of magnificent streets, and roads and houses, gardens and tombs innumerable. Secundra was evidently a part, and perhaps the most considerable, of the city of Agra. For to Secundra and far far beyond it the ground is covered with ruins and traces of a regularly laid out streets, one of these of a breadth equal to Portland place in London. We passed through for above a mile it must have been the grand West approach from Agimere as I saw one of those pyramidal obelisks, erected by the Emperor at every 2nd *koss* from Agra to Agimere. At an angle formed by another street with this I saw and inspected narrowly the statue of a fine Hindoostanee-looking horse of red and erected, they say by the Emperor, to commemorate the death of an Emperor who was killed at this spot when returning from hunting by a fall from his horse. It is better executed than any representation of life I ever saw by a native, but a very difficult part *viz*. the knee and all below is omitted as the horse stands on four stumps. If the body alone is executed the head, strange to tell has no ears but on the whole it is a good representation of the kind of animal intended.

We hear at Furrah, twelve miles on this side of Muttrah, his infantry and 150 guns are in a position at Bindrabund, six miles beyond Muttrah, said to be almost impregnable. With a deep marsh on his right and rear and impassable ravines to his left. For all this we shall beat him I doubt not but it will be, probably a tough contact, with him failure is nothing with us ruin. We hold him and his 50,000 men in far too great to contempt. I hope we shall wait for the reinforcement of 300 Europeans which will be here in a few days.

September 26th—I rode with my comrades this day, at an early hour, to visit the celebrated mausoleum of the Great Akbar that Emperor of Hindoostan.

The gateway through which we entered into the garden, where it is situated, is grand and very Saracenic, consisting of a noble pointed arch of entrance with four similar niches in two storeys, of a dome within the sides of which are scooped out into numberless pointed niches and windows with balconies and communicating to each other. And below by staircases and galleries on the four angles of this square building are four minarets of white marble, fluted about halfway to the top where, as usual pavilions have been but of which not a vestige remains. The rest of this gateway, being of stone of a red colour, curiously filled with mosaic work of every pattern and colour. The white minarets have a marvellous bad effect and look, as if they were of a different date from the rest of the building.

On the opposite side of the square garden, in which the tomb is situated, there was once, a similar entrance to this but it has now in a great measure fallen to pieces. To this regularity of corresponding parts, by the bye the Moosulmauns seem to pay great attention and I believe they call it by the name of Juab (answer, anglice) a similar expression with our own. After passing paved walks and the remains of what were *jets d'eau* we arrived at the mausoleum, placed in the centre of the garden. To describe this without singular building, so as to convey an adequate idea of it, would be impossible. Volumes or without a plan, on paper, of the disposition of it's parts being before me I spent a good while in looking over it all, yet I have not collected even a good general idea of it's form.

To the eye nothing is presented but a mass of cupolas, pavilions, columns, vaults, arches, screens, mosaic work, gilding, painting, carving all in the most diversified forms and variegated colours. Red pavilions on white foundations. White superstructures upon red. Amid all this, I must be evident to the observer or even reader of moderate taste that there can be no general effect, no real grandeur nor magnificence while in every corner and spot you meet with individual beauties and are delighted with pieces of sculpture and decoration truly exquisite in themselves. Yet the fatigued eye in vain looks for that symmetry of parts necessary to constitute pleasing whole.

On the ground storey are two rooms to the right and left of the entrance, where are interred the son and daughter in law of this prince and opposite to the door is a low dark vaulted gallery on a gradual slope at the end of which is the grand vault, where rest the remains of the Monarch himself. This dome, by the fineness of the echo, seems to be of vast extent but to give greater solemnity to the scene there is but one aperture to admit light which seems now almost choked with rubbish and a single lamp kept alive by a few faquirs scares even makes darkness visible. This vault and the gravestone are of polished white marble or alabaster and on the whole inspires one with that pleasing awe, which a visit to the ashes of the dead in our own cathedrals usually excites especially when, as in the present instance, the imagination conjures up to view the former grandeur and state and dominions of the occupant of the narrow house of death! What was written on the gravestone, I could not see, most probably the name and titles of the deceased.

On issuing out of this vault we ascended three or four storeys, not by a grand flight of steps, but by mean and concealed winding, narrow, staircases, a defect in this building which it has in common with all Mahommedan structures. At each of these storeys the flat, paved, roof of the one below on which we walked out was decorated with pavilion and piazzas and rooms of the mean dimensions, some of red stone, some of marble and at the top of the whole edifice, exactly above the burying vault I have before mentioned, we arrived on a fine square of white marble. In the centre of which, on the key stone of the dome underneath is a second tombstone of the finest white marble, covered with a profession of flowers, and foliage in the finest relief which surpasses any carving I have ever seen anywhere, not merely in correctness but in the real elegance of the stems, leaves and fruit represented the curves of which, with the bends of the falling leaves, seen in every point of view are done with all the grace and attention to what we call the flowing line of beauty that characterises the Grecian and a modern European style of executing the same subjects. I am much mistaken if this part is not the workmanship of an European hand. We know that about the time when this was erected several Europeans were at Agra, some of them artists patronised by the Emperor and there is a tradition that the Taj is the work of one of them.

However this may be this tombstone is truly beautiful, around it are inscribed, in different compartments, the ninety attributes of God in Arabic characters. This square is surrounded by verandahs, or as we would say cloisters, of pointed arches and instead of a wall surrounding the outside of the cloister the corresponding arches of it, to those within are filled with alabaster screen work of an infinite number of patterns and which looks light and beautiful. The whole of the windows in the tomb and entrances are or have been filled with work of the same kind, all of it elegant. The four angles of this square were crowned with marble pavilions, one is now disappeared and another is fast following.

The cloister and pillars seem to have been most highly finished with inlayed or I rather think painted compartments of every fantastic form. As however this square is exposed to the weather the stains alone remain to show what was and perhaps this very circumstance it is that by taking away that disgusting gaudiness of colouring makes this part of the building please so much. The floor is composed of squares of white and black marble alternated, as with us in Europe, and under the cloister the white is interspersed not with black but a rich ground marble.

To finish my observations on this remnant of Moosulmaun magnificence I have only to add that the whole building is in a miserable state of decay, fast hastening to ruin, yet the antiquity of it to us who have cathedrals of date, to which this when compared with them is but of yesterday does not seem warrant such rapid decay. But the truth is that these kind of buildings in this country, although fair to look at on the outside, consists of brick and mortar badly enough put together and faced only with a crust of thin weak stone or a still more perishable husk of tawdry mosaic so that a short time brings down this shell, weak from it's numerous dove-tailings and joining, and there remains only the mean substance of coarse brick not worth preserving.

I should have mentioned, when speaking of the Mausoleum of Akbar, that there is a fine engraving from a painting of Hodges of the entrance and which I first mentioned, in which the gateway with it's four minarets looks much grander than I may be thought to have represented it. But this engraving although correct enough is very deceitful chiefly because this disagreeable effect of the contrasted red and white is lost in a proforma which represents *chiaro scuro* only and also because the minuteness of a print's size, not admitting of, nor accurately discriminating the varied and endless inlayings of mosaic work of the front, the effect of the whole appears what it really is not, simple and grand.

September 27th—Lieutenants Hay and Swiney returned at 1 a.m., with eight guns, (one 12-pounder and seven 6-pounders) and fifteen tumbrils, into camp. And singular to relate although our camp is in front of an active and enterprising enemy with myriads of horse and some of these, only a few miles off, yet such is the negligence of the sentinels or the remissness of the persons in charge of outposts and piquets, that this train of artillery, at the dead of night and with all the shouting of bullock drivers, smacking of whips, rattling of wheels and clanking of chains that a line of guns always occasion, were not challenged by a single person of any description from the time they left the riverside, until having lodged their guns safe, in the park they returned to their tents. In our lines we were busied in receiving ammunition and stores from the park and storing them.

Our four too, which we were forced to send into the park for want of horses and men, were this day returned to us and His Excellency, who during the two months we were at Cawnpore and where we had time to prepare for the field by disciplining men and training horses or would give us a single additional man, horses, or gun, has now, when our original sixty men, are by sickness and death, reduced by a third and many of our old horses, rendered unfit for further service, graciously augmented us to four guns and two howitzers the necessary horses for which have in part been sent us by the agent, fresh from the dealer, puffed and blown up, fiery and un-broke and the men have been supplied from the 2nd Native Cavalry untaught, unaccustomed and driving ignorant of the gun exercise and though last not least unused to work along with European! Yet from this whimsical corps, this melauge of knowledge and ignorance, this magpie work of black and white, we are told great things are expected! I must fear they will be disappointed! God grant it may be no worse! If the blame fell on the authors of it alone, on the pitiful projectors of such a parsimonious plan who are so ignorant as to be unable to distinguish between necessary economy and absurd parsimony who are saving just when and where they ought to be liberal and extravagant where prudent frugality would be wisdom, then should *not* much regret it but well I know that it is not to distinguished or opulent guilt that censure ever attaches but:

Clothe it in rage, a pygmy straw will pierce it!
—King Lear

An example more in point could not be adduced than what has this day occurred. In General Orders the army is organised and brigaded and Lieutenant Colonel Monson has the right brigade! The post of honour! Above all others! And Colonel Gordon of the Company's cavalry for having expressed a fear that a Regiment (the 2nd) would mutiny and not cross the river Jumnah, in short for irresolution, it reprived of his brigade and sent away from camp to Pertaubghur to compare notes with poor Fawcett. He, too, a company's officer, because the court martial would not make his life, a scapegoat for an infamous and cruel government was degraded as far as malice could by not being allowed to join his regiment in Bundelkund any more! Lieutenant Colonel McGregor (4th Cavalry) has it is reported confidently being written to by order from headquarters and received a notification, that because he happened to be sick in the beginning of last campaign and of this he was not to think joining his regiment when recovered, but to retire to some out of the way quiet place allowing these two last numbered offic-

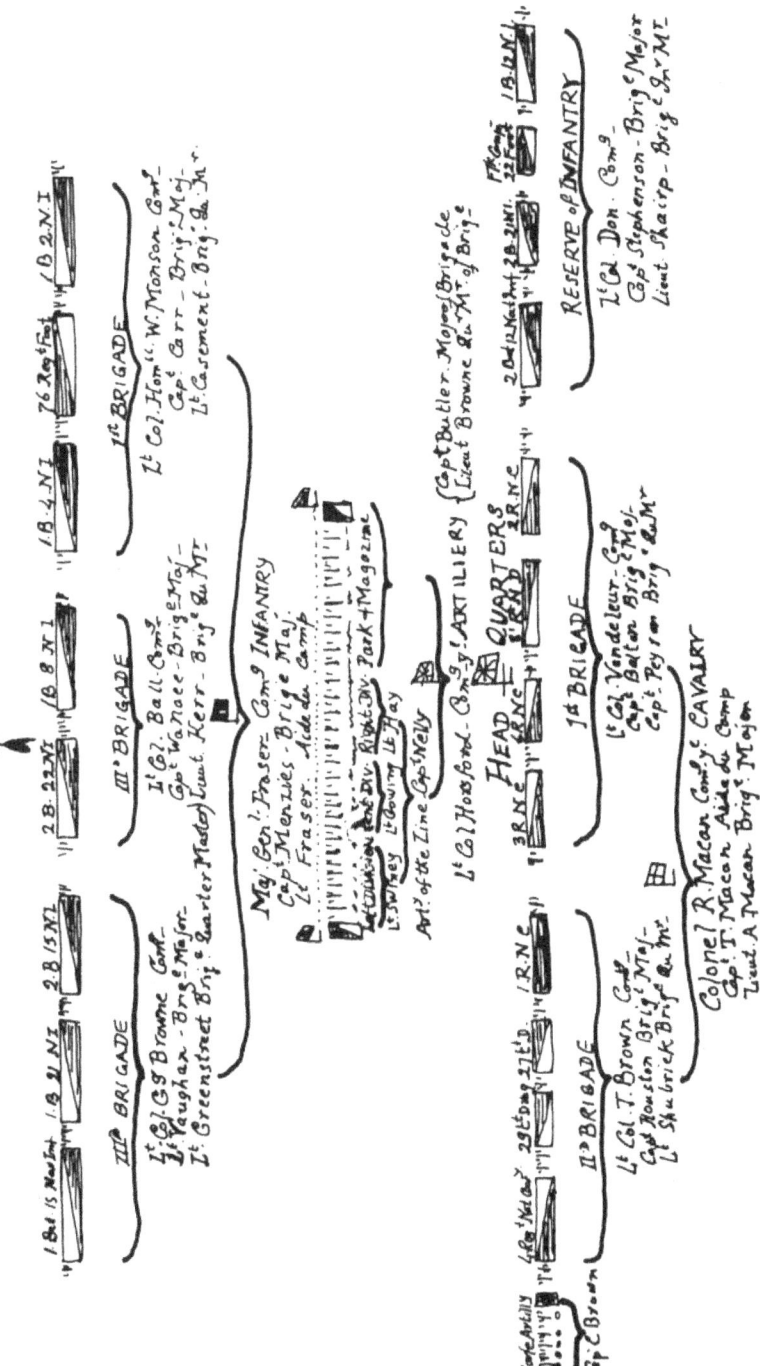

ORDER OF BATTLE AND ENCAMPMENT

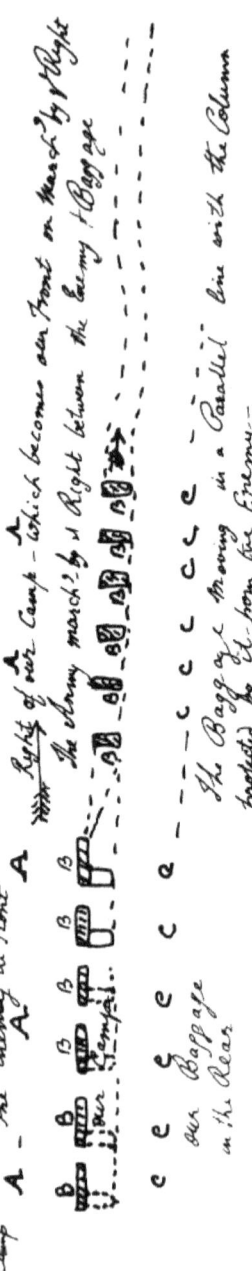

BAGGAGE MOVEMENT

ers to be guilty of what they are accused. Monson, I know to be, from the testimony of every officer and sepoy in his party, ten hundred times more criminal yet they are sent away in disgrace and he without court of inquiry or court martial or any attempt to clear away the stain on his character is appointed a general officer commanding a brigade! But they are soldiers of fortune without rank or connections and in the Company's service while he is son of an Earl, is related to the Governor-General, is a good companion of the commander-in-chief and lately is in His Majesty's Service.[3]

---

3. Sketch on page 47 shows the order of battle and encampment.

CHAPTER 3

October 1804

October 2nd—Very early in the morning, three or four horsemen were descried on our left (or fighting) flank[1] Colonel Lake (General's son and *aid de camp*) went out with a squadron of native cavalry and soon drove them away without discovering any more. Soon afterwards a small number were perceived on our baggage flank, who were driven away in an instant by a troop of cavalry. But about 7 a.m., Captain Stevenson Brigade Major to Lieutenant Colonel Don who commands the reserve and leads the advanced guard, came down to the commander-in-chief with intimation of a large body of apparently 1200 or 1500 horse appearing on our right considerably to the front.

As we had moved very slowly that the infantry, guns and baggage might be well up, which was the case, our line was very compact and on the commander-in-chief riding up to the front and seeing that the enemy appeared in a very great force on our front, right and left, the cavalry were extended out to cover the baggage and park. One brigade to the right and another to the

---

1. I shall explain this difference of fighting and baggage or reserve flank. Let A be the enemy in the face of whom we are to march. Our front while encamped at B is of course turned towards them and our baggage in our rear at C. If our march is to the right the corps on the right leads and the enemy is on it's left while marching whilst the baggage is on the right of the column, which if attacked wheels up to the same front as it kept, when encamped. Thus always being interposed between the enemy and it's own baggage. If the march is to be to the left the column will form the same reason, have the enemy to the right and baggage to the left. The column, which if attacked, wheels up to the same front. (See sketch on page 48).

left. The gallopers of the right brigade commenced the action by firing at the enemy while the cavalry formed the line to the front and the guns of each regiment began firing as soon as they came up. We, following the left regiment of cavalry were last up and at about 8 a.m. of my 22nd birthday, on clearing the rear of the last regiment, did I, James Young, Gentleman, first see the face of an enemy and first hear a hostile shot fired.

The circumstance of this coincidence is rather extra ordinary but I really had somehow or other a presentiment for some days before that it would be so or to speak more philosophically and perhaps more truly, I knew the 2nd October to be my birthday and also pretty well guessed that about this time the first skirmish must probably occur. The event turned out so and as we are all more or less superstitious however we may affect to be free from it, I instantly set my self down for a prophet or at least as favoured with a glimpse of the second light, may as it so happened that I was not killed on this my first day's action. I have marked it with a white stone as an omen of my good fortune on future occasions, although so far from having had a wonderful scape, the real wonder would have been if I had been killed when there was scarce a resistance but to return to our battle royal or soon as our guns formed up.

Captain Brown, (as well as myself) immediately observed that it was perfectly absurd to fire at the enemy who were near a mile off and accordingly our right hand howitzers alone, which came first into line, fired once. The shell burst in the air, short of the mark. The enemy were really in great numbers, I think not less than 3000 or 4000, all along our front in a parallel line with us and standing their ground. Colonel Macan who commanded the cavalry line ordered us and the gallopers of the regiment out in front and the line followed us ready to charge, drew their swords, which really had a most grand effect. The instant we advanced, the enemy retired and dispersed in small bodies among the grain and under-wood. The line, as it was not worth while pursuing such a fugitive enemy, heeled again to the right and continue their line of march. We, protected by a squadron of cavalry, keeping out on the fighting flank about 400 yards from column and after marching in this manner for about two or three miles we halted on a high spot of ground, whence we had a view of the enemy, while the quartermaster general marked out the ground for encampment.

The Maharattas, who were all horsemen now collected not far from the place where we had been engaged in two very large bodies. I am but an indifferent judge of numbers but I do not think that all round there could be many fewer than five or six thousands. Seeing our indifference they got exceedingly daring and bold and when we at last marched into our camp, which for greater security was in the form of a square. They came even within 100 yards of the camp carrying off Banjarrahs,[2] camels, elephants, whatever they could lay their hands on until our picquets were posted and even after that, so numerous were they, that the inlying picquets were several times in the course of the day sent out to reinforce the outlying picquets. According to the report of a prisoner taken, Holkar means to fight us on the grand scale. I shall conclude this long winded account of my first affair by observing that the enemy seemed more afraid of our horse artillery than of anything else and that if instead of running out in front of our line and firing we had been masked, by the lines advancing before us, within 400 yards of the enemy and then opening out to let us fire when we were ready, I doubt not but we should have done great execution among them.

October 3rd—We marched this morning at half-past 5 broad daylight lest the enemy's horse who were all round the camp, should take advantage of the darkness to carry off any of our baggage. We had not proceeded a mile from camp before we heard a smart cannonade, which lasted about a quarter of an

---

2.Banjarrahs, or as they are frequently called *Brinjarries,* are a most useful tribe of wandering grain merchants whose sole business is to follow to journey to great distances, with their bullocks loaded with gram (a kind of vetch eaten by horses instead of oats) wheat, peas etc., etc., which they exchange for money and buying merchandise, return to procure a fresh supply of grain with it's produce. Those who pay best of course will always be preferred by the Banjarrahs if they are protected also by them from danger on account of their usefulness, their lives are commonly spared by enemies.

hour, occasioned, as was apprehended, by the enemy endeavouring to cut off some of the baggage, in which they were very little successful being beaten off by the rear guard. As we proceeded on our march we perceived that we were accompanied on the left flank, by a string of horse, who kept a very respectable distance and were to all appearance but few in number.

After marching very slowly indeed for about six or seven miles we approached a village, built among very deep gullies and ravines and as there was but one narrow road along which the troops proceeded. A great stop and confusion was created among the baggage, who could only proceed by pressing in on our road. The cavalry who led the column, no sooner cleared the village than they pushed on at a gallop to regain the advanced guard and our guns were from an unusual hurry and confusion that on a sudden took place among the baggage prevented from getting on to our station in rear of the cavalry. The cause of this soon appeared for we had scarce got clear of the ravines when a party of horse, who must have preceded our march and doubled back on the baggage flank, rushed out from behind the gullies and cornfields, where they lay *perdue* on seeing the cavalry run on without leaving any face to protect the baggage, and got among the camels and Banjarrahs, when they began to kill the defenceless followers and Banjarrahs and to carry off multitudes of bullocks loaded with grains. Luckily the commander-in-chief's bodyguard (a troop of the 3rd Cavalry) under Lieutenant Martin happened to be in our rear.

This body charged the enemy instantly, who as quickly fled, leaving several killed and wounded men and horses behind but carrying off numbers of Banjarrahs' bullocks. The whole of the baggage, I do think would have been lost from the imprudence of the cavalry thus abandoning them without protection but for the exertions of this officer, who lost a *havildar* (sergeant native) killed and two horses and who only returned from a vain pursuit, when he saw the infantry in our rear come up.

Our guns, meanwhile, proceeded for more than a mile at a gallop to overtake the cavalry and in real danger, had a spirited enemy known it, of being cut off for want of protection. When we joined the column and squadron of 4th Cavalry and a galloper were sent back at Captain Brown's representation of the state of the baggage, from whom, in a few minutes we heard a cannonade begin and as the enemy were now all round us we unlimbered a gun and a howitzer. On perceiving a party of horse, with elephants and streamers on the outside of the baggage to the right a shell and two shot were fired among them, they instantly dispersed in alarm but to our surprise rode into the column and proved to be some Hindoostanee Horse, escorting a native prince, who is our ally, but who by his imprudence in going on the outside of the baggage and in not having his men so dressed as to be distinguishable from the Maharattas was near losing his life, one of the shot having passed close to his *howdah*.

As it was no mischief was done except that a fragment of the shell took off the hand of a washer-man belonging to our camp. The enemy whom Lieutenant Martin dispersed returned afterwards as we learned and played the same part among the infantry baggage, which, like ours, was left defenceless. They succeeded in carrying off many people's effects and more grain and bullocks. Nay so audacious were they, as, seeing the rear of the park, forsaken by the battalion who should have remained with it, that they cut off a howitzer, and six ammunition and store carts, all of which, excepting two carts, were recovered however, by a few sepoys returning.

The native of rank, whom I have mentioned, offered to go out with his party of horse to drive off the enemy who were thus hanging about us and he accordingly went but such pitiful cowardly work as they both made of it, I never saw. They would ride up brandishing their spears and matchlocks with looks full of ferocity, threatening and *behaudouring* (bravadoing) until they came within 30 yards, when they pulled their horses up on their haunches and discharged their matchlocks without taking any aim! It was truly playing at soldiers. At last after marching between ten and eleven miles without seeing any serious enemy as we were told we should, we encamped about a mile below Muttrah. The reserve, under Lieutenant Colonel Don were pushed into the town, of which they took possession without opposition.

Holkar, we now hear from prisoners and *hurkarrahs* (spies) was in the action of the 2nd, and as soon as the firing began, set off for this place which he left today to join nine guns and some infantry which are four *koss* from here. But so far from intending to give us battle here, his infantry and guns left this seven days ago and his cavalry remained to cover his retreat by impending our march, in which it must succeed in a miracle! Numbers of people have lost more or less baggage this day. The general himself, two elephants! But the chief loss was of grain. I think, I saw fifty or sixty bullock loads laying on the road plundered or deserted, all of which is loss to the Government and on the whole, perhaps 200 or 300 might be cut off. But it is said, how truly I know not that the person whose business it is, to supply those articles has charged for several thousands! *Aimi va le monde*[3] but to us old Indians this is nothing unusual. In truth it is the only way, now that officers established pay is so reduced and clipt of making a half penny and however a fresh man might stare at such conduct yet vice itself every one knows loses its deformity by habit.

October 4th—Captain Wellesley, this day crossed and took possession of Muttrah. Colonel Don returning to camp, still, I suspect the real cause of the halt to be ignorance of Holkar's proceedings, or of what line of conduct we are to pursue. All this day were in perpetual alarm. The enemy's horses who hover round us on every side, are grown so bold that they do not mind our vedettes at all. This day they were constantly driving them in and the piquets, menaced by superior bodies, were obliged several times to send to the inlaying (or in line) piquets for assistance. At 10 at night, by a foolish mistake, we were all turned out of bed and made to stand to our arms for two hours, not a little angry at the disturbance, especially as we received no orders for turning out and indeed so far from the line getting under arms to resist a night attack it was a single troop of the 8th Dragoons going to patrol on our right that made Lieutenant Stark, of our's, take it into his head, without reflecting on the impossibilities of

---

3. Loved throughout the world.

a night attack from natives and at an hour when people were scarce gone to bed that we were all in the greatest danger and must turn out to protect and save ourselves!

October 5th—The in-line picquets of cavalry and a battalion of infantry were sent off to bring to camp a party of 150 recovered sepoys from Agra, who were at some distance, and surrounded by Bungeez Khan a Patan and *Sardar* (Chief) of Holkar's with 4000 horses. At 12, two regiments of cavalry were ordered out to support the first party, but met them returning. The unfortunate sepoys, after expanding all their ammunition were cut up by the enemy. Many, miserably mutilated by the cruel Holkar straggled into camp, some with arms, others with noses or ears cut off by the barbarian Mahratta who treats in this way all the poor creatures who fall into his hands, whether soldiers or followers. What a pleasant idea, to serve against an enemy at whose hands if taken, I am sure to meet torture and death! As to the fate which these poor creatures have met with it is entirely to be attributed to the misconduct of a Colonel Blair Commandant of Agra who sent them off without any European officer and through a country covered with hostile cavalry at whose hands he well knew from experience, they would find no mercy, whilst he might have sent them up the other side of the river when Captain Wellesley did not meet with a single enemy.

Captain Wellesley, in his progress up the Dooab, was ordered to procure grain from the Zemindars paying for it religiously but if they behaved hostilely to him or refused supplying him, with what they could spare, to hand them in terrorism to all other rebels. All this, in the present distracted state of our affairs is absolutely necessary and I hear that Wellesley in consequence of positive refusal to assist us or him, where they had plentiful magazines of all grain, actually did hang several.

October 6th—A requisition has been sent, we understand, to the Rajah of Bhartpoor, demanding of him a formal answer "whether he chooses to attack Holkar in cooperation with us or not?" Poor devil! He is in a said dilemma. He has hitherto stood neutral and consequently Holkar has strictly respected his fields, villages and property. If he assists us Holkar instantly plunders his country. If he does not we shall, by and by and by the bye his refusal is the only chance we have of getting any prize money.

Symptoms of starvation in this day's General Order, camels, public and private are reduced from three seers (6 lb.) of gram daily to one and a half and horses from six to five! In short we now for the first time are entering on a real Mahratta War we fight an enemy numerous as the flies! And who always retire at our approach but never leave us always tormenting us, always infesting us, who cut off our supplies and thus by starving us prevent us from taking any measures of effect, towards concluding the war For aught I, see it may last these ten years! And we shall after all have to patch up an inglorious peace! Colonel Murray, too, who ought to leave by this time, being on this side of the Chambal, writes on the 6th *ultimo* that the monsoon (or as the wits in camp say the *Monson)* has set in his neighbourhood with great violence and prevented his coming.

October 7th—I was yesterday wondering that we did not give them a night attack, no sooner wished than done for at 4 a.m. the army advanced, (leaving the camp standing) in profound silence. Day broke just as we came to a village about a mile from the enemy's camp and three miles from our own. Here was a post of horsemen, who instantly perceived us and leisurely retired to their main body, firing their matchlocks.

The Maharattas lay on a hill 4 miles in front of our camp, a marsh covering their right front, without any regular encampment although plentifully supplied with bazaars but the only tents we saw, were one or two of their chiefs and among the rest of Holkar himself, who, as we certainly knew from previous information and the report of prisoners was in person there and fled at our approach.

When it was quite broad day we were yet half a mile, nearly, from the enemy who instead of retreating covered the hillocks to the amount of 10000 or 12000 at the lowest computation and sent out in front 500 or 600 men who (all horsemen) came very close and fired their pieces incessantly but with little or no effect on the heads of our columns. In consequence of their audacity the Light Infantry of the 76th which led our left column ran out to the flank and fired singly at them. The distance though sufficiently near for their matchlock balls was too great for our muskets and the 76th only killed or wounded one man or two. At this instant we were ordered to charge! Supported by His Excellency's guard under Lieutenant Martin. The enemy, who only saw our horses, took us for cavalry and stood firm enough on their hills and grounds, not less than 10000, until in wheeling round (to bring the muzzle of the guns to bear towards the enemy) they perceived the guns.

That instant and without waiting till we even fired a shot off they scampered as fast their horses could set foot to ground over the hill. An evident proof of what I have said before that if we had been behind and masked by the cavalry instead of being in front of them the enemy would have let us get near enough to use our grape-shot. As it was we could only have a few shells which (owing to some fault, no doubt, in the officer who had charge of them, Lieutenant Stark) burst for the most part in the air and a few useless enough long shots which however, no doubt killed or wounded a good number of the enemy.

Just after the first firing, when we were again moving on, we saw greatly to our right the cavalry in a long line moving slowly forward in the rear, as usual, of their guns, which were, like us, unavailingly running out in front and throwing away ammunition to no purpose. At one time I am convinced the cavalry were near enough to have charged the fugitives with great effect but strange to say they seemed to leave it all to be done by their gallopers.

When we had pursued, as I have said to about two miles beyond their camp, we halted for a little and then slowly returned to join the infantry. As to the good we have done by this clumsy attack I know of none, save that it will frighten the enemy from re-camping so near us. Yet such is their boldness, or rather the nature of their warfare, that although thousands had but just fled from one third their numbers like a flock of terrified sheep these very fellows were bold enough, in our return to camp to hang on the flanks and rear of the columns firing incessantly. Query was this business intended as a surprise?

Some say that at headquarters they had certain intelligence of Holkar in person, with fifteen guns being then encamped and intending to make a stand and that it was meant to offer battle and not to surprise. Why a surprise should be thought less preferable than a battle in due form because the enemy were more on an equality with us, I am really at a loss to understand. But if a surprise was meant, it was most clumsily managed indeed. Does it not seem likely that if instead of forming a 3rd column parallel to the infantry the cavalry had marched an hour sooner, and gone a circuitous route so as to get behind the enemy that multitudes of the latter, would have been destroyed and their retreat cut off? And again if a surprise was meant, why was it so ill timed that we arrived at the enemy's camp a quarter after broad daylight? Those very fifteen minutes would have done our business effectually, for as it was, we completely surprised them and pushed them so that they left on the ground multitudes of clothes, brass and copper plates and dishes, bullocks, horses, *tattoo*[4] and no less a thing than the palanquin of, as we heard from the prisoners, Holkar himself. A sumptuous affair it was of scarlet cloth and gold fringe and tassels etc., etc. Several of the enemy were taken, one in particular a man well dressed and seemingly of consequence.

October 8th—The prisoner of note, whom we took yesterday, turns out to have been a deserter from the 1st Regiment of Cavalry, when the corps was ordered to the coast in Lord Cornwallis War (1792) and at present, was a commander of some hundred horse in Holkar's service. In consequence of this he is to be hanged tomorrow in terrorism to all traitors and deserters. The enemy have collected again in the very same spot where we attacked them, we can see two tents again. By the bye we took a tent yesterday and a *Guthries Geographical Grammar* with several things no doubt taken from Monson's unfortunate detachment. All our servants, lascars and *syces* (horse keepers) got quantities of plunder.

---

4. A small, ugly, weak-looking pony of India that is the most useful little creature I know, carries a load of incredible weight and a rider also frequently and lives on what it picks up. The natives and European soldiers, generally have them to carry their clothes and cooking utensils, etc., etc.

October 9th—Halt again! I fear grain is scarce and that this causes the delay, these infernal Maharattas even cut off all communication with our friends at the gates of Agra.

October 10th—This morning we gave the enemy another alert, much in the same style as on the 7th inst. only that an attempt was made to surprise them by sending off the column of cavalry an hour sooner and round to the rear of their camp which was posted on the individual spot from whence drove them on the 7th. This plan of surprise, I (J.Y. Gentleman) recommended (to myself at least) in my narrative of the affair of the 7th and although no one sees my journal, yet as it was attempted to be pursued this morning it is clear that my speculations on the aforesaid topic were those of an excellent general whence it may be plainly inferred that were these, my lucubrations, perused at headquarters, the army and the public service would be immensely benefited thereby. But "true merit is always neglected"!

It is a singular thing that in every expedition made by our army where, as in the present instance, there is something of an idea of a plan and God knows these kind of expeditions are few enough in number some part or other of it always goes wrong. I do think it is to be attributed entirely to the want of sufficient number of staff officers, in the quartermaster general's and guide department. In our service at home they are far more numerous than in India but on the continent and specially in the French armies, not a brigade, not a wing of an army, but has an intelligent and professionally educated officer of this kind. These officers, previous to an attack reconnoitre with and assist the quartermaster general in laying down the plans and routes and one of them, conducts every column to it's point of attack. Whereas in this present Grand Army of Bengal, there is but one individual (Major Salkeld, Deputy Quartermaster General) to conduct the whole business of this department, of all others in an army, the most important.

It is not therefore matter of wonder that when the guidance of several columns proceeding by different routes to the same point of attack is entrusted to the officers commanding these corps who have no correspondence with each other, nor knowledge of the plan and it's details, nor acquaintance with the route, either from personal observation or collected from surveys and maps, such attacks should fail. There is no unity of cooperation, one part of the machinery, acting in a wrong manner spoils the effect of the whole. It is not the main spring alone but anyone of the minutest wheels going wrong that ruins the clock work.

The infantry and our light guns advanced in precisely the same order and manner as on the 7th, only a little earlier, we nicked the time to a minute but the way Holkar, who had not forgot the last business, was not to be a second time surprised. The instant we approached, after firing at us a few matchlocks, the enemy retired with precipitation. Their camp and bazaars having previously been sent off, we advanced over the hill, and descended on the other side. The whole horizon was covered with horse in one prodigious line with innumerable standards. At this time we turned to the left to encounter the largest body of seemingly not less than 10,000 or 12,000 and now we wanted the cavalry column but could see nothing of them. The general was very impatient and vexed to lose the opportunity of attacking this body who seemed to stand very steady at last with the 6th Regiment, who were covering our guns and his own body guard. Our guns advanced.

The enemy did not wait for our approach, but fled with the utmost speed. We now saw the whole of the horse on the right and front of the horizon, galloping at utmost speed off to the left and looking back saw it was occasioned by the cavalry column which at last we saw about four miles off (they having gone much too far off to the right) charging and following up the enemy. Had they, according to what I know from hearing the commander-in-chief say so was pointed out to them, kept less to the right and got behind the enemy they must have killed vast numbers and even as it was although the body of the cavalry never could come up with the foe, yet they steadily pursued them for five or six miles detaching flankers to skirmish with and cut up all they overtook by which the enemy it is supposed lost near a hundred killed and several prisoners and horses taken.

By the time we and they had got about five or six miles from our camp seeing that there was no possibility of overtaking this truly dastardly enemy the general ordered us to return which we did, harassed by the Maharattas in our rear the whole way. Of the prisoners, one was a *Sardar* of note, who expected that the general would treat him as his barbarian master treats his prisoners. Instead of which, to his infinite surprise he and the other captives were told that it was not the English practice to maltreat or kill their prisoners, were decried to go and tell Holkar so and were conducted safe beyond our picquets to return.

October 13th—We encamped at Chatta, a large town with an old but strong fort of stone, on a commanding and picturesque situation. We now have learned that at 11, on the night of the 11th October Holkar and his principal force quitted their camp opposite our's at Muttra and it is supposed went off to Delhi to which place it is said, his Infantry, with no less than 170 guns, are laying siege and whither we are hastening after them. There is no part of the art of war, in which we are so superior to the natives, as that of besieging. Indeed they are utterly ignorant of it and therefore seldom succeed in ought but blockading.

October 14th—A foolish *zemindar* of a village fort which we past today refused to open his gates to the general, or to supply us with grain and kept Holkar's colours flying. Observe this is no country of Holkar's, but of the Bhartpoor Rajah, our supposed ally. A few hints from the Deputy Quartermaster General Major Salkeld upon the efficacy of a 12-pounder in opening gates, bagged by the appearance of some of these very arguments, with the army, passing by wonderfully enlightened his understanding. But scarce had we passed by when a film came a second time over the poor man's understanding and he called in 500 Pindaries, who as usual were hanging about our rear to convince a guard of a few sepoys, left with him to bring grain that they had the worst of the dispute. Before these able seasoners, however, arrived the sepoys dissipated, the delusive mist that danced before this refractory *zemindar's* eyes by bringing him off to camp bound hand and foot. Happily for the finances of the subalterns of this army and of none more than J. Y. Gentleman poorest of the poor we are likely yet to have some prize money. A *dawk* (post) of Holkar's has been intercepted, by which it appears that our faithful and magnanimous ally, the Bhartpoorian, has not only assisted Holkar with money and provisions, but with guns and troops, so that after beating Holkar or driving him from Delhi we are off at a tangent for Bhartpoor and it's three *crores* of rupees

October 15th—This morning sixteen miles to Bominakupa, we did not get to the ground till past 2 p.m. and then were not a little tired. This marching so long, so slow and so late is a terrible drawback on journalizing so far from being able to enrich my journal with observations or news I think myself exceedingly diligent if I even spare so much time from my couch as to keep an account of the marches and dates. We are out of bed before 4 a.m., come to the ground by 2 p.m. Eating our breakfast takes up another hour, the happiest by the bye we have from 3 to 5, we lay down to rest or if we have a book, to read, it is then evening and time to dress for parade and dinner, then to bed till 4 again. Thus it is we spend our time, not merely spend, but waste it say their *ami Lecteur!* Can you in justice expect entertainment from a journal written as such a time as this?

October 18th—Marched to the banks of the Jumnah, close under the Imperial city of Delhi. We could only distinguish the approach to this city, once the greatest and richest in the world from the surrounding country, by the nakedness and sterility of it. It is indeed a perfect desert of rocks and stones, with ruins interspersed plentifully far as the eye can reach.

The prospect is the same on this side of the river and yet the side of Delhi, on which we lie, is not for horrible desolation and ruin even to be named in comparison with the opposite side above the river. This I have not yet seen, nor am I likely this time to do so, as Holkar's guns and Infantry left this only three days ago and have only got ten *koss* off from want of grain and badness of the draught bullocks. Holkar is therefore obliged to make a stand, compelled to it as he is by despair. I doubt not but it will be a most obstinate one.

All the *Banjarrahs,* 12-pounders and heavy park stores, tents and camels, public and private, with the exception of a very small proportion to each corps are to be sent into Delhi. And tomorrow morning, without even a day's halt to arrange matters, we set off after him.

Who is to take care of our cattle and tents or how the animals are to be provided with forage or food is a consideration, I suppose infinitely, of too small moment to be even thought of by those who provided themselves in all camp equipage at the public expense. Never reflect that all the little fortune of an unfortunate subaltern is vested in his camels and tent and his little stock of liquor and cloths and that if these are lost or destroyed he must be ruined, and unable to replace them.

I wish we may not be going on a goose-chase after this man. I fear the ten *koss* will turn out nearer twenty and if he betakes him to the direction of the Punjaub, where water is almost as scarce, as in the desert of Egypt, and as he leaves an encampment, poisons or fills up the few wells there are, we shall be in a most awkward predicament. If however we can take his guns before he escapes into that inhospitable country, he will then loose the terror of his name which his artillery supports and every Rajah will turn against him. Still the war will not be at an end. Far as Indore his country is already taken by us. He has no kingdom to return to and must go into other's possessions, plundering for support and, if he can weather it out till our army recrosses the Jumnah, he may return again to plunder the very country from which we have now compelled him to retire.

As I may not again return to Delhi I take this opportunity of mentioning that we passed by the celebrated Mausoleum of Humaion, one of the Emperors who died. It is much in the plan of the Taj at Agra, a large square platform with the octangular tomb in the centre surrounded by a dome. As I had not it in my power to see the inside at all, nor to view the outside but at a distance, I cannot be minute in description but one thing I must say, that like all the buildings I have seen in India, except the Taj itself, this is of red stone and marble intermixed which is to me always disagreeable. The dome alone is of one white marble, in the rest the red predominates. I saw the remains this day of two bridges, the only ones I have seen in India. One was plain and of four arches, the other, near Humaion's tomb, highly ornamented, in good repair and of eight or nine pointed arches.

October 20th—After breakfast, I went to visit the Imperial city of Delhi. Once the proudest metropolis in the world if we are to believe the native accounts, or even those of the few European travellers, who visited it in the last two centuries. That it's present mean and miserable appearance is to be attributed entirely, or at all, to the ravages of it's successive conquerors and plunderers, or to the decays of consuming time, is I am convinced a mistaken idea. To the eye, accustomed to regard as a standard of taste, that simple magnificence in public building and that general uniformity in private houses. That width, and regular intersection of streets which we see more or less observed in every capital of Europe. The narrow and mean streets. The incongruous mixture and proximity to each other of magnificent mosques and filthy hovels, common to Delhi with every Indian city I have yet seen, never could have appeared other than paltry and mean. It's extent however, when viewed from the minaretes of the grand mosque is truly wonderful. The ruins of old Delhi extend "far as the eye can reach" on all sides but the S.E. towards which quarter of the horizon are to be seen.

The old Fort of Delhi, strong, and a square of considerable size flanked with round towers, built by Sher Shah and in which stands the building, down the stairs, of which Humaion fell and lost his life. About a mile from this fort stands the Mausoleum of Humaion himself, encompassed with bridges, serais, tombs and remnants of departed greatness, of every description. Above the town of Delhi, in proud and solitary magnificence, frowning upon the hovels which rudely press to it's very ditch, stands the Laul Qilah, or Red Fort, the residence of the old and blind Emperor of Hindoostan, and beyond it but connected by a bridge, is the Citadel, or Fort of Selimghur. Both these forts are situated close on the banks of the river. Selimghur seems very old and ready to tremble down. In the Laul Qilah stand the royal palaces, situated close on the river, of white marble and having gaudy domes and pavilions of copper gilts. All the etiquette of the Mogul court, when in the zenith of its splendour and power, is yet rigidly adhered to by the shadow, who yet represents the house of Timour and we could not obtain admittance to any of the royal apartments.

In the Zenanah are said to live many hundreds of princesses of the blood royal, descendants, to the 4th or 5th generation of former Emperors and condemned by the cruel policy of the reigning Emperors, to spend their days in confinements. To which, at last, as is said, they are from habit, an intermarriage with their royal and imprisoned relatives, so totally reconciled, as to prefer remaining in their splendid confinement, where without exertion they are supplied with food and luxuries, to a precarious liberty, a scanty meal, earned by themselves. However a detester of tyranny and lover of freedom must regret the necessity of this state policy. Yet a perusal of the massacres and revolutions and assassinations, of the patricides and fratricides which make up the history of the Court of Delhi for centuries past will convince them at a glance, how necessary to the happiness to the lives of millions in the present state of society in India this arbitrary measure is "The more's, the pity"! His aged Majesty, blind as he is at 78 years of age, still continues to observe the scriptural precept to increase and multiply with all the devotion of a good Christian. 300 issues of the royal loins being now in the land of the living and their number, as we hear, daily increasing! The Laul Qilah, is full of the remains of the splendour of better days, of squares and arched ways and palaces of painted brick work and rich mosaic all, all in decay!

The Jamma Musjid, or Grand Mosque, is in the centre of the city nearby. The approach to it on four sides by streets somewhat more regularly than usual, in right lines for 200 yards before they meet at right angles at the Cathedral. The ascent to the grand platform on which the mosque is built is in front, to the right, and left, by three magnificent and truly noble flights of steps of broad red stone. These introduce you to a spacious platform of the same materials, surrounded on three sides by a cloister and on the fourth by the Mosque and having in the centre, a basin of

The Jamma Musjid

water. The Mosque is constructed, as usual with a large dome in the centre, and a somewhat smaller on each side, so that the depth of it is very small, in proportion to it's length. The entrance is by a grand pointed arch and the whole of the flooring of white marble beautifully inlaid with black. The appearance of the pointed arches which form the vaulted roofs of these mosques is very much like that of the aisle in a European cathedral, and is grand and solemn. The extreme angles of the front, to the right and left, are continued up to a very great height, forming two minarets or columns, crowned with octagonal pavilion of white marble.

The minarets are of black or red and white stripes and the interior of the Mosque of white marble or alabaster, while the exterior is of red stone, variously chequered with white marbles. But for this admission of different colours, this edifice would be nearly faultless, and it is on the whole the finest Eastern building I have seen and worthy of it's distinguished home. The view from the minarets is truly astonishing. The extent of the city within the walls, and still more the ruins of what was without occupy the horizon, on three sides as far as the eye can reach, even from the great height of these towers. There are in this city numerous other mosques of all sizes, and decorated differently, in scale, however and richness of workmanship and materials, alone do they differ from each other. The plan, and general effect, is much the same in all. In passing under the city walls we see numbers of practicable breaches made by Holkar and where the miserable ruined suite of the walls, the extent to be defended.

The immense force of men and artillery of it's besiegers and the men, handful of a garrison that had to defend this place, it becomes more and more a subject of astonishment that it was not taken. Nor can sufficient praise be given to Lieutenant Colonel Burn (14th Regiment) who commanded and his brave garrison, for their defence of it. Nor should it be omitted to mention, that for the first time since Delhi existed, it was now defended, and by a British garrison.

Lieutenant Colonel Burn, by a most spirited, and necessary act of severity, contributed as much perhaps to saving the city, as by the bravery of his troops. The armies of the native powers in

India are accustomed, on every occasion of danger, of difficulty and danger, when they perceive how necessary they are to their employers, to refuse compliance with orders, until pecuniary demands are complied with, frequently unjust ones and at any rate ill-timed. Colonel B had some corps of native infantry and horse in his garrison, on the approach of the Maharattas, having ordered a part of them on some service, they refused to stir until two months arrears, due to them with the rest of the army, were paid up, and two more given in advance.

The colonel judging it best to stop in the outset so dangerous a mutiny especially at such an alarming crisis, when with a mutinous garrison within, and a besieging force without all hopes of raising the siege would be fruitless, paraded his regular troops and the artillery opposite to the irregulars, required formal compliance with his orders and on reference seized fourteen ringleaders. He informed the chiefs of the irregulars of his intentions and his reasons for so doing, then from one of his six pounders, without further ceremony, blew away a *jemidar* and *duffadar* the mutineers of highest rank and to twelve others gave 1000 lashes each. The irregulars astonished and terrified submitted without murmurs to their duty and Delhi was saved by this act of severity, in the eyes of military men and those who knew the native character, not only justifiable, but in the highest degree laudable.

October 22nd—The cool, or as from contrast in this burning country it is called the cold season, seems to be set in. The same sun, which on the 18th was scarce bearable, is now quite tempered by the coolness of the wind. At 11 this forenoon, a party of us rode to see the splendid mausoleum of the Emperor Humaion, situated about two miles from camp and become from the weakness of the Mogul Government, the frequent residence, as well as all the surrounding country to the very walls of Delhi of the Mewalties or Goojars. A whole nation of professional robbers and banditti who inhabit all hilly or desolated countries of Hindoostan, sally out armed on all travellers or even army followers, plunder and commonly murder a like friend or foe, European or native, Hindoo or Moosulmaun. Many attempts have been made by Ackber and Aurangzeeb, especially to extricate them root and branch, the only way to remove this pest, as their children are regularly trained to the business and even their wives and daughters, go forth to rob and murder. But these attempts have as yet failed, both from the numbers of the Goojars, and from their taking to their inaccessible fortresses among the hills and rocks. Should we ever gain a firm footing in this neighbourhood, some similar attempts must be made by our Government if we would either ourselves live in peace or with our *ryots* to cultivate and the merchant to travel in security. Horrible idea! Of extricating a whole nation humanity revolts at the measure which, however imperious, necessity loudly demands, when life and property to the unoffending are at stake and when all attempts to conciliate have failed.

The tomb is at present deserted by its usual tenants and few sepoys placed in it, both to keep it as an outpost, and to prevent their returning while our camp is so near. The edifice is a very grand one upon the usual plan of tombs here and immense and spacious platform of twenty feet high or more a square and vaulted below. In the walls are deposited, besides that of Humaion, the bodies of several Emperors and many royal children, some of the present King's among the number. This terrace, is of red stone and wherever a grave is below a cenotaph of white marble rises exactly above on the platform, which is thus studded with many white stones. In the centre of the platform rises the main body of the building, octagonal, of red stone chiefly crowned with a lofty cupola of white marble considerably higher than that of the Taj. The interior consists, besides the central room under the dome where is the large block of marble pointing out the grave of Humaion, of eight surrounding chambers, most of them occupied by the frail memorials of royal personage. The interior of the dome is lighted up to the very top by tiers of windows filled with screen work of red stone of capital workmanship.

A canopy of gold or silver, is recorded as in the Taj at Agra, to have been suspended from the centre of the dome by a chain of the same materials and numerous musket spot holes are seen yet in the stucco and the screen work of one of the highest windows, is demolished, when, they tell us, the Jats fired their pieces at this desired canopy until they broke the suspending chain and it fell. Of all the parts of this grand structure, that which pleases me most is the flooring, which is done in mosaic work of different geometrical figures in partly coloured stones, with much taste. One monstrous fault in the platform is, that instead of a grand access to the terrace, as to the Jamma Musjid, the only ascents to this magnificent square are by four pitiful flights of steps, at the centres of the sides and from which you pass through trapdoors, or rather trap ways, on the summit. This building, although it has in common with most others the fault of mingled colours of white and red, has yet much less to chequer the uniformity of the red ground than usual and is one the whole a grand magnificent edifice.

October 23rd—We hear the Bhartpoor Rajah has made his peace with the general, "*tant pis.*" Whatever seems he may come down with to purchase his peace and well I know on those terms alone, we ever forgive the army will get none of it.

October 25th—This morning Lieutenant Colonel Burn and the 2nd Battalion, 14th Regiment marched from here into the Dooab, with the ultimate view of restoring quiet at Sehaurunpoor, in Lat. 29 N., one of our acquisitions by the Scindian peace, last year and where, notwithstanding the profound peace and tranquillity which certain addresses, (received by certain Governor General as containing authentic matter of congratulation) affirm to reign in all the ceded and conquered provinces.

The Seiks have made an irruption and the people have rebelled, burning and destroying the cantonments and even compelling the judge and civil servants to take refuge in a fort. Lieutenant Colonel Burn is besides to reduce some towns and forts in his way, for which purpose he has taken, besides his field pieces, two or three 18-pounders. Judge all, who by reading or experience, know how the ordnance department are conducted in France, in England, in Europe how they are carried on here and what a corps of artillery we have in Bengal. When I tell you that with this train, there is not a single artillery or engineer officer, the five or six with the "grand army of India" being already too few to spare even one, but what is even worse, these 18-pounders have no ammunition, not shot I mean, and are to depend for a supply of that rather necessary article for a siege on what they, or the resident at Delhi can procure.

October 26th—The General Orders of this day, (when we halted again) were taken up, first, with most handsome thanks from the commander-in-chief to Lieutenant Colonels Burn, and Octerloney and the garrison of Delhi for their gallant defence of the city. And secondly with the necessary arrangements for carrying into effect and order of the Governor General in Council, for raising four additional regiments of native infantry of two battalions (or 2000 men) each for the Bengal establishment. This is said to be only apart of what is intended to be done towards increasing the army of this establishment. Three more regiments of infantry and two of cavalry, are confidently talked of, but not a single artillery man!

The force of Bengal will then consist of, besides four regiments of European Infantry and three of European Cavalry, of 60,000 Native Infantry and 4000 Native Cavalry to do the whole of the garrisons, field artillery duties, which army and of five or six forts and garrisons. There are nominally 2100 European Artillery. *Really!* (For they have never yet been nearly complete). About 600 or 700 Europeans and about 200 or 300 Golundauze, (or native) Artillery men.

No state in the civilized world has nearly so small a proportion, France and the great continental European states, are out of the question. England, during the last peace, had eight battalions of 1000 or 1200 each and seven troops of Horse Artillery. Their Majesties even of Portugal, Naples or *ci-devant* Sardinia had far more with regard to cherishing and fostering what is, or ought to be, a scientific line of service, as it is one, acknowledged, in the ignorance of European ideas, to be of the greatest *use* of any, in the act of war. The French, Austrians, Prussians, the English even are weak enough, to encourage this corps, (the artillery) by giving him every advantage, in point of rank and honours, over the other lines of the service where talents are not expected and scarcely necessary.

According, however, to our more enlarged Indian ideas on these matters rank-enrolment and command go in the inverse ratio of utility to the state. Thus, whereas in England, the artillery battalions have a field officer (a colonel in second) more in proportion than the infantry, so in India the artillery have two in proportion, fewer than the infantry and three fewer than the cavalry! But the depression under which our service lies in this country, from this, and a 100 other similar causes, is too serious a subject for joking. In February 1802 an addition of six companies of artillery was made to our regiment but not a single field officer was added with them.

If we and the officers of the infantry or cavalry were on a footing formerly, (when the army in 1798 was re-organised) if it was intended that we should not in future be deprived of our equality in this grand respect of promotion, both which points were contained in the spirit of the orders of 98 and were besides, at the instance of the artillery representatives in 94, five and six stipulated for and agreed to by our masters of Leaden Hall street and His Majesty's Ministers. Why, on augmentation of the inferior ranks, was not an equal and fair proportion of the higher, or the field officers, also given to us? What political or military sin has our unfortunate corps singly committed, to be singly excluded from the benefit of our equal chance of attaining a field officers rank and consequent pension! That object, of all others the first in the prospects of an Indian officer and on account of which alone the equality of chance to promotion to the higher ranks was bestowed on all branches of the army alike.

Our unfortunate captain, stands at the head of the list of captains in the army, while captains two and three years their juniors have become lieutenant colonels of infantry or cavalry. For when these corps have been increased, they have always had the proportion of field officers added also. As Colonel Greene, the Commandant of Artillery, at the presidency is a selfish man, devoted to himself alone and totally devoid of *espirit du corps* or the most remote ideas of public spirit. We have never been able to interest him in our cause, but our present commanding officer in this army, Lieutenant Colonel Horsford, an officer of the highest professional ability, as well as the most general knowledge and literature whom it were injurious to name in the same page with the former man, sensible of the cruel injustice under which the corps laboured, both from immediate supersession and ultimate retardation of promotion, presented in October 1803 to His Excellency the Commander-in-Chief, then before Agra, a memorial, stating our wrongs and begging redress from Government through His Excellency's mediation. The general professed himself sensible of our wrongs and declared he would forward the memorial to Government.

A year has since elapsed, no notice has been taken of us or our petition, yet daily additions are made to the infantry to the cavalry and every such increases but adds to the injuries we have sustained! Captain Harowick of the artillery, the senior Captain of the Regiment and the principal sufferer, on going home in 1802, was furnished by Colonel Horsford with a similar memorial, to be presented to the Court of Directors. He printed it, signed it on behalf of himself and his brother officer in Bengal. The Court were graciously pleased to declare themselves penetrated by our hardships and sensible of our wrongs. They then consigned it to oblivion, we now, as the last resource have some thoughts of asking our Colonel (Horsford) to press His Excellency. the Commander-in-Chief for at least the honour of an answer from Government at least a Yes! or No! A favour we have not, in twelve months been able to obtain.

October 27th—The Dooab is all in arms, even our own provinces which we got from the Vizier, in 1801 are all in rebellion. The cantonments and officer's bungalows and property, at Chandoussy and Khassgunge are burnt among others by the inhabitants. This day Lieutenant M. W. Browne, Quartermaster of the artillery in camp, and I, met at his tent, to frame a letter to Lieutenant Colonel Horsford, to be signed by the artillery officers in camp, requesting him to obtain, if possible from the commander-in-chief some answer relating to the artillery petition of last year on the subject of field officers. This letter was meant to submit to the artillery officers, now in the army, for approbation and signature. God grant that it may succeed!

October 28th—News, that in addition to the other disturbers of peace in the Dooab, the Begum Sumroo, whose history is well known, has turned out against us with four battalions and 20 guns of her own troops of celebrity, at least among the natives, having been originally raced and commanded by Europeans.

October 29th—Yesterday Captain Nelly, the senior artillery officer in camp delivered to Colonel Horsford a letter signed by all of us except one, who although no doubt he will rejoice to benefit by our exertions, does not choose to take upon himself, even the small share of responsibility, that would attach to his share of the address were it either criminal, or unjustifiable. Whereas it is the humblest, of humble petitions merely requesting the commanding officer to put His Excellency the Commander-in-Chief in mind of petition forwarded by him, on our behalf to Government a whole year ago and to which even a Yes or No has not been deigned. The officer to whom I have alluded, knows well enough that the request will not be the less or more granted or denied for want of the signature of so insignificant an individual as he, for more reasons than one is, and should it be granted he will without danger of trouble, be one of the first to benefit by it. Should it be refused he will not doubt pique himself vastly on his penetration in seeing the folly or impropriety of subjects, using their undoubted rights to humbly petition their Governor for redress.

Another for this generous and public spirited conduct in the person alluded to I have heard alleged, *viz.*, that he had not common sense enough to discriminate between modest request, and mutinous remonstrance but had declared "that he would never put his hand to anything," "is a second denial!," "a very solemn this!" "With regard to these different opinions", as Sir Roger De Coverby says "much may be said on both sides." Be this as it may, Colonel Horsford, in his observations on the subject to the officers has handed him down to recorded and deserved contempt.

I blush to add, that the officer I allude to, is a particular brother officer of mine in the troop of horse artillery. His name! sicken with envy, hide your diminished heads, the abject time servers, the sycophants and courtiers, is in mercy I erase his name.

The colonel forwarded his officers request to headquarters in a most nervous and manly letter in his very best style, particularly dwelling on the aggravation to our distresses and supersessions, occasioned by the total refusal of even a simple answer. And the serious loss of a whole year, to the artillery, during which time, their petition would have been sent to, and answered by the Court of Directors, and the numerous supersessions we suffer by the additions to the infantry, cavalry either not have existed, or have been patiently born, as irremediable!

October 31st—As I dined this day at headquarters, I was in great hopes of being able to pick up the cause of our late movement. I could not however succeed, certain it is, that Holkar with a large body of horse, crossed about fifty miles above Delhi, on hearing that Colonel Burn had marched for Sahauranpoor with so small a body of men. He attacked the colonel, at the very time too, when sepoys are least prepared to resist, while cooking their dinner after a long march. The colonel repulsed him, with very great loss, but as must ever be the case in fighting, without cavalry, against an enemy abounding with force of that description, he lost part of his baggage, and it is feared, all his camels with provisions.

We shall probably go as far as Sahauranpoor to drive away the invading Seiks but as to the *begum,* we apprehend no resistance from her, indeed we have left her, I hear, behind us so that all co-operation between her and Holkar, is effectively couped in this case. This *begum,* for the benefit of the Country Gentlemen I tell it, is not one of the princesses celebrated in Burkian Oratory, but the ruler of a fief nominally under the Mogul though like other feudatories, she long ago made herself independent. *Sommers,* or as the natives called him, *Sumroo,* was a deserter from the Company's service. A German, of most atrocious character, infamous for having been the only person, the natives to a man declining the business that could be found to conduct the celebrated and horned massacre of the English gentlemen at Patna, He was at this time in the Nawaub of Moorshidabad's service, afterwards passed into Sujahdowlah of Oude's. From this he was driven on our compelling that prince to make peace in 1764 or

1765. He went into several other services after this and at least into that of lady in question, whom he converted to Christianity, by mere force of argument no doubt, for she immediately after married him. He died several years ago but his or her troops, from his great military abilities, were the best in Hindoostan.

The lady herself is an Amazon and more than once has headed her own troops in person. On one memorable occasion, she saved perhaps the life of the present Emperor by her personal heroism. She was last campaign, in the confederacy with Scindia against us and the very battalions, against whom we are said to be now marching, were in the battle of Assaye and conducted themselves with great credit. We detached her afterwards from her alliance and she withdrew her troops. Now again, I doubt not, from some rough diplomatic treatment on our parts, she is if not hostile, at least strongly suspected.

CHAPTER 4
November 1804

November 1st—All India sounds the alarm of war again. A correspondence is said to have been intercepted between Scindia, the Berar Rajah, our late enemies and the very man in whose behalf we pretend we took up arms, the Paishwah. I wish the Nizam and our protege the Mysore Rajah may prove staunch. Our conduct, in honest truth it must be said, does not deserve they should. Our treatment of native powers in peace, only differs from that in war in as much as, one is open attack, the other insidious aggression, under the hypocritical masque of friendship. The end, is in both cases, one and the same, that of despoiling them and enriching ourselves.

Major General D. Campbell, of Madras has taken the field with a strong corps of observation in Mysore and Colonel Barry Close, of the same establishment, an officer celebrated equally for diplomatic and military talents has put himself as the head of the united subsidiary forces of Hydrabad and Poonah. In case of a rupture with Berar, our whole frontier from Allahabad to Cuttack, including the prospect of the rich cities of Benares and Patna, is open to his pillaging horse, as it was under Aliverdy Khan in 1743, 1744, 1745 etc., etc. and from the small number of our troops requiring all we had to be collected in the Dooab, to oppose Holkar.

In that enormous extent of frontier, within the provinces there are not 10 battalions and no 2 together. I tremble to think of it. To add to our domestic disturbances, the turbulent Rohillas, in the ceded provinces, are emphatically said in the language of the natives to be sharpening their swords! In Europe, this might admit of the question whether the swords were to be used for or against the Government. We in India, no better, and our conscience tell us against whom the swords are getting ready! A *zemindar* of these people at Burrelly the capital of the ceded district, has it is said, refused his tribute to the collector, insolently adding "He was keeping his money for Holkar!" All the country around Gwalior is up and villages are mightily burning around them. When will all this end?

November 2nd—This morning at half-past five, we commenced a march the severest and longest by far that ever I have yet experienced. The cause of this hurry, was that Holkar, burning perhaps with the shame of the defeat his troops sustained at Delhi from brave old Colonel Burn, had, on hearing of the march of this single battalion, hurried with numbers of horse to cut them off. Old Burn, in the unequal conflict and totally without cavalry, lost all his provisions, and after repulsing the enemy at all hands, took up his ground under a fort and village named Shamley. The inhabitants of which refused to give him an atom of grain, being secretly in the interest of Holkar, who was there in person. Holkar is perpetually harassing the Old Boy and as often beat back but the detachment is totally without provisions of any kind and blockaded on all hands. This has been the case for three days.

November 3rd—When we were starting in the morning before sun rise, we heard several great guns firing and supposed *"Old Burn and Cyclops"*[1] to be hard at it. As however we expected momentarily to be pestered with our old our old friends *Pindaries*, we were obliged to move on slowly, that the baggage might keep up well with the line.

About 11, as we approached Shamley we were surprised with a sudden cannonade seemingly quiet close but by the regularity and number of the explosions (17). We soon found that it was a salute to the general fired by old Colonel Burn, from the little enclosure, scarce deserving the name of a mud fort, where his brave little detachment were shut up and had been besieged for five days. During which time the Hindoos, and especially

---

1. Holkar has but one eye.

the higher *castes* who may not eat sheep nor goat's flesh, were reduced to the lowest state of weakness by hunger not a particle of grain having been with the detachment all this time. Colonel Burn, for two days before he arrived at Shamley having been kept in a perpetual skirmish by 12,000 or 15,000 horse daily increasing, in numbers and boldness, took possession on his arrival of the city and Fort of Shamley having led Holkar to imagine he was proceeding onwards, while in fact he was returning into the place and thus giving him the slip.

Finding the city of too great size to be defended by his small party, and what was still worst, every man in it an open or concealed enemy, the colonel withdrew entirely into the fort in hopes Holkar, after plundering, would go off and let him pursue his route to Sahauranpoor. But finding that Holkar sat fairly down before him, and having no means of holding out, nor expectations of relief, he called his officers together and acquainted them with his resolution of storming the enemy's camp that night, and of cutting his way through them to Delhi or dying in the attempt. At this critical moment a *hircarrah* from Colonel Ochterlony at Delhi, arrived with the joyful intelligence of our army being on their way to his relief and the starving sepoys exclaimed that since the general was coming, they would hold out for five days more with pleasure, they had already parted for four.

Holkar's troops took possession of the city as soon as our troops left it and they, with the town's people, got on the tops of their high houses and gateways, that quiet looked down into the little fort, whence they kept up an eternal firing at individual officers or men. Night and day every now and then however, a ball from one of the 6-pounders used to bring down the slender parapets and the Maharattas behind them. As our army passed the fort, we saw the bodies of two Maharattas, half-eaten by the dogs and putrid, close under the walls. These fellows had the imprudence, with many others, constantly to be coming to the walls and attempting to reduce our sepoys, who in return shot them. The language the enemy used was remarkable.

"What are we and you fighting with each other for? Are we not all brothers? natives of this country! Yet you are fighting for a parcel of foreigners, of *fringies*,[2] who have no business in our country at all. Come and serve the *Maha Rajah* (Great Prince) Jaswunt Rao Holkar you shall have 16 rupees a month and a woman for nothing. Only just seize the *Old Fellow* (Colonel B) and throw him over to us, we'll teach him to defend places! The Maha Rajah will give 10,000 rupees for his head and 1,000 for that of every fringy you give up to us."

The enemy lost many men and several horses we saw their graves about the fort and when they heard of the great general's approach. In reward for the treachery of the *zemindar*, or headman of the Shamley, they plundered the city and scampered off in all directions. On our encamping here the general having heard of the treacherous conduct of the headman in refusing us provisions, trying to betray us to the enemy and finally firing on our men with his troops (observed, he is our subject, and submitted to us a year ago), His Excellency ordered a gun up to blow open the town gates and ordered also some battalions to enter and put to death every armed man and to seize all grain etc. they could find. On the gate being opened the town was discovered to be deserted by all except old men, cripples, women and children, and all the shops and property open to anyone. The sepoys and Europeans accordingly were permitted I believe, and at all events certainly did, plunder at a fine rate all that day. Shawls, cloths, sugar, cattle, thread, pickles, sweetmeats and all sorts of grain were as plenty this day as rubbish in the camp. The grain was reserved for the public use. The rest anyone got who chose to take it. One dragoon, got sixteen pair of shawls.

November 4th—The Commissary of bazaars, Captain Morrison, and the Gram Agent, Major Campbell, were all this day busied in collecting grain in the city, and a few bold plunderers, still found a few gleanings. Well! a town delivered over to the fury of an enraged soldiery, after an assault, must be truly dreadful. I judge of it by what was to be seen yesterday in a comparatively peaceful sacking, when no resistance was made. When

---

2. *Europeans, Franks, Frangies* in Turkey and Egypt. The word is the same and though of itself, no term of abuse, yet it is so applied by custom to Europeans by *enemies,* in lieu of *Sahib* or *Master.*

were none but women and children, where not a life was taken nor a woman violated yet the distress and lamentations of these poor creatures, robbed probably of their all and deserted by their fathers and husbands and sons, were truly dreadful.

November 6th—Marched on the high road to Sardanha or Saldanha, the *Begum's* capital, on our way, we passed a very large walled city of that princess named Boorhana, which was surrounded with the richest cultivation, and seems to have been, or indeed still to be, a very considerable place. It's situation is good, and there is in the centre, a very tolerable mosque as for as we could judge at least by its appearance, from without the town , for, to prevent the rascally camp followers entering and plundering the places we pass, a guard of sepoys is placed at every village till all the army and baggage is gone by and the gates of all are shut. By the bye the least collection of houses, scarce deserving the application of village, is surrounded with a mud wall to prevent plunderers, so frequent here. This country is indeed a very fertile and fine one, although it abounds with the thickest jungle, yet wherever cultivation is *viz*. for a good way round all villages and towns the crops of sugar, canes, cotton, indigo and all kinds of grain, are most luxuriant, The first of these, affords I should mention, a most delicious feed to weary marches, the sweet of the growing canes, being not only most agreeable to suck but quite uncloying to the stomach.

This evening, late at night Mr. Grethise, the Civil Magistrate of Sahauranpoor, so long besieged there by Seiks and rebels, arrived in camp from Saldanha. He was pent up at the former place for several months, and was totally without hopes of relief when the *Begum* sent one of her battalions to bring him off safe and so far from being in the least degree hostile to us, this prudent lady, not only treated Mr. Grethise with every kindness, but so late as yesterday, gave a positive refusal to a demand of Holkar's for assistance.

November 8th—A *dawk* from Delhi, of the 4th arrived here today, the first we have had, A letter from General Fraser's army mentions that they were to march next day on the Muttra road, against Holkar's guns and Infantry, which are we hear at Lasswarree or Kassowly, the very spot where a year ago the decisive victory, that ruined Sindhia, was gained by us, *omen hand malum!*

November 10th—Marched to the neighbourhood of Malaghur. Our camp was pitched on the banks of the Kaly "Nuddy" or "Nullah." A tributary stream which falls into the Ganges, between Canouge and Futtyghur. The Fort of Malaghur was on the opposite bank of the river. It seems very strong and built of mud. The chief man of it, saluted the commander-in-chief, on our pitching our camp here. From the irregularity, and prodigious time between each discharge, I apprehend one gun only was used, probably there are no more.

A report prevails in camp that a *zemindar* of our's at Anopsheher, known of old, for a disaffected fellow, has, on hearing that Holkar was ravaging the Dooab, collected five guns, and 5000 or 6000 men and given battle to a small detachment of sepoys, under Colonel Grueber, who has beat him with considerable loss on both sides. By way of set off I should now mention, that a *zemindar* or chief of a considerable town and district through which we passed this day, came to meet the general with some of his horse and to pay his respects.

His name was Mahummud Khan and he took great credit to himself, I hear, for having in answer to a demand of Holkar's yesterday *en passant* for contribution fired at his troops, and beat them off. Holkar's 12000 Horse, are now reduced to 5000 by the desertion of 7000 Seiks who joined him at Shamley, but left him some days ago, disgusted with and even reproaching him, as is said, for his cowardice! Cowardice! That term is misapplied. Holkar acts upon system and to tell a "Melancholy truth" has found out the true secret of how to fight with the English.

All former enemies of ours, from the days of Lord Clive, to those of General Lake so late as the last war, met us in the open field, with vast—nay incredible—advantages in numbers, and in artillery yet have we always beat them and again would do so from our great superior knowledge of the art of war. Holkar, has had the singular penetration and good sense, to see his inferiority at regular warfare and in casting about for some other way of going to work, he has hit upon the only safe and true expedient to annoy us. Letters of his to Ameer Khan, intercepted in Bundelkund last campaign, declared his intentions of trying to ruin us and knock up our troops by constantly avoiding fighting, by perpetually harassing our camps, cutting off our supplies, carrying of our baggage, cutting up all detachments and small parties. Making irruptions into our own country, whither we must of necessity follow and to use his own remarkable words, knowing as he did, impossibility of Europeans resisting the effects of hard work in this baneful climate "compelling us to march wherever he lead, until the very legs of the *Fringies* should swell, and they be obliged to give it up!" In what one part of these his intentions, has this man failed of performance? In the last alone.

Our legs, as yet have not literally swelled, but if we have to undergo the fatigues we have experienced since we left Delhi for any long time, even that part of his plan will be realised, and that too soon. Here since we left Shamley, have we been pursuing this man all through our own territory, when he has subsisted himself and followers on our lands and towns. We have scarce ever gone less than twenty miles a day and are exposed for seven or eight hours to the sun. Our battery is knock up, our servants tired of it will soon follow the cattle and we must follow then to overtake him we need not attempt marches, which to a regular army, encumbered with necessary baggage and artillery, are long and fatiguing, to a predatory army of light horse, without a tent in their party and depending for subsistence to themselves and horses, on the casual plunder of every village, are mere child's play, thirty or forty miles are nothing to such an enemy, while to us they are positive impossibilities.

If 5000 fellows keep the grand army, thus employed, I cannot help wondering what we should do if there were a dozen such parties all over the country, and seeing how successful they are in this sort of war, I cannot but tremble at the thoughts of when the English possessions in the Dooab, perhaps in India, would now have been if Holkar's Horse, had in the Mahratta confederacy of last year, been added to the more regular and as we found them, formidable, forces of Sindhia! Could we but succeed in getting this man's guns and infantry, his name would dwindle in the estimation of all the natives immediately. He would scarcely know where to go as our troops under Murray, are already in possession of his best territories and his capital. Were he but reduced to this grass, the petty princes of every district, would probably in revenge for injuries which almost everyone of them has suffered at some time from this common plunderer, attack him and his vagabond troops if any, indeed, would remain to him in his distress, a thing not likely, as prosperity alone can secure to them plunder, the almost only bond of union between him and them.

November 11th—On our arrival at Kooncha-sheher, where we crossed the Kaly Nuddy, we struck off further to the eastward on the road to Coel and Allyghur, on account, I understand of the information received from the poor villagers, of Holkar's motions. He had left this unfortunate town, exactly 24 hours before we passed it, so that we seem to tread pretty close on his heels. The remains of his horses forage and litter, with the numerous carcases and skins of sheep and goats, showed us the spot where he had encamped. His troops had plundered the wretched inhabitants of their very clothes, and on his setting off from hence, he is said to have divided his force into two parties. The chief body, of whom, with which he himself is, went with an intention of plundering the large and populous city of Coel in the vicinity of the Fort of Allyghur, of noted memory. In Allyghur, we have a considerable garrison but, I fear insufficient to defend Coel also. The more especially, as the inhabitants of that place, have been more than once in rebellion against us and, but a month ago, were brought under only by force of arms.

Yet, that the Allyghur garrison ought to try and defend so valuable a place as Coel is, seems to me admit of no dispute. The place has even the shadow of a mud wall, which I hear it has a very small infantry force, will be able to defend it against all Holkar's Horse. Even if the inhabitants were ill-disposed to us, what could they gain by admitting Holkar, who, when forced to abandon the place at our approach, would most certainly plunder them and leave them to our vengeance. And lastly, our proximity to Holkar, our pursuit and his flight for so long a time before us, leave the inhabitants nothing to hope, and everything to fear from an insurrection and give Holkar but little estimation in the eyes of anyone. What can this man intend? What are his hopes? His people already are deserting him. A *sardar* and forty men came into camp last night and were taken into service by us.

They say that great discontent prevails among his people, that the Patans in his service, will never recross the river with him and leave their own country. And that besides our cantonments in the Dooab, at Cawnpore and Futtyghur etc., he means to join Ameer Khan, of Bundelkund memory, and proceed down to Mirzapore, above Chunar on the Ganges, one of the best and richest cities in India. But how is this scheme to be executed? If he goes on a day's march after tomorrow, he leaves himself but one place to cross the Muttra and cross he must, to get at Mirzapore, besides long ere his plan could be executed, his guns and infantry would be destroyed and his name and power with them. As it is, he is foolishly by running about here, abandoning them to their fate. General Fraser is joined by the European Regiment and has certainly gone against them.

Naya Bazar report this day prevailed (*i.e.*, among the servants and followers in the market) that Fraser had taken the guns. But this is not Holkar's sole impolitic act. As he daily descends the Dooab he gets into the net which we, from the geographical situation of the country daily contact round him and in which he will at last be taken if he continues to move downwards. For below Muttra, there is not one other ford on the Jumnah, at his season (the Ganges is out of the question). He passed yesterday, the best he could have gone to, and which would have led him to his guns, that at Secandara twenty-three miles below Delhi. His guns and infantry would surely fight with more spirit and despair were he present to animate them, to fight with them, nor will their spirits be the more raised to hear that he is a fugitive from such inferior numbers.

November 12th—We passed by the Fort of Kameena, or Kamoon, belonging to the notorious rebel to our Government Doondee Khan. On our passing, he sent to the general to beg forgiveness for his past offences, and professing ample supplies of grain if wanted. The general refused both and added that it would be for Doondee's interest that none of our followers or baggage should be plundered as they passed and His Excellency with, I think, a most happy prudence, called in our flanking parties, for fear of quarrels, or skirmishes with 2000 men, the garrison of Doondee's Fort. In the event of which, he should be compelled, he said, to take the place, which, considering how important time was at present, to him he could not afford to do. A rebel at Khassgunge, who sometime ago burnt the cantonments then, having collected some thousand men, has committed ravages and invited Holkar, who is gone thither. Major Bowie, with the Sebundies of Futtyghur (two marches distant only) has marched against him.

November 13th—It is actually said that Holkar holds his forces together, by the extravagant promises of crossing the Ganges at Furruckabad, into Rohilkund and Oude. They scarce can be brought, one would believe, to give credit to ideas of this kind. Strong hopes, however, are necessary to be set before the eyes of a disheartened and jaded army such as by this time his must be, for even our horses, regularly and amply fed, are scarce able to hold out this fatiguing war of marching and what must be the situation of his cattle, who depend for a precarious supply of food, upon what they can obtain out of towns without walls, of which kind the number is very small indeed.

November 14th—Marched to the neighbourhood of what were the cantonments of Khassgunge and of which the remaining walls of roofless houses, and barracks and stables, but point out that here they stood. I should yesterday have mentioned that at about the ninth or tenth mile of our journey of that day we re-crossed at a ford, the Kaly Nuddy, from the East to the West bank. This day under Khassgunge cantonments, we returned to the East bank over an excellent new pucka and stone bridge, of seven large, and two small pointed arches. This fabric is very strong and seems new, built evidently by a native. It was a beautiful object to us, as were even the desolated bungalows of the cantonments, as we had seen nothing European like for so long a time. We are evidently going to Furruckabad, whither Holkar has beset his steps. He took a trip, *en passant,* to Sooroo, a Hindoo Temple on the Ganges, where he performed his devotions, an act, notwithstanding his daily murders and devastations, not a whit more impious or absurd, than our *Te-Deums* on similar occasions.

Major Bowie, with his Sebundi battalion came into camp to night from Khassgunge, where Holkar had not molested him and in the neighbourhood of which he defeated the rebel *zemindars,* and took a fort of theirs. He is not to accompany us. Holkar keeps his usual distance of 24 hours. He decidedly is pushing for Furruckabad and Mow, the first the capital of the Patan[3] of that name, and a large populous city, the second filled, as well as the capital, with these ferocious Moosulmauns, ever ready to take arms, for plunder and riot. Our appearance, so close in the rear of the enemy, may probably keep them down, but if they do rise, they will do it *en masse* as one spirit commonly actuates them, revenge and desire of booty and what is as bad, most of Holkar's force consists of the brothers and relations of these people. If, however, the inhabitants remain quiet the same circumstance, will cause many of Holkar's people to desert him, both from a wish these men always have, to sit down and spend whatever plunder they acquire in every enjoyment of luxury and dissipation and from an unwillingness to re-cross the Jumnah leaving their native country and relations, to follow the fortunes of a vagabond.

November 15th—In the villages we passed this day, besides the usual circumstances of total emptiness of inhabitants as well as effects, we had to observe with sorrow, that they had been burnt down. We are certainly getting closer to the foe or some of his people are knocking up. Early this morning some fugitives were observed at the distance on the left flank, against whom a squadron of the 6th Native Cavalry were detached to take or destroy them, but without effect. When we arrived at our ground the rear of his army, was got only a mile or two ahead, as we perceived

---

3. Patans or Pitans, the descendants of the first Mohammedan conquerors of India -afterwards supplanted by the Mogul dynasties and now very low as a nation in the political scale, but retaining all their original spirit and ferocity, the subject to the depressing genius of our Government.

from seeing some of them hastily making off from the front of camp, on our arrival and from the report of a miserable faquir the sole tenant, of a considerable town, who assured us they had but just left the smoking ruins an hour before. I suspect that Holkar, with the best, or least fatigued part, must be greatly farther on and that those we saw, unable to keep pace are following as they can.

We are all in great anxiety about General Fraser, last night late, a letter from him came to commander-in-chief, mentioning his having arrived at the Fortress of Deeg, belonging to Bhartpoor, on the 12th after a long march and finding drawn up in a most strong position, under the guns of the fort with their right to a marsh, and their left to the *pettah* (or walled town). All the enemy's guns and infantry, from the report of a Captain Jenkins, formerly in Holkar's service, and who escaped a few days ago from confinement in their army, the guns in number are 320 and the infantry eighteen battalions of 500 or 600 each! Considering their strength of position, and that his army were fatigued with marching, the major general with great prudence and propriety, judged it right to encamp out of gun shot and to reconnoitre their position previous to giving them battle on the 13th. It is probable the business was settled if they fought with but ordinary bravery, our handful of men, 1100 Europeans, 3600 sepoys and 600 cavalry, with twenty or thirty guns, must have had dreadful hard work of it.

Every hour we look for the news which will decide the fate of the campaign. If the guns of Deeg assist the Maharattas with a goodwill, it will be a most murderous business and the success of an attack, against such a force supported by guns, which planted beyond a ditch and wall, cannot be stormed, may be dubious forbid it heaven! Forbid it genius of British valour! Forbid it the recorded victory! Of Lawrence, Clive, Coote, Cornwallis and Lake! Hope I have and a great one, that the Bhartpoor Rajah will from irresolution, timidity, or policy if you chose, not given effectual support to a falling foe. It would be a good time for us to hint to him oblivion of past faults for present benefits and even to negotiate with the Maharattas themselves, who are said to be thirteen months in arrears and in a state of mutiny, unsupported by the fort. I am confident of our success. Even with all it's aid, I do not fear defeat!

November 17th—We arrived soon after 1 a.m. at Nawabgunge seventeen or eighteen miles, from Allygunge. At the entrance to this town, we halted for a quarter of an hour, while some people went to ascertain, if there were yet any of the Mahrattas here, but there were none. The last of them had departed many hours before, and Holkar, with the main body had left it at 9 a.m. of yesterday after vainly attempting to plunder the place. We now moved on for Furruckabad, thirteen miles farther on, about halfway between which and Futtyghur cantonments we heard he was encamped.

I would to God I had the power of expressing in adequate language at all times, what passes within me. Description in my hands fails when she attempts the finer emotions of the hearts and spirits, excited by suspense, hope and fear, mixed in various degree, contending for the mastery in the mind recollection and surrounding circumstances and worked up to increased urgency by each moment as it passes and brings nearer the event, which is the cause and object of these contending emotions. The fineness of the night. The fortunate event of which we had just heard. The hazardous nature of the enterprise in which we were engaged and the moment of deciding which every moment more and more approximated. The glory we should acquire by success and the happy consequences that might result from it. Yet the little real probability of our surprising so watchful a foe and the disgrace of the failure of our attempt. The fear too, that the mischief to prevent which we were now going in hopes of preventing was already accomplished. All these ideas crowding in my mind, caused a variety of pleasing, mournful sensations, heightened beyond belief as the first faint blush of morning, scarce distinguishable from the pale steady torch of the moon, began to tinge indistinctly the distant horizon, as we approached the groves of Furruckabad.

The most profound silence now reigned, interrupted only by the noise of the horses' hoofs and of the gun wheels. It was just daybreak the Futtyghur morning gun fired. The report from it's loudness, told us that the moment of action approached and everyone on the "tiptoe stood of expectation."

Orders now came down the column for the regiment to form column of half squadrons and for the horse artillery to move up and lead. We obeyed, not a breath of wind was stirring to dissipate the clouds of dust which this manoeuvre occasioned and which, added to the darkness that yet prevailed, prevented us from seeing the badness of the roads, the high dykes and deep ditches, which we were compelled to get over as well as the exhausted state of our horse would enable us, At this critical moment and just as we were about to enter a thick mango *tope* (grove), at the extremity of which the enemy were supposed to be, owing to some violent concussion in getting over a hard, deep ditch, the tumbril in the rear of our line or guns, and more particularly attached to the brigade under my command, blew up with a tremendous explosion. three natives were considerably scorched, but no lives, luckily, lost.

Notwithstanding the interesting situation in which we at that moment were placed and the unluckiness of such an accident just then, I could not help noticing how grand and sublime this explosion was in the midst of the thick woods surrounding us, and in such total darkness. It only, however, caused us to push on the faster. In about three or four minutes our four guns and two howitzers formed line to the right, at the distance of forty or fifty yards. There was just light enough, indistinctly to see them seemingly scarce alarmed and unconscious of our approach.

We instantly opened a tremendous and quick fire of grape, every shot of which must have told, about thirty or forty rounds were fired when we ceased, and the cavalry followed it up by a rapid charge through our intervals upon the astonished and unresisting Mahrattas, who fled in terror, screaming and howling, with the utmost precipitations in every direction, leaving their baggage, bazaar, women and children, swords and spears, horses, tattoos and bullocks on the ground.

The scene that ensured an eye witness alone can believe nor by anyone else can it be conceived. We followed up the cavalry in the rear. They dispersed in troops and squadrons on all sides to cut off the flying enemy. All from this time was a scene of confusion. Daylight which now became stronger, found Lieutenant Stark, myself, with two guns and two howitzers, separated from Captain Brown and his two guns, with a squadron of the 8th Dragoons, one of the 6th Native Cavalry along with us. The enemy's horse, were all around in large bodies and infinitely outnumbered our parties, one of these bodies appearing in front. The cavalry along with us instantly charged them, leaving our guns without a man to protect them. A line of conduct almost uniformly observed towards the unfortunate artillery by cavalry and infantry, which may be attended with the worst consequence, which caused the whole of General Wellesley's artillery, at the battle of Assaye, to be nearly cut to pieces, and which, on this day, had the Mahrattas been so many French dragoons, would have caused every man of us to be cut to pieces and would have deprived the world of the benefit of these memoirs.

Our poor horses, nearly worn out by a march of almost sixty miles, in 24 hours, were scarce able to get into a trot, far less to accompany cavalry on a gallop. The dust raised by the charge of our attending cavalry which I have above mentioned was scarce laid and we were slowly moving on in their tracks, when Captain Belton (Brigadier Vendeleur's Brigade Major) with about ten or twelve of the 8th Dragoons and as many native troops as came galloping down on us in great confusion, pursued close at their heels, by a large body of the enemy. As they came nearly in the same direction that a similar party of our's had just gone by we concluded that they were coming back, nor from the dust, did we perceive how matters stood, till Captain Belton exclaimed to us that an immense body were charging us and begged us to fire.

They were by this time so near, that we could distinctly see their very features and they were coming furiously down brandishing their spears and swords but the instant we turned round to unlimber, and that by the dragoons clearing away from our front, they perceived the guns, they turned about and fled with the utmost precipitation, spouting as they went off while we gave them two or three benedictions, as well as the uncertainty of aim in such clouds of dust, would permit us. If these fellows had resolutely come on in one minute, and with the loss of a very few men, they would have got in among us and destroyed us all, before we could have fired above one or two rounds at them. The pursuit and flight continued as before, nowhere, except in the instance I have mentioned, was resistance attempted, however great the disparity was of the pursuers and the pursued. The charge and carnage, lasted from peep of day till 9 or 10 o'clock, when unable to continue it, from the thoroughly jaded state of all the cattle, and the gun in particular, we slowly returned, having since the action commenced gone over eight or ten miles of ground.

In the above actions the Mahrattas are supposed, from the best guess that can be made, to have lost above 3,000 killed, besides numbers wounded.

On our part, we lost two European dragoons killed, thirteen wounded, no natives killed, nine or ten wounded, several horses killed and wounded and more missing. These lost were chiefly led horses, whose conductors most probably left them to go and plunder the dead and dying.

We took Holkar's own elephant, twenty or thirty camels loaded with grain, tents etc., etc., bullocks and buffaloes, horses and tattoos innumerable besides twenty hackeries loaded with grain. The fruits of Holkar's plundering trip in the Dooab, so many brass cooking and eating utensils and dishes were taken, that the camp followers were absolutely loaded with them, scarce a lascar, or follower but provided himself with a horse or *tattoo*, a shield and spear and sword and many dozen *tattoos* and bullocks and horses were afterwards shot, no one appearing to take them away.

Upon the whole a better planned, timed and executed business never was performed. Half an hour, a quarter of an hour, sooner or later would probably have spoiled all, we arrived at the precise nick of time and came by surprise on an enemy who has always vainly boasted, how impossible it was for the English army to overtake them, or even come near them. We have taught the enemy that distance is no security against antagonists who can march with guns sixty miles in 24 hours. We have saved a populous capital, and large cantonments, from a foe that was at their very doors. In fine, we have out-marched and surprised the most enterprising chief of the Mahrattas, the most vigilant and active nation of Hindoostan, by a march perhaps the longest and most rapid of any recorded in the British annals of this part of the globe, and our efforts have been crowned with the most complete success.

In this business, several of the enemy when attacked by our people and overtaken, defended themselves with courage, bordering on despair. The two Europeans we lost, were both cut down by one man and an old, reverend Patan, with a flowering grey beard, overtaken by the commander-in-chief and his bodyguard, although dismounted, drew his sword, flourishing it round his head and challenging them all to "come on!" Lieutenant Martin and several of his troopers attacked him individually but were not able to hurt him nor was he killed, until a dozen pistols were fired at him, when he died resisting gallantly even in his last agonies.

As the Holkar himself, from certain intelligence, we learned that he was asleep after a late debauch at the moment of our approach, he had not a single alarm post, guard or picquet, nor were any precautions whatever taken to guard against a danger which no one supposed even possible to be at hand. Holkar's caste which is that of nearly the lowest Hindoo does not preclude him from drinking spirits and it is said that all the wine he took in Monson, and Brown's retreats was reserved for his own use. He arrived here yesterday morning at 10 or 11 o'clock and notwithstanding that many of the people of Furruckabad well knew of our being close at his heels, yet the Nawaub Regent and courtiers, with the principal *shroffs* (bankers) went out the same day to visit him and supplied him with grain and some money, most of which, with an elephant which the Nawaub made him a present of we afterwards took.

The Nawaub afterwards sent out a set of dancing girls to amuse Holkar, who sat up, debauching, till late at night, when the news of the destruction of his infantry and guns at Deeg having been brought in by a *hircarrah*, the assembly broke up. In the morning when we commenced firing Holkar's friends placed him on a fleet horse, ready saddled, as those of the Mahratta chiefs usually are and off he went. We have since heard that he and 4000, the remains of his force, some without horses, some without clothes, spears or swords, crossed the Kaly Nuddy at a late hour, on the road to Manpoory.

November 18th—The cantonments of Futtyghur are very extensive and extend along the Ganges which runs in the rear. The magazine and depôts are contained in a mud fort on the right, where the infantry cantonments and artillery barracks are. A large and deep natural chain of precipitous gullies or ravines surround and well defend the right, front and left of this part-joined by a bridge and at the distance of more than a mile on the left, are the cavalry lines, containing stables, and huts, for six troops of native cavalry, besides the officer's bungalows.

The whole force in this station consisted of about 600 recruits, who on Holkar's approach, for the first time had muskets put into their hands, artillery, they had in abundance, but no men to work the guns. This defect and the want of officers, to the miserable sepoys they had, was supplied by the spirit of all the sick officers and European merchants, not above eight or ten in all, including two Officers, Major's Smith and Armstrong late of Scindia, and Holkar's services. two 12- and two 18-pounders were brought from the fort, into which the sick, the women and children and a few of their valuables were placed.

Captain Royle, who commanded, saw that it was impossible to defend the whole line of infantry and cavalry cantonments especially as the last, lay quite open. He therefore judiciously withdrew himself to the infantry lines, and with his guns, kept off the Mahrattas, who at 3 p.m. of the 16th attacked him but were obliged to sheer off, after however, plundering the cantonment bungalows and burning all the wood work and thatch of them and the stables. Our appearances, so unexpectedly, next morning, in all probability saved the remainder of the cantonments from sharing a similar fate.

The regent of Furruckabad, is, I hear, in confinement for his conduct, the Nawaub being a minor is not. The Regent will probably either be hanged or sent to compare notes with Vizier Ally in Fort William, for his treason, this being a province of ours, and the Nawaub our pensioner. Many think it would be a good plea for discontinuing even the shadow of sovereignty that the name of Nawaub gives this man in the district. It is a kind of *imperium in imperio* certainly and the natives of the place, as in this present instance, will always follow the example of their nominal Lord. Still more think, that as the Furruckabadians assisted Holkar with money, provisions and men, and even conducted his men, torch in hand to burn the cavalry lines, that they should either have been given up to plunder or have been fined in a large contributions for the benefit of the army.

Certain it is any natives, in our place, would have plundered the town and put every soul in it to the sword. Our, uniformly opposite conduct, on like occasions, not only is not gratefully felt, not only does not secure their allegiance, but on the contrary, excites the contempt and decision of these perverse people, and makes them the more ready to rebel from their assurance of escaping punishment. I do begin to think that these people, from all I have even yet seen, must be governed by an iron rod.

November 19th—Halted again this day. We were all most busily employed in laying in a little stock of liquor, our old one being perfectly exhausted and we, not likely again to visit a cantonment in a hurry. From further particulars of Major General Fraser's engagement, which have arrived, we learn that the enemy, with 150 guns, in several rows, or tiers, lay in an exceedingly strong position with their left to the Fort of Deeg, a large deep marsh covering their front and rear. Their right alone accessible, on the 13th at 3 in the morning the 76th and European Regiments, the 1st Battalion of the 2nd and 2nd Battalion of the 4th and the 1st and 2nd Battalions of the 15th marched to attack them. The 1st Battalion of the 8th and a Battalion of the 22nd Native Infantry were left to defend the camp and baggage, while the 2nd and 3rd Cavalry kept in check a numerous body of horse which threatened to fall on the rear.

As day broke the troops were yet two and a half miles from the enemy, whose line is said to have extended above three miles. The Europeans, formed at the head of two lines and they traversed the enemy's line, under the successive fires of their guns, from right to left. But when they had driven all before them and got to the left, the treacherous *Killahdar* of the fort opened a most terrible and deadly fire on them which could not be silenced by exposed infantry unable to attack guns placed beyond a deep ditch and high wall. They were consequently compelled to abandon part of their prey and to fall back. They however brought in eighty-five guns from the marshes, into which the enemy had dragged them. The Mahrattas have, with the remaining guns, taken up another position on the opposite side of the fort. The work is therefore evidently incomplete, nor, as long as the enemy are protected by the guns of the fort, can they be attacked with a prospect of success.

Should General Fraser die of his wounds I tremble to think that his successor is Colonel Monson of retreating celebrity. With regard to him and to the battle, as I have above related it I shall make no comments, but merely mention two remarkably striking points, which, if true, deserve and require elucidation. The one is that the action ceased, whereby General Fraser losing his leg, he was put *hors de combat*. Query? Where was his successor? The other is how came they at daybreak to be still two and a half miles miles from the enemy? To these questions time will answer, till then, I shall say nothing.

With regard to the loss of the enemy, we are ignorant of it's amount in killed, wounded or prisoners. We have suffered much, as all accounts agree that greater bravery, under such disadvantages of situation and disparity of numbers never was seen. The 76th have lost 170 killed and wounded. The European Regiment 75 ditto, one native battalion 96. The others probably in the same proportion. In addition to the perfidious conduct of the Governor of Dig, it is said that the Bhartpoor Rajah, with 15000 men, was in the engagement.

November 20th—We passed over an angle of our late field of battle and saw the putrefying carcases of hundreds and hundreds of Mahrattas and Patans strewn on the ground. One or two poor wretches, unable to move, yet lived in the momentary hope of relief from death. I know not how it is but such shocking scenes as witnessed this day and on the 17th would once on a time have affected me and disgusted me. Have it overcome all things but to a reflecting mind, it is melancholy to think that the human heart, formed as it is for the reception of every noble and tender feeling of love and mercy, should even become steeled and callous, and should even come to witness the destruction and death of thousands of fellow creatures with indifference, bordering, even (in the moment of battle) on pleasure! I cannot think, or dwell on this humiliating truth without thinking that the vanity of man has assigned himself a much higher rank in the scale of creation, than he has any right to do, but a little lower than the angels! To substitute a more correct sentence, but a little higher than the brutes!

November 21st—Holkar, is said to have divided his force, part having gone to Etawah and part towards Muttrah, with which last party it is said he himself is.

November 22nd—Marched at half-past five, West by South, eighteen miles, to Manpoory. We are now on the Great Agra road and on known ground which I have now travelled on for the 5th time, within twelve months. It being almost to a day, one year, since with Captain Wegudin's European detachment, we first came by this road, to join the great army what chopping and changing since then! Who would not be a soldier! During a space of more than thirteen months, since we left our boats at Allahabad on the 2nd October, I have been about two months, out of the tented field and have experienced a pretty variety of climates and gone over a tolerable quantity of ground! No wonder a man's constitution so soon bears out in India.

I am, however most heartily sick of campaigning and do not in a hurry again wish to renew these scenes. It may all be pleasant enough, to the ignorant and uneducated or to boys just arrived and desirous of novelty. Those who have no resources within themselves, no way of passing their time but eating, sleeping, visiting, annoying quieter people or hunting and shooting, may no doubt have all these enjoyments in greater perfection in a crowd such as a camp always contains, but for me, give me my barrack or bungalow, where I can stay at home if I incline or spend a rational hour in select society. Give me my books, my colours, my music and I will leave it to more adventurous spirits, to sally in quest of pleasure forth among camps and the din of war. Everyday I spend in this country I feel my disgust increase. My longing for my own country grows stronger, yet vain is the longing, hopeless are my signs and wishes.

How is it possible for a man, knowing himself condemned to an inevitable servitude for twenty-two of the best years of his life, years that should, if any ever are to be, years of gaiety and pleasure to feel any ardour, to be other than careless how he passes the miserable term of his purgatory? All other considerations, with me at least, are absorbed in the one grand and never ceasing idea ever uppermost in my mind, that of eagerly looking forward to the happy hour which shall put a period to this state of banishment and slavery.

November 24th—Marched to Aitah or Eatah, a very large town, enclosed by a wall and bastions, of mud, of above a mile in circumference and situated on the borders of a geel or marsh. It has besides a quadrangular citadel or inner fort of a small size and the whole place is filled with trees. This is on the direct road to Muttrah and Allyghur and was recognised by the officers now with the army, who went with the general at the beginning of last campaign (August 1803) and on the expedition against Sassney, Bidgighur and Kutchourah, (in December 1802), all which forts, as well as that of Hattrass, belonging to the celebrated Diaram Rajah, of suspected notoriety, are within two or three marches of it.

About eight miles on their side, Baubupore, we passed through the town of Sukeet, chiefly remarkable for a singular mud fort of considerable size, but now much ruined, which was besieged and taken with the Nabob Vizier's permission, from it's refractory chief, by Mr now Major Ouseley, then an Indigo planter, and now in the service of Vizier Saadut Ally and his *aide de camp* and Factotum, at Lucknow. Mr Ouseley afterwards established extensive Indigo works here. The fort is situated on a commanding eminence, or hill, as in these dead flat countries are style every rise in the ground, formed, as most of the hills, on which I have seen flats built in the Dooab, of the rubbish accumulated, of perhaps a series of forts and buildings for ages.

Eatah, has fallen much to ruin, at present the inhabitants seem busied in patching and repairing it, probably from seeing that even here, they are not free from ravaging incursions.

November 25th—Marched to Poorah, a town enclosed by a miserable mud wall. We passed the ruins of an old Fort, called Bukussar, once very strong, now totally destroyed as a fortification. To our astonishment we learned this day, that poor General Fraser was much worse, by the last accounts from Deeg, and that the command had, in virtue of seniority, devolved upon, of all other men, Colonel Monson, of retreating celebrity, who had left his position before Deeg and actually retreated to Muttrah. This is certainly very singular, to speak of it in the most favourable, possible, manner. By the testimony of the grain officers of both armies, we well knew that on the 17th there were twenty-one days' provisions in that army. They might therefore have held out till the 7th or 8th long before which time, we should have joined them with supplies in abundance.

One would suppose there is something fatal and flighting to the British character, in the name of this officer. He no sooner succeeds to the command of a victorious army than it becomes a retreating one. Yet, I am inclined to hope that fatal as this measure must be, it is yet necessary for in the first place General Fraser, if sensible, must have been consulted on a measure of such importance and if he was not sensible, Colonel Horsferd, a Brigadier, Commanding the Artillery department and next in rank to Monson would certainly, with the other brigadiers, have remonstrated, and even prevented its executions had it not been positively necessary. For if the remainder of Holkar's guns and infantry wish to retreat, our going back leaves them free to do it, without interruption. Every officer in camp, His Majesty's not excepted, is growling at Monson and prayers for poor Fraser's life, are most earnestly preferred by every one who wishes well to that army.

November 26th—Marched to Meenoo, a large and seemingly populous village, which belongs to Diaram, Rajah of Hattrass. In the neighbourhood of which, it lays, I have heard it is peopled by

Mewatties, a plundering race of people, inhabiting a large district of the same name, nearly opposite to this part of the Dooab on the other side of the Jumnah but who have emigrated in bodies to this bank. Unless what I rather suspect, is the case, that the *cis-and trans-*Mewatties, have no other connection but the name, which from the character of the original inhabitants of Mewat, has come to be applied to any village of thieves by trade.

We were all equally alarmed and indignant this morning by a premature report of Monson's having retreated to Agra. This report, strengthened by the aggravating report of some natives that Monson had left the captured guns behind him, prevailed all day, the more readily from Monsoon's character, and former exploits in the retreating line of the service, being so well remembered. The evening however brought positive despatches to the commander-in-chief and many letters to individuals. Poor General Fraser, is dead! He expired on the 24th. Monson was preparing, having arrived at Muttrah, to pursue his route to Agra, where positive orders arrived from the general couched I doubt not, in language none of the mildest, for him not to stir a foot farther till our arrival. The orders, I hear, for marching, had actually been issued, but were now countermanded. It is said that Holkar in person with his remaining infantry, cavalry and guns is gone off as fast as he can to Joudpoor. This he could not have done, had our army remained at Deeg! Monson in his retreat, was menaced by numerous bodies of horse which were however repulsed, we hear that some baggage was taken by them.

November 27th—Soon after daybreak, and at the distance of about three miles from our last ground, we passed close under the celebrated Fortress of Hattrass, with it's adjacent *pettah or kuttrah,* the latter, in Indian fortifications being the town and the former, the citadel of the place. The *kuttrah* of Hattrass, is fortified with a very strong mud wall and deep ditch seems to be of an irregular form, with circular bastions at every angle and many gates, without the walls is a considerable bazaar as if the town was not of sufficient capacity to contain the overflowing inhabitants. The whole place seems to be indeed very populous, and the inhabitants whom I saw, in great crowds on the walls and roadside, gazing at our guns as we passed, appeared to be better clothed than the people of most villages that I have yet seen in this part of the country. As to the fort it seems, as well as the imperfect view I had of it could enable me to judge, to be of considerable extent and very strong consisting, apparently, of fort, or rather wall within wall. the innermost, in which is the Rajah's Palace, being of great height. The whole of the works, except the gateways, seem made of mud, consolidated by age and the numerous bastions are all round.

The ditches, I hear are very deep and the mines, numerous in every part. A minute inspection of these and other interesting parts of the works, was not permitted us, sentinels, at every corner almost, warning us to keep off.

The state and military greatness affected by this Rajah, who is to us, nothing better than any large proprietor or *zemindar*, are very great. Several thousands of his horse were encamped in topes, and all round the fort and one battalion of regiment sepoys, clothed and disciplined in imitation of our troops was encamped on the glacis. The Rajah has many others, I understand, in his service, and in great order. He is also daily increasing his forces, as if aware of the rupture which inevitably must happen, between powerful masters like us and as overgrown subject as he is. It is indeed impossible, with any kind of safety, to permit this *imperium in imperio*. This solecism in modern European ideas of politics, a military force in the heart of our own country and shut up in one of it's strongest forts, both under the sole command of, paid and raised by a subject.

How dangerous it is, that a disaffected person should have this power in his hands, especially in time of war, is evident from the uncertainty and distress which this very Diaram's treachery has caused us in the present campaign. How difficult it is to extricate or crush such a man. Let Sassney, Bidgighur, and Kutchourah testify, each of which were, in the cold season 1802, attacked and destroyed, for this very reason and none of which were stronger than Hattrass. Diaram's *Zemindary*, did not then belong to us, it was not in the ceded, but in the conquered provinces, as was another very strong fort, which we passed to the right this morning, about four miles from our ground, and called Kamona, belonging to Bugwaunt Sing Rajah of Sassney and to which he fled, on the fall of that place. Bugwaunt Sing has been since pardoned, although Sassney Fort was not returned to him but from our custom of introducing our own judges and collectors, into all our provinces, he and Diaram, know well they will be, at the end of this campaign, if a successful one, attacked and deprived of their forts and troops. This accounts for all Diaram's treachery to us when he thought he could do it with impunity, and for his abject submission, when we come near his fort, or when our armies are successful. He must wish success to anyone who is hostile to us.

The introduction of our really mild jurisprudence, presents to him every prospect that is hateful, from a petty prince affecting independence. he will fall into the safer and humble situation of a common *zemindar*. Nor will the immense riches, which he will then possess in greater abundance than now, in as much, as he will have no channel of expensive forts and armies into which they can be diverted, console him for being put in regard to armies committed by him, on a footing with his meanest subject, and subject to be called to an account, tried, and even executed, for putting to death a fellow subject, a privilege of his present Royalty, which he possesses and considers as one of the dearest prerogatives of his rank, to use with impunity.

It is said he sent a *Vakeel* (ambassador) to the commander-in-chief, professing submission and hypocritically congratulating him, on the double victory, proffering at the same time any assistance we should require as to supplies. As it is said this man was well received, I suppose expressions of satisfaction on our part, were exchanged with equal sincerity. As in worldly politeness, too, in common life, each well knew that the other lied, nay that the other did not believe him. The 13th and 17th of November have made a wonderful change in Diaram's policy. I doubt not but we have a long account to settle with him, for his behaviour when we were somewhat low. independent of the necessity of crushing him in a political point of view.

Diaram holds his property of our government on a tenure

nearly resembling that which we style feudal and his conduct, is quite that of a turbulent baron of the 7th or 8th century. He carries his feudal ideas too, farther than most Indian proprietors of land, for all his tenants, hold of him their lands as vassals on the tenure of military service for a portion of the year and the usual rents or proportion of the land produce during the rest. This does not apply to his infantry, who are mercenaries, but to his immense militia. as it may be called, of horse. who are all obliged to attend, in addition to the stated periods whenever the Rajah is in danger, or at open war. Hattrass will cause many lives before it is taken and but for the real necessity that exists of getting rid of so formidable a thorn in our side, this Rajah.

I should really regret any change in the government of this district which from it's fertility, cultivation and populousness, has every appearance of being as well governed as the state of society in it will admit, and certain, I believe it is, that however better, in theory, our municipal Government would be, the inhabitants would far prefer remaining as they now are.

November 28th—Marched to the banks of Jumnah opposite Muttrah, a bridge of boats being here prepared for our crossing. We marched quickly across, and proceeded three miles farther to join Lieutenant Colonel, Monson's (late M. G. Fraser's) Division of the grand army, which lay in the neighbourhood of the city. The city of Muttrah looks large and grand from the opposite bank, filled as it is with Hindoo temples and flights of steps descending down to the river, for the convenience of the Brahmans and the many devotees, who come hither to bathe. This however, like all other Indian towns, mean and dirty when you arrived at it, and go through the streets which are crooked and narrow and crowded up, everywhere with falling and fallen houses.

We were most happy this day to rejoin our old friends and fellow-soldiers after a month's tedious absence, in which time both parties have done and suffered much. Though theirs has been by far the most dangerous and severe duty of the two, of both the utility has been great to the state, yet here, perhaps we have gone beyond them. They have only done what has been done for 50 years before, in beating and taking hostile infantry and guns, while we have exhibited a spectacle to the wondering native powers, unexpected by them, unexampled to world. We have shown these plundering powers, whose whole strength lays in light cavalry, whose mode of warfare is to overrun a whole province with fire and sword with incredible rapidity, that even at these, their own weapons, we are more than a match for them. During the time we have now been absent from the army we have seen a pretty variety of country, have seen some of the severest marching and for a longer continuance than any army in India before us had. Our friends on this side have on their part, seen some as hard fighting as probably ever was witnessed and now that we are again met, it is no small pleasure, to compare our different exploits, to pit our marching against their fighting.

November 29th—Upon talking with Colonel Horsford on the subject of the retrograde movement, I learnt from him that it was absolutely the effect of necessity. They could not in the first place, for want of battering train and stores, as well as the diminutive size of their little army, either break ground before the fortress had they been so inclined, or even partially invest it.

The number of captured guns, which required their whole force to protect them, cramped and logged every hope of continuing operations against the enemy's remaining forces, which moreover were protected by the Killahdar of Deeg. It was necessary then, to lodge their guns in a place of safety and equally so to send the sick and wounded where they could be treated, as their situation required. No detachment from so small an army could be sent to escort them, without endangering the safety of both parties. It was therefore as necessary for the whole to go, as it was useless for them to remain idle before Deeg. To these arguments must be added the cogent one, want of specific orders from headquarters, regarding the line of conduct intended to be pursued towards the Bhartpoor Rajah.

In excuse for his conduct on the 13th, the Killahdar of Deeg and the Rajah urge that we began hostility, by insulting the fort and that when our Europeans came so close to the walls, they within, thought the fort was intended to be taken by storm by us. This accusation, or rather recrimination, on their part is no doubt false and were it even true, the attempt would have been fully justified, from the evident and notorious partiality shown by the Rajah to Holkar from the beginning of the war, and in the flagrant instance in question, of sheltering a force hostile to us, under his own walls. But whatever justice there may be in the Killahdar's assertion, as our conduct subsequent to it, must have involved the Government in a fresh war with Bhartpoor by at once commencing hostilities on the spot.

Poor General Fraser, at the instance I hear, of the shrewd and penetrating Colonel Horsford, ordered, that until instructions from headquarters arrived, no act of hostility should be committed on our part towards the fort and that the cannonade which they kept up on our advanced post, for so many days should not be returned by a single shot from us. Thus leaving by this judicious and politic line of procedure, the grand question of peace or war, to be decided by higher authority and cautiously doing nothing on our part, that could possibly shut up the avenue to reconciliation, should such be the wish of Government.

Doubtless General Lake would have been better pleased, had we, without leaving the decision of this important question to him, at once, in the heat of passion and stimulated by revenge, plunged into war, for now the responsibility will rest with His Excellency. And for the same reasons, if the commander-in-chief has submitted the question to the final decision of the Government below our Lord, would have been much better pleased if the general had at once gone into the war. But such shoulders are far able to support such a weight of responsibility, than those of simple officers without interest, and who in-case of the war turning out unfortunate or disgraceful, would without remorse, I fear, have been made the scape-goats of these great men, as poor Colonel Fawcett was near becoming but a few months ago.

Chapter 5
December 1804

December 2nd—Report says that Holkar is gone off from Deeg with 2000 horses. I am of opinion that if Holkar's person, or his guns, have ever gone into the Fort of Deeg (which we are assured they have done) the Bhartpoor Rajah would not easily let them escape from his protection, at least if he has got them fairly into his clutches. The Bhartpoor Rajah (Runjeet Sing by name) knows full well what a scrape he has got into and while we will certainly make the guns, a *sine quanon* in granting him peace, the person of our Cyclopean foe would be a peace-offering in value so high to us, that we would considerably abate in our terms, for the sake of having their formidable opponent in our possession.

December 3rd—About 3 p.m. intelligence was brought to the general that a line of march was perceived from the picquets and particularly from the village of Omrah, on a high hill, about half a mile in front of camp, and where we have an advanced post. The 1st Brigade of Cavalry under Colonel Macan, were ordered out to give chase, and about half-past four farther reports having been made to the general by officers, who saw or thought they saw, guns and tumbrils moving off. The remaining brigade of cavalry and our guns went out with the old general at the head.

We marched forward, in the direction of the supposed enemy, until dark, and as it was firmly believed that the enemy, with his guns, was affecting his escape we fully expected to have gone on after him all night. At the thoughts of which, we were not a little annoyed, because from ignorance when we left camp, of where, or for what purpose, we were going out, not an officer or man in the detachment had brought a warm coat, a drop of water or liquor of any kind, nor a biscuit.

All these things, joined to the coldness which began to come on at nightfall, made us feel most wretched, when, to our infinite joy and relief, our guardian angel appeared to us in the shape of the 1st Brigade of Cavalry, returning from the chase and bringing in prisoners, the fugitive enemy, which proved to be seventeen *hackeries* (Hindoostanee carts) empty! Upon this we all came to the right about, and by help of a fire which the general ordered to be lighted up at Omrah we with some difficulty found our way back to camp, then about five miles off.

December 5th—From the village in the centre of our camp and still better from the hill on which Omrah stands and where our advance picquet is, we can distinctly see that fort and town of Deeg with troops apparently to the number of 10000 or 12000 exercising. Chiefly infantry, who are practising platoon and file firing and the formation of columns and lines, manoeuvres in which they must have been instructed, either by some of the deserter sepoys from the 9th and 14th Regiments, who were with Monson's detachment or, what is strongly suspected, by some renegade European or half-cast in the Bhartpoor service. Certain it is that all the 76th and European Regiments to a man swear that they saw two Europeans, or men in European clothes on the walls of the fort and Lieutenant Swiney of the artillery, a particular friend, when on duty at our advanced post on the 15th ultimo saw, he assures me, a person of the above description, directing the firing of one of the fort guns and afterwards, some repairs of the fort.

December 6th—In the evening I received a letter from Cuttack, from Lieutenant Parker of the artillery, a friend of mine, full of bad news. First of all, as more nearly concerning us, I learnt that the army in Cuttack is in the field. At first Colonel Harcourt, who commanded, gave out that the object was to reduce a refractory Rajah so indeed it was, but that Rajah is no less a personage, if one may judge by the force going against him, than the Rajah, of Berar himself. This we know besides from other sources.

A letter to Colonel Monson has been received, it is credibly reported from the resident at that court mentioning, that his situation, in consequence of Holkar's successful feats, has become so disgraceful that if matters did not shortly assume a different tone, he should in a few days be compelled to quit the court. A proceeding always tantamount to a declaration of war. A proof, too, that a rupture with the Western Maharattas, at least, is expected by us, is that the Ramghur Battalion and a Battalion of the 20th Native Regiment have taken the field on the Western frontier of Bihar and Bengal, where they await further orders.

In truth the Berar Rajah Sindiah were more frightened than hurt by our brilliant last year's campaign. They are recovering from the shock and begin to see from Holkar's success, how far mistaken they were in regularly fighting us our own way, instead of adopting the sure, and as they now perceive, the successful mode of desultory, plundering war. What the consequences to them would be if they again engage in war with us, it is not easy to say, impoverished and humbled as they are by their present connection with us, one cannot see how their situation could be changed for the worse.

As for us, by the same argument, we could not well be gainers by a war. Our hands are, with the single enemy we have to fight, quite full enough. What would be our situation, if Moodagee Bhoonsla, who, by his territory stretching all along our frontier to the West, for hundreds of miles may penetrate when he chases, should pour in a deluge of predatory horse upon our fertile and hitherto peaceable provinces of Bengal and Bihar? We have not a single horseman, nor above three or four battalions, in any part of that prodigious extent of country, so interrupted has their tranquillity been for sixty years. We could not offer such an enemy even the shadow of opposition.

These districts, the resources of which, in men, money and grain, have, in my humble opinion, been the sole means of enabling us to conquer Hyder and Tippoo. Indeed to domineer over the whole of India would by an incursion of this kind be ruined for years to come and our sinews of war withered beyond recovery. That such an event is neither unlikely nor impracticable. Let the history of Bengal during the Subahship of Aliberdy Khan, predecessor of Surajah Dowlah, and the ablest sovereign, as well the most active general that ever governed that Kingdom testify. (*vide* Orme).

December 7th—The other piece of bad news, which the letter I yesterday received contained, was a disaster that had befallen a detachment of the Ceylon army. And which is so just a punishment on the Government of that island, that the only thing to be regretted in it, by an impartial and unconcerned person, is that the unfortunate involuntary tools of our scandalous ambition, are the sufferers and that the weight of this misfortune has not fallen on the guilty heads of the adviser and movers, who quietly sit in their cool palaces, calculating with apathy on gaining their object, at the expense of a certain probable number of lives. And, as they feel them not, taking not, into their account the miseries worse a thousand times than death itself, which their schemes, cause to the poor soldiers and their parents, their wives or brothers.

When I was at Colombo in Ceylon in September 1801, I recollect hearing persons high in power, even the Governor himself, make no secret of their intentions to pick a quarrel, as soon as matters were in sufficient forwardness, with the Candians, (the original inhabitants of the Island, and who possess only the interior, while all the sea coast, is our's).

The experience, of the Portuguese and Dutch, who several times, and with many more troops than ever we have had these, had vainly attempted a conquest of the whole Island and had as often been compelled by this Parthian foe or by the slower but more certain influence of a climate baneful to European constitutions did not weigh with these vain schemes. The bad success of their predecessors, seemed but to enhance the glory to be derived from a conquest, before found impracticable and Mr North appeared to flatter himself, that what the ferocity of the Portuguese and the sagacity of the Dutch Government, were unable to achieve, was reserved to adorn the annals of his administration, singular for being the first Royal East Indian Government. The King of Candy whose small and insulated territory showed him what was to be expected from European connection, had steadily resisted all our insidious attempts to negotiate further points we wished to gain. He was strictly neutral, but would not hear of any closer connection, in other words, would maintain the integrity of his dominions, and the independence of his Government.

Nor could all the humiliations to which, at the period above mentioned, even General McDowall Commanding the forces, submitted, when he went as Ambassador from our Government prevail on the Candian to permit a road, to be made between our two chief settlements of Colombo and Trincomallee. A measure, to which one would suppose none but a madman would ever assent and scarce-less than a madman propose. In consequence however, of the refusal to this extravagant proposition, His Majesty's Governor in Ceylon declared war against the Candian monarch in a magnificent manifesto, which alleged some pitiful quarrel between some merchants of either power about a Bay of Areka (or Bette) Nut! as the cause.

The fate of our first campaign is too well known. We obtained un-resisted but nominal possession of the capital and territories of the Candians, but in a very short time, the unceasing skirmishes with the Candians and the dissolution of a pestiential fever so thinned our numbers, that we were glad to abandon everyone of our conquests and the last of our armies in it's retreat was cut to pieces, or taken by a barbarous enemy. The destiny of many of the wretched prisoners, and among others of Captain Humphries of our regiment is yet unknown, most probably they perished miserably. But ambition, stimulated by disgrace and desire of revenge, had not yet been satiated with enough of victims. The war on our part ceased from inability to carry it on. But in a year supplies of men arrived from Europe and to the surprise of all here, who conceived the war at an end, after more than a year's cessation, it is again renewed and again have the invaders been driven back with disgrace.

A detachment of 300 Europeans and sepoys marched lately

from near Colombo to Candy, with orders to pillage, burn, kill and destroy all they met. At that place they were to be joined by similar parties from our other coast settlements. According to the invariable practice of the wary Candians, they met with no opposition in their way and even took above a *lack* of rupees about seven miles from Candy. But they had not arrived there many days before they began to find their situation alarmingly uneasy, especially, as the expected cooperation from the other side of the island did not take place.

They now thought it high-time to retreat and they took the road to Trincomallee as the safest and most expeditious. On the road the Candians, in ambush behind their jungles and rocks, picked them off with their matchlocks like dogs. They were forced to abandon their captures, and even their own artillery, ammunition and baggage and my letter says "The miserable remnant of this unfortunate detachment, marched into Trincomallee with little more than the clothes on their backs" and it is said, two officers of the Bengal Volunteer sepoys serving in Ceylon cut their own throats when wounded, to prevent their falling into the hands of a barbarous, and it must be added justly incensed enemy.

December 10th—A reward of 1000 rupees has been published several days continually, for whoever will apprehend any of several native troopers who deserted from picquet to the enemy, with the horses and arms, an excellent and necessary order! I omitted to mention that on the morning of the 8th, His Excellency the Commander-in-Chief and Staff, accompanied by the horse artillery and all the cavalry, went at daybreak for the purpose either of reconnoitering the ground about Deeg, or as was believed by many others, of surprising some guns in a village of the enemy's some miles from that place, or lastly, as others affirmed, of drawing out, and seeing the force of cavalry the enemy had.

If we went for the first purpose, we did not go by two miles near enough for any observations to be made. If for the second, we failed, as no guns were found or seen and if for the last, we were of but little use, for nothing happened but that we and the

Mahrattas acted over again the old scene. They were retiring while we advanced, harassing our rear when we were returning home, which we did about 12 o'clock, after having made, in six and a half hours, a circuit of seventeen or eighteen miles, rounding several hills and villages considerably to the westward of Deeg and returning by a village (terminating the great lake that trashes the fort) over Ough the village on a hill, where the severe cannonade on our Europeans was made and when General Fraser, lost his leg.

The enemy, mounted on better horses than I have yet seen, were seen from one of their camps, abandoned on our approach and situated on a hill, to an incredible number, covering the whole of the triangular recess formed by the hills and lake and extending to under the very fort walls. Never did I see so many created beings together! As we retired homewards they pressed on our rear and their hold beyond belief while our backs were turned, but the instant the guns killed a few by the grape-shot, they fled in all directions.

December 11th—We marched to Ough. We took possession of several posts round about on hill without opposition. The foraging guard were obliged to cannonade the enemy's horse pretty smartly, before they would allow the foragers to pursue the occupation and when obliged to retire they burnt all the villages and dug forage in the vicinity so that the whole horizon was covered with fires, all day long. In those cases, the immediate sufferers, the poor villagers and peasants, are of course infinitely too mean to deserve to have one thought wasted on them. But if Holkar thus burns and destroys the country of his magnanimous ally of Bhartpoor, the revenues of the latter will feel a sensible diminution I apprehend, especially as this is the precise time when the second crop of the year is planted and watered , occupations in which all hands are required.

Our camp being close to the village which terminates the Great Lake, about three and a half miles from the fort, I went, in the course of the day, with my telescope to look and saw numbers of troops as usual exercising under the walls. It is said that we are not to attack the fort up by the Isthmus between the lake marsh, where General Fraser fought, but that we are to go round the lake, and it's bordering hills, and to attack the place from behind. Our encamping here today must leave the enemy in doubt as to our intentions. They are now very busy at entrenching themselves on the right of the lake (the old field of battle), all which works will be useless if we go to the other side and if we (as it is said we shall) cut the embankment that keeps the lake from overflowing the adjacent neck of land, we cut off the retreat of guns or treasure at least, by that outlet. The view of the lake, hills and fort with the embankment bordered with trees, is highly beautiful. The extent of the lake is very great, though the water does not seem deep. It is perfectly covered with wild fowl, the larger of which (a kind of stork especially called the *Paddy bird*, from living in overflowed rice fields) were able to wade over every part almost of it. It sweeps away greatly to the right of the fort so that we must make a very great detour to get round by our left.

December 12th—We this morning marched, completely round the lake and outside of the hills, until we could see the back of the chain of hills, terminated by an old ruined fort and by Gopaul Ghur. A small but strong fort which is joined to the town wall of Deeg, although enclosed by a stronger wall of its own. The shape of the town, we understand, is flat and here it sends out a long, thin arm round the head of the lake until it meets with the rising hills about three-quarters of a mile from the fort in the centre of the town, and here it terminates in this Gopaul Ghur. A place of evident great importance to us, as being somewhat higher than the town and as high as the Grand Citadel, whoever is possessor of it, is master of the town and can carry on his approaches to the fort, under cover of the fire from this place.

December 13th—We expected to have commenced operations this day against the place, but as the camp was certainly too far off from it (at least five miles), we, by an after order of late last night, moved ground at 8 this morning to a fine plain about one and three-quarter miles from Gopaul Ghur. We perceived from a height, the largest body of cavalry I ever yet saw, apparently marching in a line parallel to, but in the opposite direction to our own, from near the town of Deeg, to an extent of four or five miles, skirting along the bottom of a range of high hills, which, running parallel to those under which our camp is from a long and finely cultivated valley, of five or six miles in breadth. There were, with this prodigious body, hundreds of standards and many camels and camel *hircarrahs*.[1]

From the number and colour (red and white) of a cluster of triangular flags and from the number of attending camel-men, we saw Holkar himself was there, at least so we believed and we expected to hear that he was moving off to put in execution a threat he made, that the instant we sat down before Deeg, he would recross into the Dooab again and compel us to go after him, or let our province be plundered. How wise such conduct would be, no one can doubt, but whether his troops would second his wishes, in again exposing themselves to miscarriage and defeat I question much, as I likewise do whether the Bhartpoor Rajah, who must sink or swim with him would relish such a mode of employing troops that should be occupied in assisting to defend his country. The troops we this day saw whatever their future intentions may be, discovered no symptoms of anything beyond their usual employment of plundering in the present instance and as to their march it was necessary for them to move away, if they meant not to dispute possession with us, from the ground we were about to occupy in the neighbourhood of the fort while the breadth of the valley, yet allowed them room to do it undisturbed.

On seeing their line close round our rear the horse artillery guns went out about 500 or 600 yards to the left flank to salute them *en passant*. They did not however, come near us, but on pitching the camp and when all but the forages were quiet in their lines, these plunderers began to be excessively troublesome, nor were they quiet, until the 29th Dragoons and some light guns went out, when they, not liking the reception they usually meet from white faces, speedily moved off to their camp, or rather stationed, some miles off to the left of our line.

---

1. Attendant mounted on a camel.

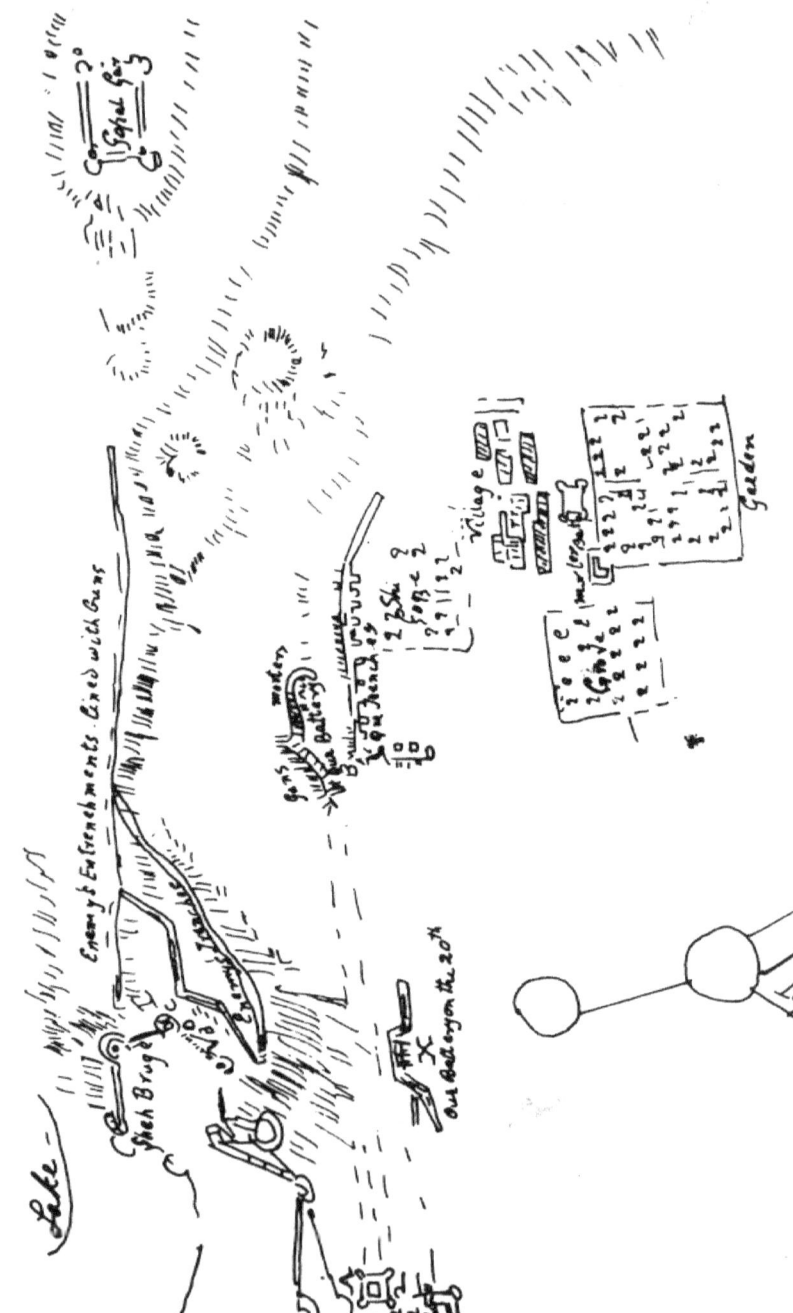

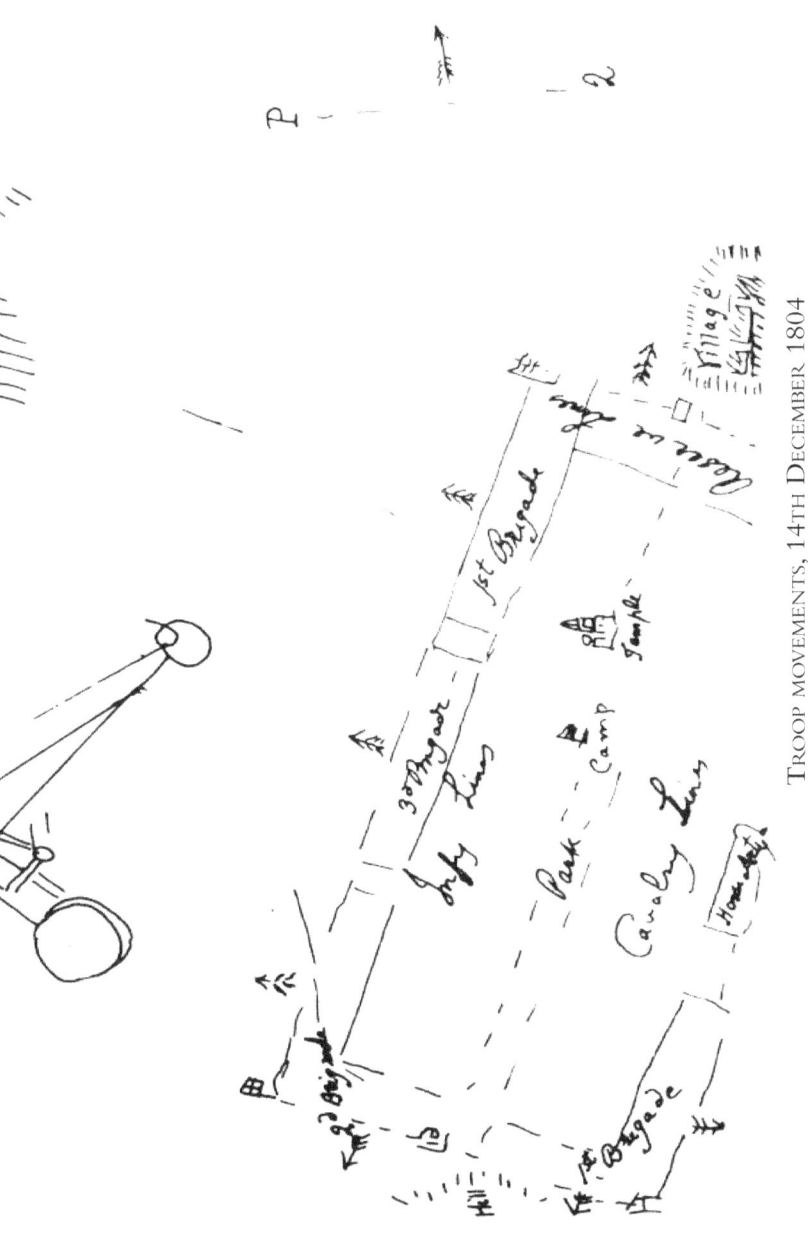

Troop movements, 14th December 1804

December 14th—Late last night, four, 12-pounders under Captain Nelly and Lieutenant Swiney, the flank Commanders of the 22nd Foot, the European Regiment, the two Battalions of the 12th Native Infantry and six Companies 2nd 21st Native Infantry, supported by the 1st of the 8th and 2nd of the 15th Native Infantry, moved down under command of Lieutenant Colonel Don with the view as we hoped of escalading, either the kind of citadel at the end of the town called Shah-bruje (King's Bastion) or the old Fort of Gopaul Ghur. The cavalry and indeed all the troops left in camp were under arms all night, in readiness to repel any attack that might be made by the enemy's horse in our neighbourhood, or to support our people it repulsed. The arrival of morning brought us the disappointing Intelligence that Colonel Don's orders were preemptory and that he was only to take post in a grove of some extent situated about 800 to 900 yards from Shah-bruje, from about 1200 yards from Gopaul Ghur and forming with these, an obtuse angled triangle, of which the grove is the obtuse angle.

This tope is about one and a half from camp, or somewhat more. The troops took possession of this place without opposition, it being deserted on their approach and it is supposed to be Shah-bruje itself which has no ditch and a nearly defenceless doorway, would have been taken easily, had we improved the occasion of the panic caused by our troops advance. As to Gopaul Ghur which is in ruins, the enemy would never dream of defending it at all and the possession of it to us would be of the last consequence to us, for all along, between the two forts and between them severally and our post, multitudes of ridges of hillock stony and accompanied of course by corresponding vallies, run in every direction, affording ample cover to hosts of the enemy's matchlock-men and musketeers, who poured in, all last night and all this day, from behind these ridges, a most destructive and never-ceasing fire.

Were Gopaul Ghur our's, the enemy would not dare to occupy the vallies between it and our post, as they would be then between a double fire and a very small force would be sufficient to keep it for us. Two companies of sepoys could do it, for it is not, for the sake of any positive use it would be to us, that I think we should have taken it, but to prevent the enemy's occupying it, as a cover to their snipe-men or snipers as here we style marksmen.

Our men made a tolerable entrenchment for themselves during the night. In the morning, a cannonade from the fort[2] commenced. Our people kept snug, being as yet in no condition to return it, growing bolder by our forbearance, the enemy drew up seven or eight pieces of canon, some of them very heavy, all along the ridges of the hill extending from fort to fort and fired away at a prodigious rate. Colonel Don thinking to disperse these gentry by a few shells, ordered to 5½ inch howitzers with the party on the guns outside of the fort, from behind cover of an old ruined village. But before three shells were fired the enemy, perceiving whence this annoyance came, directed instantaneously on the spot, a converging fire from all the guns in and out of the fort. Which, in a few seconds, levelled the mud walls to the ground and discovered our howitzers thus exposed as if they were on a plain. Colonel Don was then obliged to order them to be retired under the entrenchment, to submit in patience to the superior fire of the enemy until we should be in a condition to return it. The annoyance from the enemy's musketry was so great, that our working parties could do but little towards making picquets and fascines the object, for which we took possession of the grove.

December 15th—This day we were able to bring little more against the enemy than yesterday. The engineers were busied all night at constructing the 18-pounders battery but it was not yet near ready. A hole however, was dug for two or three mortars, which now and then gave a useful-shell, as did the single 12-pounder we were able to bring into play. One or two of the most troublesome of the enemy's guns were said to be disabled. Certain it is, they were more respectfully silent than they were yesterday, but at 4 p.m., when a royal salute was fired by us, in consequence of the capture of Gaulna in the Deccan by Colo-

---

2. When I talk of the fort I mean *Shah-bruje,* not Gopaul Ghur.

nel Wallace's army, the enemy taking it for the commencement of a general action or as a serious answer to our jokes, began a most tremendous fire from all the guns of the fort and from ten or eleven posted on the heights and behind the ridges between our post and the forts. At the same unlucky time, they got out a couple of very heavy pieces at a small *gurry* looking place (A in my sketch) under the town walls.

On hearing our salute, the enemy's immense body of horse encamped on our ground of the 12th instant got under arms and moved down, thinking no doubt the work was begun.

December 16th—A party of sixty dragoons having gone down as a working party last night, our works were in some better stage of forwardness. By the bye the whole of the three regiments volunteered for this service to a man. The matchlocking continued if possible more virulently than ever, meanwhile traverses have been erected to destroy the effect of the enfilading gun and two 12-pounders sent out from camp to divert the attention of these guns, but from the great distance, Sergeant O'Loughlin, a brave and distinguished artillery man, who commanded these 12-pounders was unable to do much.

December 17th—This morning the 18-pounders battery opened, only four embrasures were prepared as yet and of these, so ill-constructed was the whole business, two fell in from the explosion of our own guns, so that all we were this day enabled to effect was the beating down their defences a little and making some holes in the brick wall (B) opposite to and protecting the gateway. as however, when this wall is beat down another must be breached behind it. The spot for the breach was changed to the bastion (C) and recess (D). This morning at 8 a.m. our guns went out with the forages to protect them during their work from the large bodies of horse that are hovering all round. We met fortunately with forage, pretty near camp and did not see an hostile face, luckily, as I may say, for no one who has not seen the baggage and consequent number of cattle in an Indian camp, can conceive the difficulty of protecting with a small force from a plundering enemy of cavalry, such a tumult bullocks, hackeries, tattoos, asses, men, women and children clamorously shouting and screaming, and screaming to their beasts and to each other and scattering themselves, in spite of orders and attempts to keep them within line over all the adjacent country.

More than ever do we regret that Gopaul Ghur was not originally taken possession of by us. The annoyance of musketry from the sand-hills, under cover of that place, increases daily. The enemy, so far from being intimidated, have actually drawn out about twenty guns on the brow of the hills, extending from fort to fort. They have with great prudence and ability retired them so far back, that their muzzles only are above the hill top, they have actually made batteries for them, regularly and well constructed with entrenchments for their men and even approaches towards us, presenting the singular spectacle of besiegers – besieged. Nor is this all. The enfilading guns at four are likewise in battery, so that all attempts to disable them, are useless from our 12-pounders at least.

Holkar with great part of his horse, has moved away from his post. It is currently believed, as reported by our *hurkarrahs*, that Runjeet Sing (the Bhartpoor Rajah) sent a letter to Holkar, upbraiding him with doing nothing and remaining inactive, whilst his house was beating about his ears. Notwithstanding that he (Runjeet Sing) had involved himself in a war, entirely on Holkar's account and had supplied him with money, provisions and men, that in consequence of this, a grand meeting was held of the chiefs, when it was resolved to attack the British camp the instant we attempted to storm the Shah-bruje. Holkar is said to have stated in answer to Runjeet Sing, that he could not attack the English camp at present because it was a perfect *killah* (fort) in point of defence, but that he would move off and intercept a battalion of Europeans (75th Regiment) that was coming from Muttrah with treasure. For this purpose he is supposed to be now gone, but his pains will be fruitless, as the 75th and the treasure, are ordered to remain at Muttrah, till the fall of Dig shall render the junction safe.

December 19th—The batteries continued to play with effect on the breach. The battery is perhaps as bad a one, as ever yet was constructed, it is cut out of a hillock, of great breadth but little height. The sole of each embrasure is the soil alone of the hillock, sandy and dry. The merlons are this same soil, badly lined with a few fascines and so crazy and rickety is the whole affair that every explosion from our own, a shot from the enemy's guns, makes the embrasure fall in.

This night, Holkar returned to his old situation. From the short time of his absence, it is highly probable he went to intercept the 75th Regiment and the treasure, but finding them snug at Muttrah, returned. He gives out, that the instant we stormed the breach, that moment, he will move down on our camp with all his force in different directions. In short the day of the storm, will be a busy day for all of us, for we must send the greatest part of our infantry to the storm so that we and the cavalry will have a camp of prodigious extent to defend. No easy task, for so small a body as we are compared, with the enemy. I never look on the enemy's formidable battery of twenty-five or thirty guns, all along the hill, where our stormers must pass to the breach, without deploring the passive conduct of the old general. So unlike him too in not making a night attack, during this favourable moonlight weather on these entrenchments and guns, everyone of which I am convinced might be taken if we were to rush on their left flank nearest Gopaul Ghur and take them along, by the bayonet, from left to right. If we could not bring them away, we could at least spike or dismount them and as to resistance, we know they never will stand the bayonet of our troops. Before they could possibly discharge three rounds per gun, we should be in on them, and as to the fort, it seems totally deserted and were it not, it might be kept from firing by one or two shells from the 8 inch mortars thrown into it! One thing is to me self-evident, no party ever can march up to storm the breach, exposed as it would be, to be raked from front to rear of the column by twenty or thirty heavy guns, we must therefore sooner or later take these guns previous to attempting a storm.

December 20th—A circumstance has occurred which has made a great noise. A European artillery man was apprehended by some vedettes so far from camp on the road to Deeg, as to make it scarce a question but that he must have intended to desert, such is the bitter animosity, or rather antipathy, at all times, and especially in war times between Europeans and natives, that I suspect strongly he must have been drunk. It is not really credible to anyone who has been in India and marked the impossibility of any union of manners, or even thoughts, between the two species. If he really did mean to desert, it is a crime unpardonable, for it is in some measure unnatural and shocks even the lowest soldier.

December 21st—This day though not particularly distinguished by any public event, will be for ever endeared to my recollection, by one private occurrence. The communication from camp has, ever since we sat down before Deeg been totally cut off, no public postman was able to get out of camp to the place of his destination for the enemy's numerous horse surround us in every direction and as they unmercifully mutilate every poor wretch of an *hurcarrah* (postman) they catch, no man, however poor or necessitous would risk his limbs or life for the paltry salary he could earn by it.

In the midst of this darkness a ray of light occasionally breaks in on us in camp by the general's private Government expresses which now and then convey a news paper or two. By one of these we learned a few days ago, that several India men had arrived at Calcutta, having General Sir John Craddock (Commander-in-Chief at Madras) General Smith, for Bengal and the 17th Regiment of Foot, upwards of 1000 strong. All this news is good , excellent in the present state of our Indian army but yet all this sinks to nothing, when compared with a piece of news which was communicated to me accidentally, by one of the *aid-de-camps*.

That my dearest young brother Rayner was probably a passenger on board the *Baring*, certain it is that this long looked for brother, or some one of his name, *is* on board this fleet. As I have been always led to believe that my father would send him to India when an opportunity offered, I think it highly probable that this is he. No one who, with a heart wholly wrapped in domestic and social affections, has not suffered the misery, exquisite to such a heart, of a banishment from what he holds most dear and that for so many years, as to amount to a total estrangement, can conceive what a happiness, what a blessing it is to have a dear friend and brother in this state of exile in this foreign country. Who can share one's joys and partake one's griefs, in short one being among the crowd of mercenary wretches and holiday friends that swarm in India, whom one knows to be interested in one's welfare even in one's existence.

Sensible as I am of the blessings of such a dear friend, I shall yet ever give myself credit, for having indirect opposition to my own wishes, opposed my brother's coming to India. I stated to my father many times, the real state of the question as it occurred to me and always decidedly recommended, any situation that could be procured for him, among his friends and in his own country, to one in this country. But my father, the most sensible and the best of men, has like most other fathers of families in Europe, a great prepossession in favour of India, founded on the splendour of the very few who return from peculiar circumstances, with great fortunes to England and strengthened, if I may use the expression, by ignorance of the far greater number, who perish miserably here, from inability to return home. However this be, I have conscientiously discharged my duty to my father and my brother and shall enjoy with tenfold pleasures the delight of Rayner's society, of forming his young ideas, of teaching him what I know and of learning what he is better skilled in.

I borrowed Rs. 400 and sent it down to him by a bill of exchange, as I know of what use a little supply of cash is to a young fellow starting in India and what a world of future debt and difficulty he is saved, by a little timely aid of this sort. The news of this dear youth's arrival was so sudden, that I was quite agitated and womanish about it and could scarce hold my pen to write to him, nay my dreams, I declare, are occupied with nothing but his image, such as he was, when I was his favourite and adored brother many years ago. Now, he must be much altered in person, yet this auspicious event occurring at a time like the present, when I am in daily danger of losing my life, makes me positively quite gloomy and superstitious, for I cannot help thinking how it would embitter my last dying moments and many future years of his life, were I to be killed or to die, just when this long looked for reunion was on the eve of taking place yet before we met. But all this may be fallacy, I will hope so and sink the subject for the present.

December 23rd—This morning half of our troops went to forage and were out a long time from the great distance they had to go for forage. A detail of foraging duties would be thought frivolous in any narration of a war in Europe but here from the incredible number of cattle requisite to carry public and private baggage, provision and stores. How to procure food for this prodigious number of mouths becomes a question of serious import and is a consideration of no small consequence, in the calculation for an Indian army's taking the field. Especially, because in India, not even we ever dream, with all our wisdom, of the real economy that would result from establishing depôts or magazines of grain etc. in case of emergency or of war. The consequence of which is an expense of ten, of a hundred times, the magnitude when supplies are wanted, I mean the necessity which arises of buying all our grain from Banjarrahs, who of course do not sell it the cheaper. Because we must have it or starve and which leads to the necessity of our supporting and protecting the dreadful encumbrance many thousand cattle to carry this precarious supply, along with our camp.

The breach is reported practicable by Colonel Horsford, so we understand at least, and the three gun battery is ordered to batter the bastion of the Boorj, next the Town Hall, this I conceive is only a feint to make the enemy believe we shall not storm the present breach. Everyone expects the assault to take place tonight, as the relief for the trenches is ordered not to go down at the usual hour, but to wait till especially ordered!

December 24th—Last night, at a quarter before 12, our guns and the cavalry were, by private orders from the commander-in-chief to commanders of corps, got ready on our own parades. Just as we turned out of our couches, on which we had hastily thrown ourselves, dressed, in expectation of the assault taking place, a fire from the fort, the Shah-bruje, the town and the enemy's entrenchments on the hill commenced. The moon had not arisen and the darkness, besides enabling us to distinguish every flash, illuminating the smoke and atmosphere, gave a certain honour and grandeur to the scene, that is not easily conceivable by those who have not been witnesses of night attacks.

To attempt a description of this interesting and awful scene, is impossible, such a fire, so regular, un-intermitting and that lasted so long. Even those officers who have seen most service, declare they never yet witnessed. It was not a mere smart fire of musketry, with every now and then guns intermixing their deeper reports, but one eternal roar, continued all along the town and hills. One sheet or stream of fire, that seemed to have no end.

Our guns, the 8th Dragoons and 4th Cavalry were now ordered off to the right flank of the camp, to defend the angle of the camp next to our trenches and exposed to the threatened attack of Holkar's prodigious army that was encamped about one and a half miles off. We took post at P 2, barely out of reach of the tremendous fire from Shah-bruje and the hills, which continued with little intermission till our arrival at our post, when we drew up and two of our guns, under my command were sent out towards P to scour the ground towards the prolongation of the gardens and Gopaul Ghur where it was supposed the enemy would make the attempts. Soon after we all drew up the firing ceased, except from the citadel and town which now and then fired a great gun.

Never was moment more truly interesting to any set of men then was this short period of uncertainty to us. The general himself, was with our little party (the elite of the army) yet had no orderly, no *aid de camp,* brought us an account of our success or miscarriage. The enemy that *we* expected, soon after our taking post, sent a few scouts, probably to see whether our camp was guarded or not and the reception they met with seems not to have inclined them to repeat their visit, for they left us unmolested. And thus were our anxious moments rendered more painful, by inactivity, which left us nothing to employ our thoughts on but our poor fellows, of the storming party, who might, for aught we know be ere this repulsed, perhaps exterminated, by so superior an enemy. At last I perceived, just as the moon shorn of half her beams', dimly arose a distant *dooly,* slow moving along from the trenches at the groves towards camp, several of us flew towards it. It contained a Havildar of the 12th Regiment severely wounded and never was a more pleasing answer received than was his, to our earnest questions. "The Boorj and entrenchments, are all our own"! so rejoiced was the old man that in his energy of describing to us '*how the field was won*" he forgot his wounds and tried to get out of his *dooly* to explain it all, more to the satisfaction of men who were not to be satisfied but with a full detail. After him, many others, in the same condition, Europeans and sepoys, officers and men followed and as everyone agreed in the respect of success, we were truly happy. Several times however, the firing of musketry and rockets recommenced, as often were we made uneasy, as often were our fears quieted, by additional accounts of our success that barred all doubt.

We passed some hours more in ignorance of the exact extent of our success. At least we ascertained that the Shah Boorj and the enemy's entrenchments had been carried and most of the guns captured. Lieutenant Colonel Macree, who commanded the troops employed, had with great prudence, restrained his men from any attack on the town of Deeg in the night, as from it's prodigious extent and the small numbers of our troops, those too probably scattered in quest of booty, such an enterprise, might have been fatal and have robbed us of our hard-earned success.

The enemy, all agree, fought with desperation, their artillery men bayoneted at their guns. After they were driven from the breach, through the Boorj, into the town, they fired several times, attempted to retake it and when our storming parties had cleared the batteries, spiked the guns and hurried on to the breach. The enemy returned to their entrenchments and carried off many pieces. In the morning Gopaul Ghur was evacuated, as untenable by them, and instantly occupied by us. In the course of the day, the inhabitants in a body and Holkar's Infantry with their remaining guns, were seen marching off in a prodigious body, at the gate on the opposite side of the town and lake from that where we were and taking the route of Bhartpoor, were descried covering the whole Isthmus between the swamps and bunded lake where the battle of Deeg was fought, with elephants, camels, hackeries, and bullocks in crowds, laden with their effects, and probably with the treasures of the fort and town.

Our guns, and Lieutenant Colonel T. Brown's (2nd) Brigade of Cavalry, were instantly turned out to pursue and overtake them if we could, but under positive orders, to risk nothing. We had scarce got two and a half miles from camp, when we perceived the whole of Holkar's choice Cavalry, 10,000 or 12,000, drawn up, all-round, to cover the flight of the garrison and inhabitants. We knew well that if we advanced on them, they would as usual disperse and retreat, keeping up a harassing and running fight with us on front, rear and flanks, the instant we offered to continue our route, a conduct which (not to speak of the danger which our 1100 or 1200 men run of being cut up by such superior numbers) would effectually prevent our continuing the pursuit of the fugitives with any prospect of success.

In this situation, Colonel Brown, with a prudence, which does him honour, sent his brigade major back to camp to inform His Excellency of the state of affairs, and requesting instructions and the line of conduct he was to pursue. In consequence the brigade was ordered back, really to the joy of all us poor devils, who were tired most completely from want of sleep the preceding night, the heat of the day and who well knew that the object of our expedition was unattainable and that from a desultory skirmishing fight with these fellows, neither glory nor advantage could be reaped.

It is confidently asserted that although the commander-in-chief applauded Colonel Brown's temperate conduct to himself, he took other opportunities of saying that; "He thought Colonel Brown's Brigade, equal to the attack of any force". I hope and believe this is not true. In the first place, we all know Colonel Brown, and ourselves, well enough to know that we could have attacked and defeated the enemy at any time, even with such a disparity of numbers but what would have been the use of it were we sent out to fight? Or to overtake a quantity of flying baggage? The last undoubtedly and Colonel Brown was ordered to "risk nothing." He found his object unattainable and sent to say so, at the same time remaining on the spot, until he should receive orders what to do in the next place. If Colonel Brown ought to have attacked the enemy, why did the commander-in-chief order him back? Colonel Brown wisely indeed, would not exceed his orders, because a personal responsibility would have attached to him, had any misfortune happened to the detachment yet when the responsibility, was shifted from his, to the general's shoulders, Colonel Brown was ordered back.

The clue to this conduct at headquarters if true, is however very easily discovered, when Colonel Brown was sent off, we had only got an outpost of the Fort of Dig, in our possession and our camp was in so hazardous a situation, that the loss of a man could not be risked. During our absence however, a great change had taken place. The enemy had evacuated the town and all the works, but the citadel. These our troops had taken possession of quietly and the gunner had even sent in a flag of truce to propose evacuating the main fort and we by this change of affairs, were become very bold indeed. The enemy's flag, by mistake was fired on. and one of ours which was sent to them, was fired on in return. Six hundred Jats (brave Hindoos of high caste) had shut themselves up in the citadel, determined as they gone out to defend it to extremity, and orders were given in consequence, for two 12-pounders to march and blow open the gates of the only entrance, in the course of the night.

December 25th—This morning we were fortunate enough to see the Union Jack of Great Britain, flying on the walls of the Fort of Deeg, which had been evacuated during the night by it's garrison. Suspecting, from the attempts at correspondence made by the enemy, that they would do something of this kind during the night, His Excellency, most prudently, did not, by attempting to take the place by force, throw away the lives of his men.

When day broke it was found empty and instantly occupied by us. After breakfast, almost the whole camp went down to visit the fort and town. I, among the number, went over the whole of the trenches batteries, enemy's lines, forts, Shah Boorj and city. It is truly astonishing, how we were able to continue our attacks on this place under such opposition and so many obstacles as we had to encounter on all sides and nothing but a conviction of how fruitless all opposition is, to our scientific and bold approaches could ever have made them so easily give up the citadel which is a large quadrangle, with bastions and cavaliers, and a very deep wet ditch. All of excellent masonry and of a height far exceeding anything I ever saw. This very circumstance however, would have rendered it an easy task to batter it down especially as it's thickness bears no proportion to it's height, so that on making but a slight hole; low down in the mason's work the prodigious super-incumbent pressure would bring it down by tons at a time. Still however, this would have taken time to do but as there is but one entrance to this building of any kind; the garrison no doubt were fearful that all retreat would be cut off from them. A circumstance enough to dispirit a set of men, who, as they never grant terms themselves to a brave foe, think they never will receive any when in distress.

On looking at the gateway of the fort, which it was intended to blow open, I cannot but rejoice that this scheme was not put in execution, as I am convinced it would have either failed altogether or been attended with dreadful loss. The gates are three in number, one within the other. The whole of the road between each, being crooked and flanked by the fire of the fort and outworks through which it passes, and to conclude the business the last gate, was walled up a considerable way and had the garrison staid in it, would have no doubt been completely so.

The new and beautiful Palace of the Rajah, built on arches in a lake, stands just without the fort and is, with it's beautiful gardens, by far superior, in every respect, to any building I have seen in India. The grandeur and heavy magnificence, of the principal building is indeed great and splendid, successive tiers of apartments descend, with their balconies into the water, habitable, as the increasing heat of the weather dries up the tanks. The Zenanah[3] or Daftarkhanna[4] both built in part

---

3. Women's quarters.
4. Office.

of marble; beautifully worked and carved are each fine wings to the main building in their several styles, but what constitutes the superior charm of this sweet place is the complete set of jets *d'eau,* which border every walk in the garden and play round every part of the palace. There are, of these many hundreds. all of them supplied, by a large deep, quadrangular cistern, a bath, on the roof of the Zenanah, surrounded on the inside by holes, stopped with wooden pegs each communicating by long pipes built in the walls with it's jet, so that on the removal of a peg, its corresponding fountain, instantly begins playing. This cistern itself, is recruited by water, drawn up from the surrounding tanks, whilst I was there, the secret of the pegs was discovered, and we in a few minutes let most of these beautiful fountains a flowing. The effect was beautiful and gratifying beyond belief and reminded one of the Sultans, in the Arabian Nights entertainments, repairing with their favourites of women to their groves and gardens, surrounded by running streams and playing fountains, while the guest, the song, the dance, the story "went merrily round."

    These visions, again, soon gave way to the reflection of what Runjeet Sing had deprived himself of, by his ingratitude and treachery. Not merely this superb edifice and these beautiful gardens, deserted by the pomp of majesty and the fascination of beauty were polluted by the gaze and the tread of vulgar curiosity, but the immense, and once populous and flourishing city of Deeg, was now without an inhabitant of any kind, except the sick and aged, who were unable to leave it! May this reverse be a memorable warning to the other natives, how they conduct themselves towards people who can be as powerful enemies, as they have been jealous friends. Runjeet Sing's conduct to us last year was rewarded with an additional territory of five *lacks*.[5] Yet joined our bitterest enemy against us *"Tempora Mutantur Etnos*[6] etc. He has now reaped as he sowed.

    December 26th—It was intended to have marched this morning but the necessary arrangements, for the captured guns, grain

---

5. A term for a territory yielding that sum of annual revenue.
6. The times are changed and we are with them.

and prize property prevented us. The prize agents of the army[7] have been very busy in the fort looking out and digging for treasure, and selling all property. Informers of treasure, or property of any kind concealed, get half of it, if it is their own secured to them, and quarter if it is public or another's effects. Two *lacks* - 9000 rupees, have been dug up in the fort and more is expected, as by all the native accounts, fifty *lacks* of rupees were always kept in Deeg, and sure we are that on the 24th the fugitive would never have tempted the cupidity of their protectors; Holkar's ill paid Cavalry, by carrying with them any cash. Several *lacks* of *maunds* (a *maund* is 80 lb) of grain, have been found, which will be purchased by the Company and effects of greater quantity than value are selling by auction daily for the benefit of the prize fund. A Lieutenant's share, of what we have already realised will amount to about 400 rupees.

Strong suspicions are entertained, that much money is concealed in the beautiful carved and fretted walls and pillars of the palace and our prize agents, of whom two are left for the purpose of searching in Deeg, will I dare say, not stand upon much ceremony about pulling it to pieces.

December 27th—A singular fragment of a letter, discovered in the Shah Boorj, gives a tolerable idea of the conduct of this siege, in the eyes of the natives. It is written in Persian, from a man seemingly in high command to his friend and after the usual invocation etc. goes on to detail the siege; "These *Fringies* have opened on the Boorj, first six 18-pounders then three more, with many mortars. During the whole of this time we have brought to bear on them seventy or eighty guns from the fort, the town, the Boorj and from our numerous batteries. We have enclosed them in a circle of fire, yet these infidels (*caffres*) will not even deign to return us a shot. They fire unremittingly

---

7. Prize agents names are Lieutenant Hay for the Artillery, Lieutenant Pester for the Native Infantry, Captain Boys for the King's Infantry, Captain Covell for headquarters and Captain Houston for the Native Cavalry, Lieutenant Smoke for the King's Cavalry. I record their names because in general this appointment is a fortune in itself, five percent on all sales or three per cent on cash, being allowed to them.

and without regarding us on the devoted wall. Thou knowest we to be no coward (*na-mard*) (no-man) I am to and I will defend the Boorj, yet I feel that we shall be beaten and killed, that the *Fringies* will certainly prevail".

December 28th—This day it was proclaimed; by beat of *tom-tom* (a kind of drum) about camp, that as the country we were in was now the Company's[8] territory, all plunderers would be tried and punished immediately. A tract of land of some *lacks* of yearly revenue has been given to the Raw Rajah, whose territory and orders of that of Bhartpoor for his fidelity and attachment to our cause, while even we were in distress. A small fief, has likewise been given to Ahmed Bux his brave *Vakeel*, who with 400 horses has followed our fortunes and been present in all our actions, assisting where he could. This is excellent and proper.

December 29th—Yesterday a *vakeel* from Runjeet Sing, Rajah of Bhartpoor, came as far as the picquets on his way to camp. He was then stopped, until orders for his admission were received from headquarters. An *aid-de-camp* it is said, and universally believed, arrived with orders to turn the *vakeel* instantly out of camp, without hearing a word from him on any subject whatever. The orders were executed, although the *vakeel* imposed "to be allowed to say but two words to His Excellency, to be unpermitted to throw himself at his feet and trust to his mercy!"

Was this conduct on our part wise? Was it justifiable? Was it politic? Is it our policy? Is it consistence with good sense totally to destroy this Rajah, infamously, as he was behaved? If he is crushed some other must rise, who was kept down by his superior luster or power! Will our implacable conduct not rouse the jealousy and fears of the potent Jyepoor Rajah, especially

---

8. The East India Company have never yet made war in India, that they did not disclaim ambitious view, or territorial aggrandizement. Yet the East India Company have never yet made war in India, that they did not as often, add immense tracks of country to their former possessions! What means then, this farce of words? But their hypocrisy has been always punished. These additions of nominal land and revenue are gradually accelerating the downfall of the East India Company by making their seeming greatness of moment enough to attract the cupidity of ministers, who in a breath can and will destroy them.

when, by the annihilation of the formidable chief of the Jats, we become his next door neighbour? That same political wisdom that dictates to us to clip the wings of so treacherous a prince, ought surely to prevent our quite destroying his political existence and nearly extend to reducing him to such a level with his lesser neighbours, as would always place the political balance in our hands. Is it moreover like a wise general by refusing any terms, even the most severe to him, and favourable to us. to give to such an enemy that courage which borrowed from despair. must be always formidable? We have left him nought to hope for at our hands. If then he must from a great prince descend to the station of a poor man and a fugitive, will it not be his best and wisest conduct to fight to the last drop of his blood? But above all let us suppose that the terms which this *vakeel* wished to offer, as we are certain they must have been very humble, even extended to our utmost possible wishes, to all that we wished to gain by fighting it out (who shall say that these were *not* his terms when he was not allowed to propose any?).

In this supposed, and not impossible case may not the general be called to a severe account for having ignominiously turned away, without a hearing a suppliant, clothed in the respectable character of an Ambassador and for having done at a great expense of blood and treasure. What it is at least probable he might have done by treaty? And will he not be answerable for every life lost in the siege of Bhartpoor? These questions seem to me, to carry with them their own answers. I would not have it supposed that I have wished one day. one hour of precious time to have been wasted in diplomacy, or intrigue, but we knew we were to halt for reinforcements for three days certain.

The distance to Bhartpoor is only an hour's gallop for a horseman, so that from the facility of obtaining full powers, signature etc., etc., the treaty might have been dispatched with ease in 24 hours and had unforeseen difficulties arisen to be delayed, I would not on that account, have ceased operations for an hour even. The more imminent the danger grew, the readier *they* would be to concede points in dispute, nay more, I would not have consented to open a negotiation. I would have quickly turned the Ambassador out of camp, if upon hearing his proposals, they were not of the most humble nature. But to do this without even knowing what they were! A Moosulmaun of rank with a large suite of horsemen, elephants and camels, formerly resident at Delhi, from General Perron and now residing at Bhartpoor, came today to pay a visit of ceremony to His Excellency, as he had frequently done last campaign. But, although he declared he came in no public character from Runjeet Sing, he was not believed, but was turned also, away from camp!

CHAPTER 6

January 1805

January 1st—This morning, at 7a.m., the army marched on the high road to Bhartpoor. We saw none of the enemy, passed through a rich country, quite full of the stacks of the straw of that tall species of Indian corn, called Juwar or Kurbee, which the enemy have not destroyed or burnt, as they so often do, to our infinite annoyance. Where Holkar is, no one knows, most people believe however, that he is near Bhartpoor, which he and Runjeet Sing mean to defend desperately. It is said that the two monarchs, had an interview, after our turning off the *Vakeel*, and that Runjeet Sing abjectly implored Holkar's help. The only resource left for him, as we would not pardon him, that Holkar, to preserve him in his good faith demanded money, which was liberally paid, to the amount of two lacks daily and two of his sons, as hostages. With regard to which last demand, Runjeet Sing is said to have required time for consideration, before he complied. I don't much believe all this because it was not Holkar that had reason to complain of treachery but on the contrary Runjeet, who might well accuse Holkar of first bringing him into the scrape and then quietly looking on while his forts and towns were taken.

We encamped at a village not far from the Fort of Comeere, which by the native powers, has always been found a most strong fortress. The whole of this country is full of wild hogs, an animal most destructive to the cultivation, from it's voracity living entirely on sugar canes and roots but which is here a royal beast, the hunting and killing of which is reserved for the Rajah alone. We however, as may be supposed, or not at present been observant of

His Bhartpoorian Majesty's game laws and when the coast is clear of Mahrattas, the line of march is filled with the officers brandishing their spears in full chase of this ferocious animal, whose flesh, from the cleanliness of his feeding, affords a most delicate report, totally free from the rank flavour, of the domestic pork.

January 4th—The people of the fort do not fire on us at all, but some horsemen drove in our vedettes in the morning, a trick, which it is supposed they were taught by four scoundrels troopers of 4th Native Cavalry, who deserted with their horses and arms last night. A report prevails that Runjeet Sing is determined not to fire on us in hopes of getting terms, by not exasperating us.

At 9 p.m. Brigadier Maitland, with two hundred 75th Regiment and Native Infantry, moved down, and without opposition, took possession of a grove 980 yards from the place where he entrenched himself. It is reported that 5000 or 6000 men who were posted there exclaimed, as they retired on the approach of the Europeans, that "if the Rajah had not forbidden them to fire on the fringies many a one of them should be laid low"! All the valuables have, it is much feared, been taken out of the fort and sent off before our arrival. Holkar is encamped on the other side of the place. It was reported in the bazaar, and therefore deserves all the credit and no more that can be attached to a bazaar piece of news, that Runjeet Sing's mother is coming out to try and soften the general's flinty heart. In imitation of Coriolanus's mother and wife, no doubt.

January 5th—It is now said that Holkar is gone off homewards, certain it is we see nothing of him and so inactive an ally might as well be at Jericho as Bhartpoor, for any good he does. Unless good it be to burn every village within a league or two of camp, which they do not fail doing, as at Deeg. The people in the trenches are not disturbed, except now and then by a chance matchlock. The garrison even failed to take advantage of a glaring error, either in the engineer who marked out, or people who dug the trenches; daybreak discovered, to the astonishment of the troops and everyone, that one of the principal trenches, instead of being parallel to, was perpendicular to the part of the fort to be attacked and consequently liable to be enfiladed in its whole length. At this late hour they were forced to begin another trench in the right direction which they completed without molestation. If the fault lay with the engineer it is inexcusable, when it is so easy by taking the bearings of the place to find its direction, and from marks taken, to ascertain the parallel situation of the trench before it is dark.

January 6th—Holkar, it is said, is returned and with him, Ameer Khan of Bundelkund notoriety and a better man than Holkar, for instead of uniformly putting his prisoners to death, as the latter does, Ameer last year liberated two young officers, whom he had taken.

This evening Captain Nelly and Lieutenant Swiney, went down with six 18-pounders to the battery, which from the stupidity, to call it no worse, of Captain Robertson, the engineer on duty, was most abominably constructed of six embrasures. three were laid to bear on a well, in front of the battery and one bore on no part of the works. Captain Robertson had besides, so ill masked his embrasures, that the enemy, perceiving where they were, had injured them greatly.

January 7th—The batteries opened this morning, on a part of the curtain at A to the left (fronting the fort), of the centre bastion B. In the evening so fast did the wall come down, that Nelly sent to Colonel Horsford to say the breach was practicable. The colonel accordingly went down but very prudently preferred trying another day's battering on it before he would report it's practicability to the general.

January 8th—Lieutenant Hay opened this morning, a battery of two 10- and four 8-inch mortars. This officer, who is adjutant to the field artillery, and as such who cannot be expected to take subaltern's duty in tour, makes a great merit of volunteering it on certain occasions. Not of volunteering the laborious and creditable duties, as they occur but only those which an artillery officer has a pride in, and gains credit by performing, such as opening a new mortar, a gun battery, which is expected to have great effect. This practice, is in my opinion, ungenerous and unfair to the other officers, as well as in itself unjust. It is too irremediable as he happens to be the senior subaltern present, as such, if he was resolved to do duty, why does he not go down to the laborious and unpleasant duty of the trenches?

Poor Colonel Macan is superseded in the general command of the cavalry of the army by Lieutenant Colonel Wood of His Majesty's service in virtue of a new regulation, oppressive and cruel to the Company's officers. The King's lieutenant colonels having, it is said in the warrant, complained bitterly that from the rise in the Company's army being entirely by seniority, many junior lieutenant colonels. of the Company's troops were promoted over their heads to the command of regiments as colonels. H.M. is pleased to authorize the commander-in-chief, for the time being in India, of H.M. forces to grant the local rank of colonel to every King's lieutenant colonel, so superseded by a Company's. So far the regulation on the first view seems a fair one but wears a very different face, when we advert to the circumstance of H.M. lieutenant colonels. being able to purchase in three or four years, the rank of lieutenant colonel, which no Company's officer attains but after a laborious service, of perhaps thirty years. So that although the Company's lieutenant colonel may be junior, as such he is an older officer by many years and has been superseded in every rank below that of colonel, by boys of H.M. Regiment.

A stronger proof cannot be brought, than the instance in point, when an old veteran like Colonel Macan, and who has been Commandant of Cavalry for five years, is at once superseded by a young man, Colonel Wood, who is about as old as Macan has been an officer in Bengal, thirty years to will. Besides, in H.M.'s tender care of his own officers, he never has adverted once to the double supersession, which by this regulation, some of the Company's lieutenant colonels, suffer.

In our service, artillery, engineers, cavalry, infantry rise independent of each other, now an artillery lieutenant colonel stands, we shall suppose first in seniority, next stands a King's infantry or cavalry lieutenant colonel and third a Company's infantry or cavalry lieutenant colonel. The Company's infantry lieutenant colonel (3rd in rank) is by a vacancy in his department of the service, made a colonel. The King's lieutenant colonel, is by this regulation, promoted also to that rank that he may not be superseded by the Company's officer, and both, are promoted over the head of the poor artillery officer, who was, as lieutenant colonel, senior to both! Lieutenant Colonel Horsford (Artillery) and Lieutenant Colonel Kyd.(Engineers) are at present in this situation, doubly hard it is too in this army at present, when a colonel's prize money is more than double that of a lieutenant colonel.

Colonel Macan, after remonstrating to the general on the hardship he has suffered, asked leave to quit the army on the fall of Bhartpoor, intending to go home and resign so thankless a service, until the road between this and our frontier, is practicable. This old and venerable officer, colonel commanding of the Bengal Cavalry, a brigadier general, on the staff of the army under the Presidency of Bengal is appointed an honorary *aid-de-camp* to the commander-in-chief. What mockery!

January 9th—The enemy having been most assiduous in repairing during the night the damage done to the wall during the day, orders were sent for the batteries to keep up an unceasing fire of shot and shells on the breach last night. But notwithstanding all our efforts, the breach was completely stockaded in the morning and the batteries were all day employed in knocking down this stockade. But from the gabions, of which the battery is made, being originally filled with loose earth (that is not carefully beat down) and from the incessant fire and consequent concussion on the merlons, having still more beat down what insufficient earth was in the gabions and not allowed time for it's repair during the night, the battery became altogether inadequate to defending the poor fellows in it.

Our regiment has borne all the brunt of this cursed business and has suffered in officers out of all proportion to the rest of the army. No wonder indeed for despising our enemies as we do, we no sooner sit down before a place, than instead of regularly going to work by first erecting enfilading and ricochet batteries, to destroy the defence and dismount the guns of the place, and then battering in breach, we run up a hasty battery for breaching, in the midst of a plain exposed to the whole of the fire from the place, which we never attempt to take off and the consequence is that multitudes of our people are killed and the enemy remain at their defences and guns till the instant when we stormed.

January 10th—I sit down with a heavy heart, to record the events of last night, so heavy a misfortune I am happy to say, I never before had occasion to write. May I never have again!

By sunset the breach being to all appearance practicable, the whole of the European Infantry in camp with the Native Infantry, under the command of Lieutenant Colonel Maitland (75th Regiment), were advanced to the assault, at 8 p.m., in three columns, after leaving a guard of Europeans and natives in the trenches. Our guns, the 8th Dragoons, and 6th Cavalry were, at the same hour, ordered out to Z and X on the right of the camp, to protect it from any attack of Holkar's army, and to keep up the communication if necessary, between our stormers and camp. The rest of the cavalry and infantry remained round camp, in different scattered positions, to protect it. We, took up our position, just at 8 when we had well drawn up a tremendous fire, as at Deeg, of great guns and musketry commanded, and did not finish for more than half an hour. This, as we afterwards learned, was but a false alarm.

The enemy being apprised of our intentions, and completely on the alert, shortly after this a second fire, far hotter than the first, and of much longer duration began. In our anxious and uncertain situation we hailed the "Glad tidings" brought by Captain Butler, major of brigade to the artillery, and sent up to our post by Colonel Horsford, in quest of the general, to inform him of intelligence, brought by a wounded European, of our being in full possession of the place. No-one ever dreamed of disbelieving, even of doubting the possibility of our success and accordingly all gave loose to congratulations and joy.

The fire was a third time renewed and with even greater violence. The musketry being comparable to nothing but the roll of a drum, yet neither this, nor the incessant fire of great guns kept up for the next two hours from the fort, led anyone to suspect that anything was wrong. So sanguine were we in our hopes. A strange rumour now pervaded our little detachment of a vague, uncertain, even doubtful nature, of the troops having been repulsed. Still, though every moment added weight and credit to this shocking idea, we clung to the "sweet siren hope." Nor would be convinced of the folly of our "sweet delusion," till an order, at half-past one a.m., for our return to our lines, accompanied with information that admitted not of question, that our troops had been baffled and had returned to camp made us "fall from our high hopes." From the exaltation of hope to the deep wretchedness of despair.

I speak of this moment of misery as my own feelings at the time were, others happier perhaps of lighter hearted dispositions, a perhaps without vanity I say it, of less reflection, affected to consider it as a mere nothing. But is it nothing for all our Europeans to fail in an attack of that nature, in which opposed to Indians, they have been always considered as invincible? Is it nothing to let the natives see that men of our colour can be beat? To have let fall the veil of opinion, our great support, the chief cause of all our success in India? Is it nothing to boast of the vengeance we intend to take against a perfidious ally and to be baffled in our attempt? Is it nothing, for General Lake, the happiest child of fortune, hitherto by the natives deemed invincible and "whose very name" in their own words "was more powerful than any army," to be driven back with disgrace and loss, at the head of his "grand army" by the despised rebel Rajah of Bhartpoor? And to wind up the story of our misfortunes, is it nothing, at a time like this, when all the powers of Hindoostan and the Deccan trembled with jealous fears, on their thrones, when those we have forced to a hard and ignominious peace, those whom distance or strength have caused us as yet to respect, are joined together in one common hope for our extermination, these stimulated by apprehension, those by revenge.

Is it, I assert, a matter of trivial import at the critical moment, when every power in India balancing as to the conduct it shall pursue, looks anxiously to the result of the present contest that the flower of the British forces, that our collected strength should be beat off from the town of Bhartpoor. But our pride, our insolence in the day of prosperity, when we insultingly spurned the submissive and humiliated *Vakeel* from our camp merited a fall. I will say that the recollections of our conduct on that occasion, of our haughtiness, of our impolicy and folly, in thus driving these people to despair, made me, when I heard the firing begin, have a prophetic foreboding that as we certainly deserved, so we should fail.

In a military point of view we could scarcely have expected to succeed and hear our failure may be attended with the best effects in warning us, by example, how we so despise an enemy and teaching us how we again run headlong into a breach without previously taking off the defences of the place. The disposition of the attack, the causes of our repulse and the loss we have sustained, I have not yet learned.

As yet every narrative, even of those immediately and personally engaged differs, materially describe the failure as owing to the impracticability of the breach others to the disobedience of the commanding officer, and a third and I regret to say a numerous class, to the backwardness of the Europeans. Certain it is, the loss in officers and men has been prodigious. Colonel Maitland is among the killed and many men are missing, all of whom, as well as the poor wounded men, the enemy were this day seen murdering and mutilating as they lay. One chief was killed by a shot of an 18-pounder, fired by Captain Nelly as he came out to view the slaughter and triumph. Our spies say he was uncle to Runjeet Sing.

January 11th—The annexed sketch will show our disposition for the siege, and attack.

I have by this time, heard many accounts of the repulse and it's causes. Everyone, with a single exception, seems to me, undeserving of complete relief, as each throws the failure on the other. From all however, some information is to be gained, and by comparing the several accounts, with the clear and intelligent opinion of my able friend Lieutenant Swiney, (Artillery), who is impartial and unprejudiced, I have been able to form something of an idea on the subject. Lieutenant Colonel Maitland's orders, I know from the unquestionable evidence, of the adjutant general's letter to Colonel Monson Commanding in the trenches,

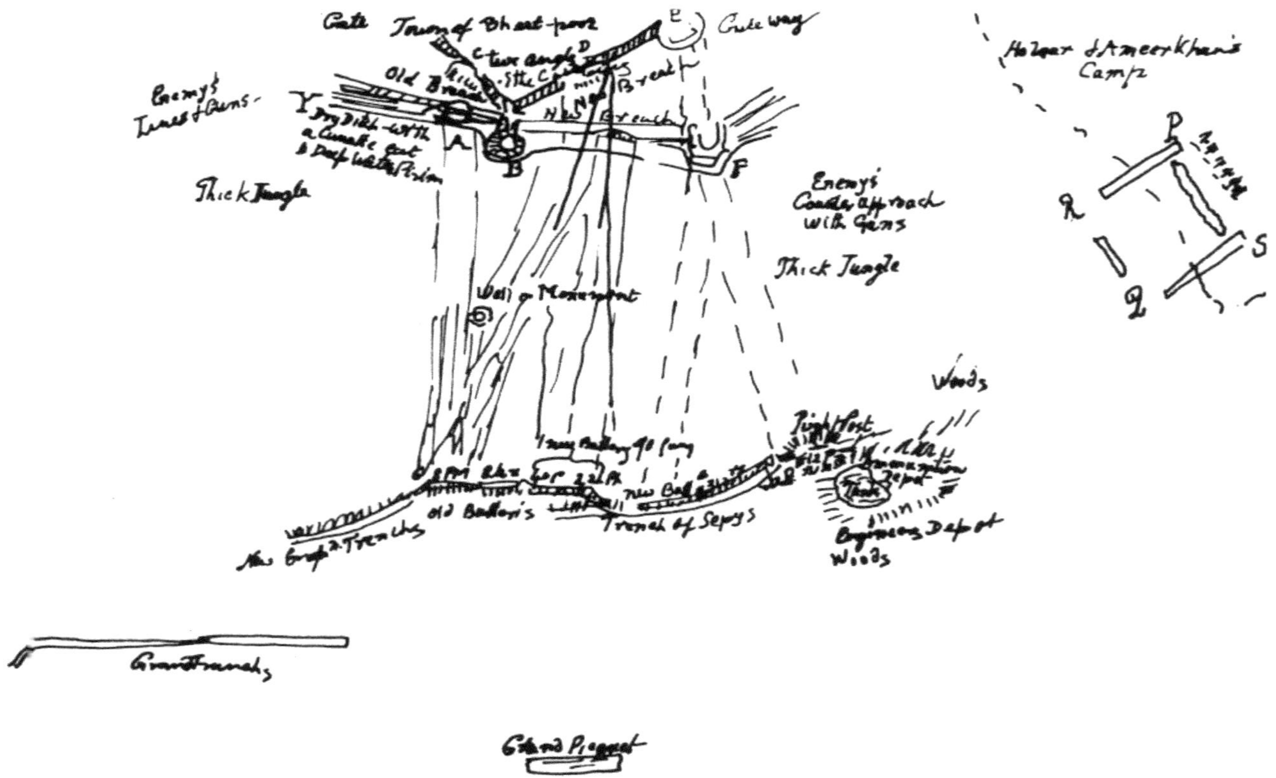
Gate
Town of Bhurtpore
Gateway
Holkar & Ameer Khan's Camp
Enemy's Lines & Guns
Old Breach
New Breach
Thick Jungle
Enemy's Covered approach with Guns
Thick Jungle
Well or Monument
Woods
Old Battery's
Trench of Sepoys
Engineers Depot
Woods
Grand Trenches
Grand Picquet

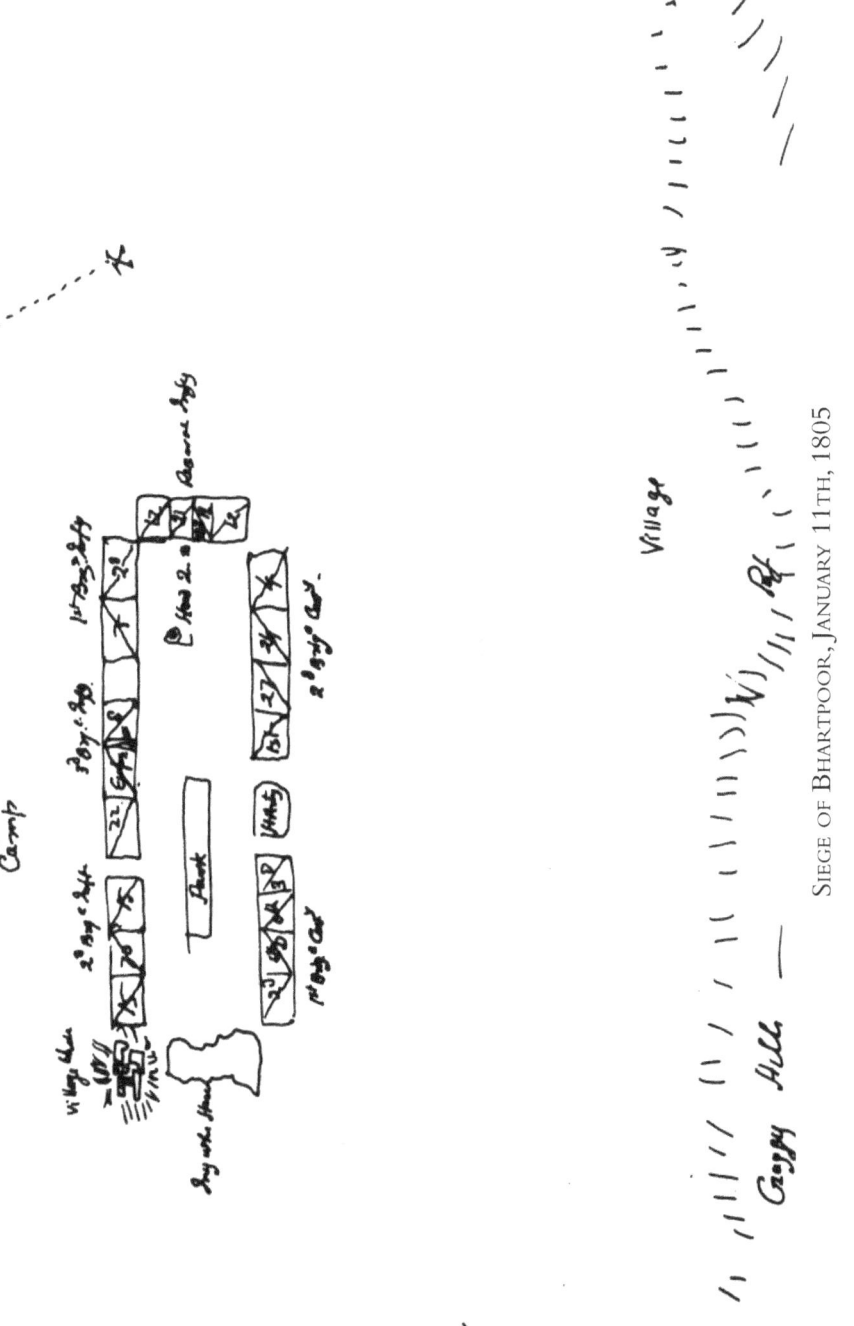

Siege of Bhartpoor, January 11th, 1805

and who was of course made acquainted with all the intended plan, and which letter, Lieutenant Swiney saw. It mentioned, that the troops were to be divided into two columns.

The right commanded by Major Hawkes *viz*. 80 of the 75th, 1st of the 2nd Native Infantry and a party of artillery were to scour the trenches of the enemy and spike four guns to the right.

The left column, under Lieutenant Colonel Kyan 80 of the European Regiment, and 2nd of the 22nd Native Infantry were to do the same to the left. And it was expected that, after driving away the enemy from the trenches, these two columns might be able to enter with the fugitive and meet the centre column within. If this was impracticable, they were, after performing the parts, to go to the breach.

The centre column, under Lieutenant Colonel Maitland and Major Campbell, was to move to the breach and after entering, were to divide to the right and left along the ramparts. four 6-pounders were to accompany the party, two on each flank, commanded by Lieuts Swiney and Pollock, to clear the breach and defences of the enemy by the grape, and to support the column.

The most clear and explicit directions as to route and time were amply detailed. The place of assembly for the whole was appointed at the left of the gun battery and the centre column was to proceed 300 yards before the others moved. A better conceived plan could not possibly have been laid down but two things in it were certainly wrong

First, the hour 8 p.m. was wrong, the enemy, from the assiduity in repairing the damage are daily made, should not have been allowed a single half hour after dusk, for the moon being in the 2nd quarter is as bright just after sunset (the time when we ought to have stormed) as any part of the night.

Second, knowing the command of water the enemy had from the lake, Colonel Horsford was always apprehensive of the making a cut and letting in deep water before the breach, scaling ladders to serve as bridges also, were to accompany the party but instead of this important duty being performed by fighting men, by a battalion of sepoys or dismounted cavalry, they were entrusted to a set of miserable coolies. The arty *bildars* (pioneers) people who are hired and discharged as they are wanted, at the lowest wages for a labouring man, who get no prize money, nor are pensioned if they lose the limbs in the service. Can such people be expected to go into such a scene as the "imminent deadly breach?" The wonder ought to be, at their folly in even going into danger at all.

As to the execution of these orders now detailed, the following is I fancy pretty near the truth, whether (as some say, but which I cannot believe) Colonel Maitland received different (posterior) orders, from what I know were once intended, it is impossible now to ascertan but certain it is that he did not parade on the left of the battery, when the guns waited for him and in consequence his 6-pounders never saw the party at all and Colonel Maitland left them behind.

The whole of the three columns were jumbled together at the outset. Colonel Maitland went away to the right, a prodigious way, Colonel Kyan represented to him, that he was wrong and that it was high time his (the left) column should strike off to their own destination. Colonel Maitland, even abusively I hear, persisted in asserting he was right to order Kyan to go. At last he found out his error and the right and lieutenant colonel left him. In trying to recover his road, Colonel Maitland now obliqued as much too far to the left and falling in with the left column several rounds it is operated were exchanged, before they were discovered to be friends! Colonel Maitland still pressed too far to the left and pushed Kyan still farther.

Major Hawkes meanwhile, executed in part his scheme, spiked and overturned three guns of the enemies but could not, or at least did not see a gate through which Bapoosindia's Infantry fled into the fort at our approach (C), as we since learned from the spies.

Colonel Maitland now approached the breach but the enemy were completely alarmed and the approach of our unfortunate troops was seen as distinctly as at moon day. Blue lights and fires being lighted up on every part of the breach and walls and burning wood and straw and baskets thrown down the breach to lighten the scene still more. All these obstacles would have been nothing to Europeans but having approached by the left of the breach (D) the head of the column came, to their utter surprise, on a cut through which water ran to a deepened, broader ditch made in front of the breach. The road admitted of only three or four abreast, some plunged in before they were aware, some were drowned, so deep was it, none could get over.

The ladders were now called for but were not to be found, the *bildars* having run away before they were at least brought up! Our unfortunate men stood for above half an hour in this horrid situation, exposed to millions of matchlocks and what was worse than all, grape from the guns in the bastion (B), just over the heads, and not 20 yards off! Over two ladders were brought, they admitted but of one or two abreast and some of them broke. Some of the men, unable to stand like Russian infantry to be murdered in this way, pressed on through a shallower part of the ditch. But not a man got to the other side with dry ammunition, a circumstance of itself enough to have disheartened the bravest troops.

A few men pressing on over these obstacles got to the breach, and twelve or thirteen men are said to have in part ascended it. But the indefatigable Jats had, during the intervals between 5 o'clock and 8, scarped away the displaced and loose mud from the bottom.(M) While at the top, above the small perpendicular remaining part (N) of the wall, a firm and lofty stockade (O) was planted, which effectively precluded any attempts to gain the top. Unsupported too, as the few who arrived at the breach were, by the rest of the column, which was all in confusion from the massacre of men and officers and the want of dry ammunition, or a passable road across. Twice was the breach attempted by this handful of men, but all was vain. *The Grenadier's March*, three cheers, God save the King were all essayed, to stimulate the men, but in truth, it was impossible to be done.

Colonel Maitland heroically leading on to a third attempt, was speared through the stockade by the enemy, who smug behind had nothing to fear. Major Campbell fell wounded. The other leading officers shared a similar fate and at last the troops retired, finding farther attempts unavailing. Both Europeans and sepoys behaved with a coolness altogether surprising, which we consider the murderous scene in which they were obliged to stand passive. Soon after retiring, Colonel Kyan who was in the rear, found that the enemy had sallied out, thinking our batteries would now be abandoned but a few discharges, made them speedily return.

In this affair the enemy have little credit for defending the breach, they were in no danger, in fact, they fired secure behind the parapets, against our men exposed and the guns that our impatience permitted to remain in the bastion, flanking the breach, are said to have vomited death to dozens of our devoted men at every discharge. Had Colonel Maitland brought up his guns, grape from them, fired at the parapet or breach would have been of essential service in cleaning those places of the enemy and keeping up the spirits of our men.

From the accounts of spies, we learn that the enemy several times abandoned the breach in consternation and on the night of the 9th, eight *hurkarrahs* came to our post, to say that all the females and treasure and effects of the frightened inhabitants were hurrying out at the opposite gates.

This day however, and yesterday, were days of general rejoicing in the city. The Rajah, Holkar and five other Princesses met to congratulate each other. It is said Runjeet Sing abdicated the Rajahship in favour of his son, the defender of the place. All the European heads were brought in to the assembled Council and the bearers profusely rewarded. The public treasures were thrown open to the *faquirs* (religious beggars) six rupees was given to every man who fought on the 9th.

The gates were thrown open to all who were afraid to stay in the place and 700 men put on the yellow dress, emblematic of a resolution to conquer or die in the breach! Had the Rajah been wise or prudent, setting humanity out of the question, he should have sent into the general the prisoners wounded, with his supplication for peace, instead of cruelly putting them to death. And on our part, I think we should have sent to demand Colonel Maitland's body, or to bury the dead, but as we are too proud, even in our misfortunes to do this, so they elated with a temporary prosperity, too weak to see that we dared not have refused terms. If they had acted in this wise and humane manner.

From the above lamentable misfortunes, I hope we shall in the end be refit by respecting our enemies, a little more than we have yet done and by deserving success, if we obtain it not. The success of the besieged will probably make them less desirous of sending off the treasure. But to efface this stain from our reputation and to prevent the dreadful political evils that may result from it, we must redouble our activity. We must take an ample and above all a speedy revenge. It is truly shocking, but it is positively necessary to our existence, that now a terrible example to the Indian nations should be made of these Bhartpoorians, and it will be done!

January 12th—We have altogether withdrawn our officers and men from the batteries at which the place continues, night and day to fire. This looks as if we were tired of the business. We should not let them suppose the blow has been so severely felt by us. We should be doubly active in appearance, after a check, for here lies the grand superiority of our military character over that of the natives.

January 13th—This day 400 or 500 of Holkar's best Horse under two or three great chiefs, all Patans, deserted from his service and came over to ours. Matters probably were previously settled with us. They encamped on our left. However good this policy may be, yet it is humiliating to our name and character to employ rebels and traitors like this, particularly as we well know they are not very fond of fighting and can only be of service to us in not fighting against us. The great Bungeesh Khan, related to the Nawaub of Furruckabad, and mentioned in the early part of these memoirs as having been our opponent at Muttra etc., is also bought off we hear and gone to Jyenagur.

January 14th—Major General Richard Jones (lieutenant colonel of the Bombay Artillery) appointed to supersede Colonel Murray of dilatory memory in the command of the army at Kotta has joined it and orders were yesterday we understand sent off for him to move forward and join the grand army. The reason of this we understand to be, that Ameer Khan with many guns and 60,000 infantry and cavalry is at Dholpoor, in which fort, Lieutenant Colonel Ashe and the 2nd of the 9th Native Infantry are shut up. Ameer Khan gives out that he is coming to join Holkar and as a counter balance, Jones is ordered on Hernaut Sing, who commanded Holkar's army at Deeg on the 13th November, and after the fall of that place, who went off with the remaining battalions and men to Khoosialghur, is also coming back to Bhartpoor, where the enemy do seem resolved to make a desperate stand.

The brave and active Captain Hutchinson, Commandant of Rampoorah, has taken Toonk, a walled town and chief of the Rampoorah district, by escalade. A body of horse were encamped under it's walls. Hutchinson marched two companies of his little garrison under Lieutenant Robertson, (2nd of 21st Native Infantry) to beat up their quarters while, during the surprise and firing occasioned by this feint, he with another party, escalated and took the place from the opposite side. Euge!

January 15th—From authority that can not be doubted, I learned at headquarters today, that Ameer Khan left Dholpoor, for this place on the 13th and he ought to be here tomorrow at the usual rate of marching. This chief lingered near Gwalior till he heard of our repulse, he now is coming on! This is one of the nothings caused by our failure. It is but the first, pray heaven something may soon happen to make it the last!

January 16th—This morning the new batteries, being completed alongside the old ones, began to batter in a new place, to the right of the bastion (B), viz. (D) in my sketch. I have given a general idea of the new works and have drawn the angle C B D E, which is nearer the true angle of the curtains and bastion (B) than my former one Y B F. The wall came down fast, and three 12-pounders in the trench to the right, directed by the celebrated Sergeant O. Loughton, assisted by two 12-pounders at the right post, were of use in awing the enemy's guns. The expectation of having a sufficient breach by the evening, does not seem to have been entertained, for the French guard was no greater than usual. In several bulletins, communicated to me frequently during the day by my intelligent friend Swiney, I learned that although the wall fell fast yet no perceptible slope was produced. A circumstance which, as he said, showed the ditch to be a very deep one and from them being larger guns in the curtain. It was, he said, most truly equally evident that the wall was very thick, allowing only for a passage behind the trail of the gun on the ramparts and scarce any for recoil.

January 17th—This day was the regular foraging day but we were not ordered out, a striking proof that something great was expected, in consequence of so large a party, as the escort could not be spared from camp. Yet, although the batteries continued an un-intermitting fire, no great effect was produced. My friend Swiney gives the melancholy but true reasons now; The garrison employed by raids of people to work at the breach in the night and operation in which, during the darkness of night, it was impossible effectually to interrupt them, so that the breach, in the morning, completely stockaded and built up, presented a stronger wall in reality, as well as apparently to the besiegers. The ditch is so deep that it swallows up every particle of earth knocked down and the same circumstance, it's depth, affords complete protection to swarms of workmen, who are busily employed in removing in buckets, the earth as it falls. Our poor fellows, officers and men, are all employed at the batteries, without hope of relief. For as I have before had occasion to remark, in this grand army of India we have not one relief of artillery officers or men for even our pitiful batteries of 25 pieces and to man even them, we have been compelled to take the men from the battalion guns. So that in case of an alarm, the only guns in camp are the horse artillery and gallopers of the cavalry regiments.

January 18th—All hopes of the brisk and sudden effect, expected from our powerful batteries, seem to be given up for this morning. We went out ten or eleven miles behind the hills to forage. We did not return till 5 o'clock. This work gets now terribly hot and fatiguing and although it has hitherto not been so dangerous as battery duty, yet for my own part, I would far rather go down in tour to the trenches. Not only because there I should learn more of my professional duty but because I cannot but pity the terribly hard duty which the poor officers and men of the foot artillery are obliged to undergo. One half of the officers were withdrawn last night, but for the poor men, who have already been 72 hours on the battery, night and day, there is no hope of relief till the siege is ended. One corps, is employed in camp duty and indeed is liable to perpetual harassing and turnings out on the least alarm. But I think that the cavalry gallopers, in such a conjuncture as this, should perform those duties and we be permitted to relieve in part the artillery of the batteries. This, but just to ourselves to record, that we volunteered our services for this purpose but the general would not hear of it, saying that he should not reckon the camp safe, if we were away!

Major General John Smith arrived at sunset in camp from Agra, having performed in 38 hours, a march of near 50 miles without halting. The direct road from Agra is not above 32 miles but to avoid the fire of the town of Bhartpoor and the attacks of the enemy's army, he was compelled to make a prodigious circuit. He was not molested but many of his men were left on the road, and a great number of followers with baggage cut up by the Pindaries in the rear. This small detachment of 1200 or 1300 men is almost seasonable relief to our jaded sepoys, who scarcely are off one duty 'ere they are put on another. Yet the un-considering majority of officers in the army, lament the arrival of a number of officers and men, who will deprive them of a portion of expected prize money. For my own part, as I would not for an instant hesitate to purchase the possession of this place with all my hopes of prize money, I therefore would be happy to hear of what is so earnestly deprecated in camp, the arrival of General John's or Colonel Martindale's armies. Besides, there is either a great deal of prize money or none at all in Bhartpoor. In the first case we can spare a little and in the other, *Qu' Importe.*[1]

January 19th—This day, at half-past 2 p.m., I took a ride down to the trenches and batteries. The breach being only 650 yards from the batteries. I could distinctly see every part of it with my glass. As usual it has been thoroughly repaired the preceding night and certainly, the repaired was stronger than the original wall, which is however very thick. It is not a mere stockade (or poling

---

1. Anywhere.

of beams) but in my opinion, a strong epaulement of fascines, (or boughs) and earth, strongly stockaded to keep it together, for the shot that struck the new part, splintered it and lodged. That the slope is now great I am certain from the beams of wood laying on it. The shots that hit the lower part of the wall have now very little effect, they go in and lodge, scarce discomposing the loose earth, a natural consequence of battering a mud wall.

The more the adhering part of the wall is loosened, the more a collection of loose sand and earth accumulates round the remaining solid part, forming an irregular cone, whose base is extended as it's height is diminished, but the lowering of which becomes daily more difficult, as the base extends. The profile (2) will explain this and No. 3 will show the daily repairs in the wall, observing that all the earth that falls into the ditch, or the cunette, is regularly carried off. During the very time the shots were flying about the ears, I observed there were people at (A) carrying away the shot as they fell and as these men were only visible from the naval upwards I am inclined to suppose that a road has been left clear, all round the bottom of the breach, since everyone agrees in the great depth of the ditch and therefore these people could not have been standing in it.

Top stockade was much shattered (as indeed it is daily) and had we not been, to use a homely word, cowed, by the misfortunes of the 9th inst. have no doubt, but we should have stormed this breach two days ago. The ditch however, is a serious obstacle. No 2 hurkarrahs agreeing as to the precise breadth and depth, although all allow it to be great, it is said to be nine feet deep and twenty wide. And we have ladders prepared twenty-eight feet long, with a kind of crutch, like supporters of nine feet length, which are to be placed in the opposite bottom of the ditch, and the ladders pushed on till they fall over on the opposite side. But only suppose the ditch to be a few feet broader and deeper, and our ladders are useless.

I have thought that the simple contrivance of empty powder, a spirit, casks to be slung in strong net work of cord, with a hook affixed and a corresponding eye underneath the extremes of the ladder, would be an excellent contrivance indeed, for the ditch

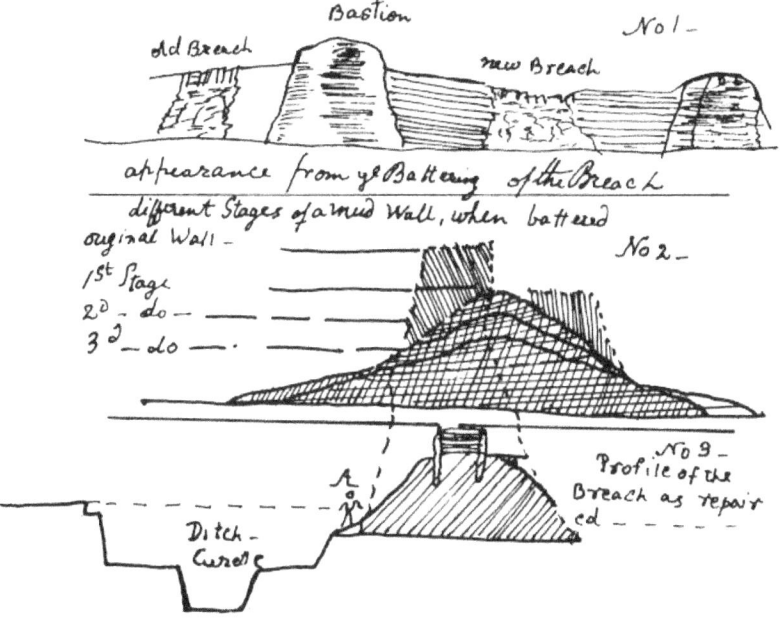

Breach and repairs

Ladder over the Ditch

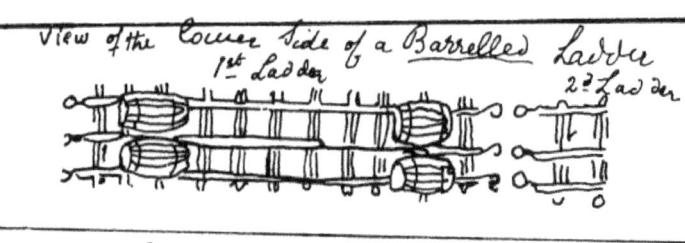

View of the Lower Side of a Barrelled Ladder
1st Ladder   2d Ladder

View of a Bridge of 2 Ladders - in Elevation

Wet Ditch

of whose dimensions we are so ignorant. For be these ever so great, a floating bridge leaves nothing to apprehend us to depth and if the ladders are made with strong hooks and eyes to attack the extremes to each other, a floating bridge may be made *ad infinitum*, over standing water of any breadth and the point of junction of two ladders, otherwise the weakest part, would here be the strongest by the united buoyancy of four barrels at this point. Four barrels, two at each end would I think be sufficient. If not, eyes be placed at equal distances along the ladder, six, eight even ten barrels, if necessary, might be hung on in pairs, for by the barrels been carried separately from the ladders the machine is in no way cumbrous. And on arriving at the water, the front pair of barrels are hooked on the bridge, it is launched to the opposite side and should the ditch be narrower than was supposed, the instant the barrelled extremity touches the opposite shore, the stormers rush on and are in an instant across, if not, a second ladder, ready barrelled, is hooked on to the first and so on ad infinitum.

January 20th—This morning I mentioned to Colonel Horsford the idea of the barrels. I could see that it had before occurred to him but he seemed to approve of it and I understand mentioned it afterwards at headquarters. In the evening I was told something of the kind was preparing at the park and took to myself no small credit for starting this idea. I am almost sure that it will succeed, if the men are previously drilled who are to carry it. We are all impatient for the storm, which some fancy will take place to night, though I should prefer day-work, when a bridge has to be made over a ditch of unknown dimensions. The breach is an excellent one.

January 21st—I am fated, once more to be the historian of defeat and disgrace! We have again tried to take this place and again have been obliged to retreat with great loss in Europeans and natives. It is one of the nothings I suppose, caused by our first repulse, that these Jats do not seem to fear us as the natives used to do, but naturally gather courage from our mishaps.

Yesterday, a havildar and three troopers of Captain Pagron's troop of the country, volunteered to go down and look at the breach and ditch. A plan was laid, that dressed like irregular Hindoostanee troopers, and mounted on excellent horses, they should gallop down to the breach, affecting to be deserters and calling out for protection from our parties and for admission into the fort, while our sentries were to fire blank cartridges at them. They were then to return. This plan was executed in every part with the completest success.

The enemy, completely deceived, though it was broad day (at 2 p.m.), did not find out the mistake till the three men returned to our lines, after having inspected the breach and ditch. In consequence of the gallant behaviour the havildar got promotion to the rank of *Jamadar* (lieutenant) and his companions, to the rank of havildars and to each of the three, 500 rupees, was presented on the spot as a reward. They described the breach as capable of being rode up and the ditch, as broad but shallow enough from the quantity of mud driven into it. In consequence of their information which, in as far as regards the ditch, proved totally erroneous. All schemes for crossing probably were not planned or executed, with that caution which would have ensured success.

At 4 a.m., the Europeans and sepoys of the storming party marched down to and remained in the trenches ready. We, in the lines, remained most anxiously expecting the signal to get under arms. At 3 p.m., the whole of the cavalry, with our guns, turned out and marched left in fronts round the rear and right of the camp, until we came between Holkar's and Ameer Khan's camp and our batteries and lines of attack. The intention of our taking up this position was, to prevent the myriads of Mahrattas there encamped, from coming down on the right flank of our storming column, or on our batteries and an excellent precaution it was.

As soon as we arrived at, or near this position, we saw the whole country on our front and flanks covered with horsemen, far exceeding in numbers, anything I ever before saw, or had yet fancied I should in my life see. The attack of the town had now begun and they had evidently been under arms for some purpose of attack when we got to this spot. They began forming into regular lines and columns of prodigious size and moved down slowly, with every appearance of a determination to eat up the comparative handful opposed to them, which without vanity, they might certainly have done with the sacrifice of a few hundred men, but for our two howitzers and our guns assisted by the gallopers of the regiments.

Our guns were instantly ordered out towards them. The right and left of the line thrown back, as they were equally menacing of every quarter, and the 8th Dragoons were drawn up in the rear as a reserve. While the 4th Cavalry drew up on our face to protect us. We fired with great quickness and no doubt considerable effect, for ten minutes, some of our shells and all our shots falling among them, and doubtless leaving the mark where they fell, among such "congregated heaps" of men. At the first few rounds they wavered and at last broke and quickly retired out of cannon shot in all directions. They had no guns, but fired many rockets and multitudes of matchlocks, few of our people, however were hurt. Two howitzers, with two squadrons, were now detached 700 yards to the left, to dislodge a crowd from a grove and square wall, where they had collected, and the first shell burst among the crowd, killing and wounding many.

The line kept it's ground, as our motive was a different one from that of fighting or pursuing, and as the guns opened at 800 yards, we had no opportunity of seeing what execution we did. Some of the sapient gentry in camp accused us of firing away a great deal of ammunition with little effect, but whatever numbers of the enemy might have been killed, is nothing to the propose our end was fully answered.

The terror if not slaughter evidently caused by our cannonade, kept the enemy at a most respectable distance from the stormers, and from our cavalry, who, if we had not sickened the enemy in the beginning as we did, would most unquestionably have suffered prodigious loss and been able to do nothing in return, against an enemy who always disperse when a regular body offers to charge them.

Just as we were flushed with our success, Lieutenant Colonel Gerard (adjutant-general) and Major Salkeld (deputy quartermaster general) arrived from the trenches with the sickening and petrifying intelligence, of our having again failed. The memory of our last unexpected defeat had never permitted me to indulge a sanguine hope of success. I therefore felt this blow less than those around me, who had laughed at me for supposing that what had happened once might happen again, yet feel it, I did, and bitterly.

As our stay here was no longer of use the line now phased about, in the same position, while we manoeuvred by the prolonge in the rear. A precaution which was of the greatest use, for the enemy hung on our flanks and rear plaguing and annoying us all the way home and kept at a distance only by a few seasonable shots every now and then. I never felt a hotter day and was not a little fatigued when we got back to our lines, which we did soon after dark, melancholy and dispirited, reading in the features of all we met, a sad sympathy of ideas.

January 22nd—From the accounts of my infallible friend Swiney, who was on the storming party and indeed from the universal testimony of all engaged, I find that our party were obliged to retreat from finding the ditch too broad for the ladders and far beyond a man's depth. Brigadier, Lieutenant Colonel Macree (76th) commanded the storming party. A column to the right of that, commanded by Brigadier, Lieutenant Colonel Simpson was to protect the right flank of the stormers from all attacks that might be made on them, and to go, destroying the enemy's guns in their posts on the right, as they proceeded to a gate of the town which they were to force and then enter and join Macree.

Two parties of Europeans carried the ladders, and two 6-pounders, commanded by Lieutenant Swiney, accompanied the stormers to defend them if necessary and to annoy the enemy with grape. On arriving at the ditch, Lieutenant Morris (European Regiment) found his twelve or fourteen feet too short. He jumped, though slightly wounded in the leg by a shot, into the ditch and swam across, to try it's depth, which, though he even tried for he could not find. This gallant young man himself ascended the breach which was perfectly practicable. He, and one or two swimmers who got to him and went up with him, found it deserted.

The enemy's wall pieces and great guns from the two adjacent bastions continued playing furiously, so hot was the fire on the party from every part of the fort, that one of the guns was disabled and numbers of the bullocks in all killed and wounded. The exertions of Lieutenant Swiney enabled him, however, to bring all safe off. The ladders, I am told, had large *dubbers* (or oil-skins as big as casks) attached to them to float them and several men jumped, I hear, on these ladders, which easily upheld them, as these skins are buoyant as bladders. But the irregular bladder, like shape of these, renders them far less eligible than barrels and the cumbrousness of the machine, if the dubbers are previously tied on to it, is a strong objection. If one ladder was found somewhat too short, why was it not provided with strong hooks and the other instantly attached to it? Tying them together, as Morris, says he thought of doing, is far too tedious an operation, to be performed under so hot a fire. While the hooking on of the barrels and ladders to each other is comparatively the work of a moment and in this unfortunate instance have, I cannot but flatter myself, certainly succeeded.

January 23rd—Early we were alarmed by a heavy cannonade from the N.W., evidently in the direction of Captain Welsh's convoy. It continued with little intermission till 8 a.m., when Lieutenant Colonel Need, with the 27th Dragoons and 2nd Cavalry was sent to reinforce Captain Welsh, from whom no news had been heard. The firing still continuing, the remainder of the cavalry with His Excellency at their head, followed in half an hour. Guided only by the firing, we proceeded till we came nearly to the ground where we foraged yesterday, when we halted.

The pleasing intelligence arriving that the enemy had been defeated with the loss of four field pieces and three tumbrils. Captain Welsh, it seems, proceeded yesterday to Toonk, a village three miles beyond the village where we foraged. He there met the convoy from Muttra of 5,000 Banjarrahs, escorted by four companies of sepoys and two guns, which then returned to Muttra.

Captain Welsh early this morning proceeding molested, as usual, by the enemy's horse, until he came to this village, where to his surprise he found posted two or three battalions of infantry and four guns, and some myriads of horse. He instantly, with great presence of mind, occupied the village, built on a cone eminence, with his infantry, placing his four pieces on elevated spots and his cavalry and the Banjarrah bullocks as many as could be placed, under protection of his guns. The enemy had a battalion or corps of *Ally Coles* (Irregular Infantry armed with swords, matchlocks and long spears), besides his regulars, while the horse separated and carried off the terrified Banjarrahs, the infantry supported by so many horse that Welsh dared not stir out, twice stormed the village and as often were repulsed at the point of the bayonet, by the steadiness of our battalion of 500 men (1st of the 15th).

Welsh offered a 1000 rupees, and a *subedar* (captain) commission, to any man who would try and reach our camp to inform the general of our situations, now every moment more perilous, for ammunition was getting low and two of his guns were dismounted. In this moment, when every man gave up hopes of again seeing us in this life, Colonel Need's reinforcement was espied from afar. Welsh, instantly sallied out with his cavalry and infantry on the enemy's battalions shouting and huzzahing "the General is come!" on the enemy's guns and infantry. The infantry on the guns, the cavalry on the infantry. The enemy were broken in a moment, the guns captured and helped now coming up.

A general pursuit of the fugitives commenced, in which most of them were killed by the enraged troops, and about fifty standards were taken, besides arms, accoutrements and clothes. The commander of them, some say Ameer Khan himself, others, Hernaut Sing, was overtaken in his palanquin, stripped himself of a complete suit of steel armour and his clothes and run off naked, but was, it is supposed killed. All these things and a fine Dollond's telescope were found in the magnificent palanquin. The march of this gallant detachment was like a triumphal entry into camp. Every man here and there carrying a magnificent silken standard, and the guns bringing up the rear.

The 1st Cavalry alone, had thirty-three standards. As the enemy had three or four hours to plunder, without interruption, more than half of the convoy were lost to us, great part of that however, was not carried off, but abandoned by them in the pursuit and scattered about among the jungles. The bullocks having thrown the loads and run away.

January 24th—The batteries do little or nothing now, so it is always with us after a repulse, we show the enemy by our silence, how dispirited we are. A few shells now and then fired at some working parties on the outside of the fort, are the only symptoms we give of being alive.

January 25th—We still continued to do nothing. Colonel Don's detachment escorted to Agra most of the empty Banjarrahs and hackeries, to bring back a very large supply of grain, which is so scarce in camp that half allowance for man and beast, we scarcely shall be able to hold but till he returns. As his convoy will be a most immensely large one, some apprehensions are entertained on account of his comparatively small escort, lest the enemy should move down with all his forces to attack him. Whilst we could scarcely venture to send him a large reinforcement from camp, lest we should by so doing, expose our trenches and camp to an attack from the fort or the enemy without. The European trench guard is reduced to 100, instead of 200, the reason for which is the increasing heat of the weather which makes Europeans begin to be very sickly and likewise, that the late attacks, has sadly thinned the few men we ever had.

January 26th—It is strongly reported, and by many believed, that the enemy are counter-mining our batteries, and that they had sunk their shaft (to commence the operation) not within but without the fort and within 400 yards of our batteries. In my opinion, there is one circumstance, which renders it impossible to do this, in this very low soil it is impossible to dig twelve or fifteen feet, without coming to water, so that their mine must be very near the surface indeed, so also must be their gallery leading to it. Thus the mine will either be ineffective, or will from it's little depth, be easily discovered by burning.

Colonel Horsford has taken a most effectual mode of preventing their doing any mischief by digging a trench round the front of the battery, until water is found below this, it is evident powder cannot be lodged and if they mine above, they will be discovered when they arrived at this trench. But in fact I do not believe they are mining at all. It is most certain that they could not commence from the other side of the broad and deep ditch full of water, surrounding the place, i.e. within the walls, and I do not think they would dare to begin the operations so far on the outside of the place, when an occasional sally from our trenches would discover all and destroy in a few minutes the labour of weeks, which a gallery 400 yards in length, must be.

I have now brought to a conclusion, the 1st volume of this journal. I had hoped to have ended it long ago and not to have been obliged to commence anew on another book, after 181 close written, and long pages. But the war, unfortunately, seems scarce nearer to a conclusion, than it was, when I began to write its commencement, five months ago.

Every fresh action, whether victory it be, or defeat, only seems to raise to us fresh enemies. To subdue the hydra-headed Mahrattas, will I fear, be found a task requiring more exertion of strength than that little Hercules, our ambitious and quarrelsome Lord and Governor possesses, even with the bravery and perseverance of General Lake and this army, at his back. Look where I will, I see not the most distant hope of dawning peace. I see nothing but a cloud of enemies, open or concealed, filling the political horizons. Each as they separately rise to view more dreadful than that which preceded it.

What consequences may attend the fall of Bhartpoor, I know not. He may fly to his other forts and keep us there for months besieging, while his ally and formerly the principal in the war, makes a diversion or two into our territories and while the heat of the season, will incapacitate us from performing any active, military operations. If however, the Rajah is desirous of peace, and we are wise enough to grant it him, after our experience of what despair will do, there will be yet hopes of terminating the war, if not with splendour, at least without disgrace.

May our late defeats, may our daily increasing enemies, may the ruinous expense of this war and the approaching consequent bankruptcy of the East India Company teach an awful lesson to the ambitious Marquis, who has caused all this ruin. Who has to immortalize by conquest, the period of his administration in India, sacrifice the interest of his employers and with the cold, unfeeling wantonness of cruelty, which politicians alone know, has shed, such torrents of human blood. May these, and the honour of a change of ministry and consequent impending impeachment, teach him that able politician as he thinks himself, he may be, he has been miserably out in his calculations of Mahratta strength and power of resistance and may a speedy peace be the fruit of his experience and of his terror. It is not yet too late.

The genius of Hastings, for negotiation and intrigue delivered him from a similar situation, (a general Mahratta confederacy against him) in 1782, brought on too by crooked and ambitious and dishonest policy of his own. The situations are much alike. The able manner in which Hastings bought the neutrality of the Berar Rajah and procured in consequence the death of that confederacy, perhaps saved him, from what might have been the consequence of his impeachment. And if the present Emperor of Calcutta is a wise man, he will, as speedily as possible, lay up in store a similar set off for his numberless demerits since he came to the Government of India. To be reserved for the hour, now not far off, when the death of the old King and the fall of Pitt and Grendville's party will make his Lordship's responsibility for his acts as Governor General more than a mere name, a *vex et preterra nihil*.

January 27th—Camp with the Grand Army Before Bhartpoor. Nothing of importance in regard to this unfortunate and protracted siege, is yet begun upon . We are daily busied in cutting down and collecting materials for our new works, whatever they are to be, but until the arrival of Colonel Don and his important convoy, nothing can be done in the artillery department, and it is certainly wiser not to begin to break ground, until all is ready for vigorously following up that measure. The General Staff and people in our trenches, are daily amused, by one scoundrelly spy or other, who come in to us. On what I cannot help thinking false errands, as they have never yet come to anything serious from chiefs of the enemy, pretendedly desirous of coming over to us with the battalions or guns. These people certainly come over on purpose to see the state of our batteries, trenches, camp etc. and, although I should not be afraid of their seeing these as often as they choose, yet there is something humbling, in being made the daily fools of those fellows. I am told that they practise many ingenious modes of knowing the distance from the trenches or bastions to our posts and battery.

One is ingenious and simple, they set out with a clew of thread, a small string, one end of which is held by a confederate. They advance until they arrive at our battery or post, calling out that they are deserters and on coming in they break the thread off, which pulled into the fort and measured, ascertains our distance to a nicety for their guns or mines or shells. We know all this, yet suffer ourselves to be daily gulled.

Today, a Golundauze came into us, who proved to be a fellow that had before deserted to us, been entertained by us, had gone away again and been absent without leave these many days. He excused all this, by saying he merely went back to bring off others, and his apology was accepted! He now said, he came with a message to headquarters from Messrs. Goman or Gowan and Sibley, two Europeans, are *mestizoes* in the Bhartpoor service, who had formerly written to General Lake, offering to bring off all their battalions. This letter of theirs had been intercepted and in consequence they were closely confined, and in daily fear of death or mutilation. They wanted now to escape and thought they had still influence enough to bring off the men but fearing to write, had employed this man, he aversed to negotiate verbally for them. This story, seemed plausible, and the Golundauze was entrusted with a letter from headquarters to these men, and again sent back to Bhartpoor. I wish any good may come of it! Who knows that he is not retorting our weapons on us and negotiating with our sepoys!

Lieutenant Colonel Martindale, with the Bundelkhand army, on the 13th was on the banks of the Scinde, north of Narwa, Amboogee's capital and next day was to cross on his way thither. He is now however, positively to return to Agra and if possible, in time enough to effect a junction with Colonel Don, for whose safety, serious apprehensions are entertained. Rumour says the cavalry are to march tomorrow to escort Don into camp. If the enemy move in great force to attack him, which if they do not do, they are blockheads, the loss of even the convoy would compel us to raise the siege in an instant

January 28th—Movements have been perceived early this morning, in the enemy's camp. It is said all the horse, have decamped, for what purpose we know well, Don marches from Agra today. Agra is only twenty-eight miles off and it is pretty certain that Martindale cannot have joined him yet. Late in the evening General Orders were sent to commanders of corps, for the horse artillery (of course!) and all the cavalry, "to be ready if wanted at 4. a.m. next morning".

January 29th—At 4 a.m. orders arrived, for the cavalry and us, to mount and close up to the left of the infantry, where we were to draw up left in front in column, rear to the hills.

Here, to our great surprise, we remained until near 7 o'clock, when we were joined by H.M. 75th Foot and the 2nd of the 22nd Native Infantry with His Excellency in person. A sure sign that something was to be done. No baggage was permitted with the detachment. The men were ordered to carry the blankets and two days' cooked provisions. The officers, carried only what little cold meat they could muster.

We now plainly saw that we were going a long way and of course knew it was to escort Don and his convoy. On the 28th most of the cavalry of the enemy marched towards Don and just as the general, at 4 o'clock, was preparing to start with us, hurkarrahs came to say that in the preceding night, most of the enemy's infantry, with thirty or forty guns, had moved for the same purpose as the cavalry, and were to take up positions on commanding village, on the road where Don must pass. In consequence of which, alarming intelligence, the infantry corps. were instantly ordered with us and the whole of the cavalry, even to the regiment, then on piquet, was ordered to join.

We now moved off and from the instructions verbally given by His Excellency to Captain Brown, relative to our part in the play that was expected to be acted that morning, we learned that the enemy's infantry and guns, in great force, were supposed to be posted in a high village, six koss off, from which we were to drive them. Had they been there, I have no doubt but we should completely have defeated them, and taken all their guns, a piece of good fortune, which we never can hope for, whilst they lay encamped, under the walls of Bhartpoor.

The Mahrattas however, seem to know our old general's penchants for promptitude and rapidity of action too well after the Furruckabad story and the rescue of Captain Welsh. To venture any thing that could not quickly run away within reach of the old general's long legs, accordingly after making a complete semi-circuit of the deep morass and city of Bhartpoor, of fourteen or fifteen miles, expecting momentarily to be saluted by some of their guns, or to descry some of their infantry, we arrived at the supposed post of the enemy a village (A) on a very high hill which commanded a view of all the adjacent country for several miles, the city of Bhartpoor and the enemy's camp.

From this eminence although not a foot soldier nor gun were to be seen, yet about a mile on our left, where the jungle was very thick, we saw a prodigious body of remarkably well dressed and well mounted horse posted thick to the amount of 5000 or 6000, all along among the bushes.

At a prodigious distance and right in our front, we could distinguish the thick, heavy, and I may say, solid dust, of some very large body of men and animals, which from it's being in the proper direction, and from the scarce perceptible rate of it's movement, we conjectured rightly to be Don and his convoy, slowly advancing. At first it was feared that the dust we saw, might proceed from the enemy's infantry and guns proceeding to attack Don, but besides the above circumstances in favour of its being the convoy.

The general knew, from the time of the enemy's battalions having begun to move at night, and the slowness of motion, necessary with guns, that they could not have possibly gone so far in this time, with a temperance and steadiness, that does him honour and rightly judging that the consideration of getting his convoy safe home was superior to any of the consideration whatever. General Lake refrained from any attack, on this body of horse. He also refrained from moving on any farther towards Don, which would only have attracted this horde of enemies then along with him. He halted the troops in the plain, below the hills, posted a body of infantry and a gun or two on the commanding spots, of the hill and village, to watch the motions of the enemy, intending of course, if they moved to move likewise and in this position we calmly remained unmoved by the petulant attacks of the enemy's matchlock-men on our flankers and column, and only now and then reminding them by a 6-pounder, of the respect due to their superiors.

We arrived at this spot about 1 p.m., and about thirty-one ascended the hill to look at what was going on. I could, by the help of a capital glass, see Don slowly advancing and through the compact atmosphere of thick dust, raised by his massy, ponderous, slow column, I could plainly distinguish our dragoons and sepoys, which put an end to all uncertainty. Looking now to our rear, towards Bhartpoor, I could plainly distinguish the dust of some large body, moving hastily out from the camps behind the city. By and by, I perceived their numbers to be indeed great as their successively ascending and descending several low hilly ridges, gave me an opportunity.

They advanced rapidly. Many of the General Staff and most of the bystanders, affirmed there were among them regular bodies of infantry, but I never could see any and in the end we found there were none but cavalry. Already their advanced bodies approached us we all prepared to repel an attack on the convoy already within two miles of us, or on ourselves, but as the former was in greater danger, from the enemy being on both flanks, the 27th Dragoons was detached under the quartermaster general, Major Salkeld, to reinforce the convoy, and to show them the way to the ground we were to occupy during the night.

From 4 p.m. till dark, the flanking parties of the cavalry, the guns on the hill and now and then our guns, kept up a straggling engagement with the enemy, who poured in, in shoals, all horse,

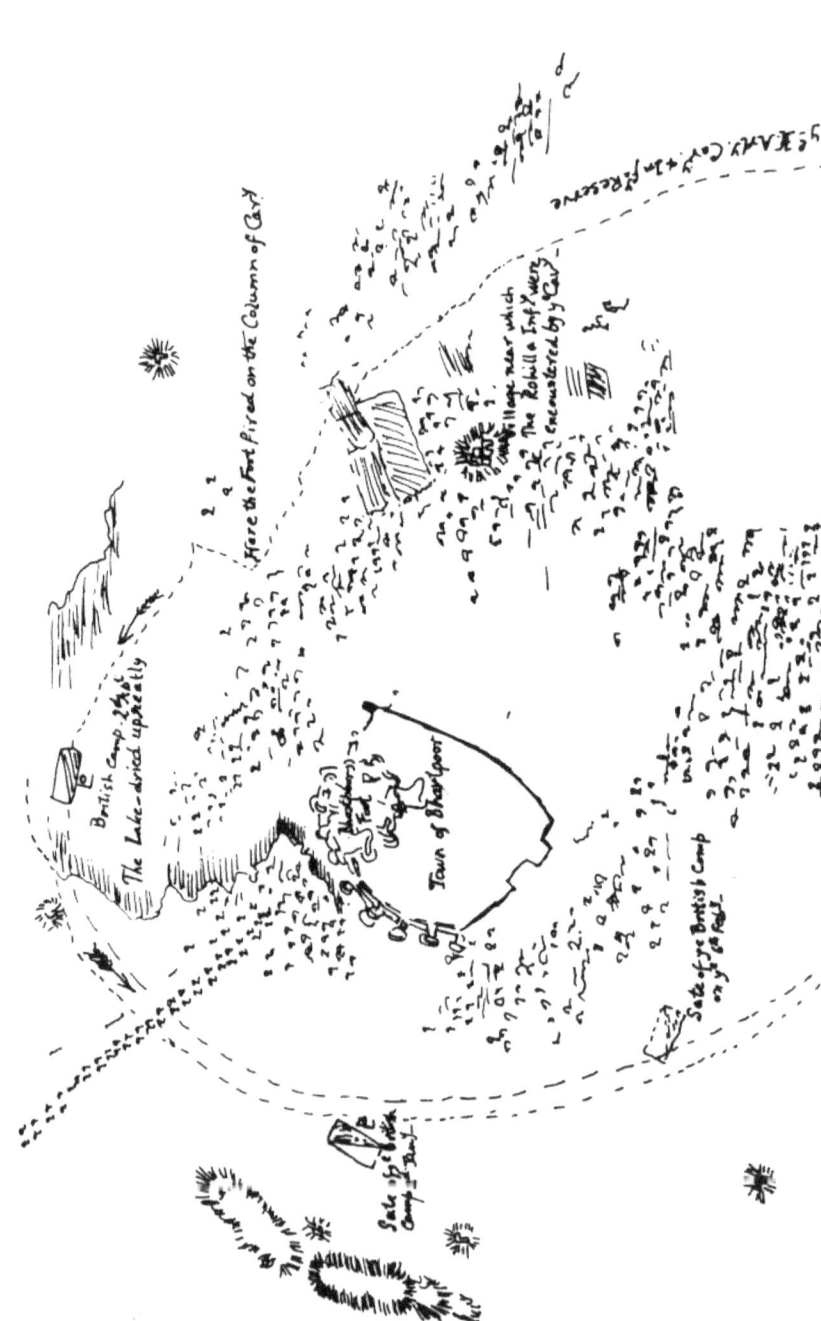

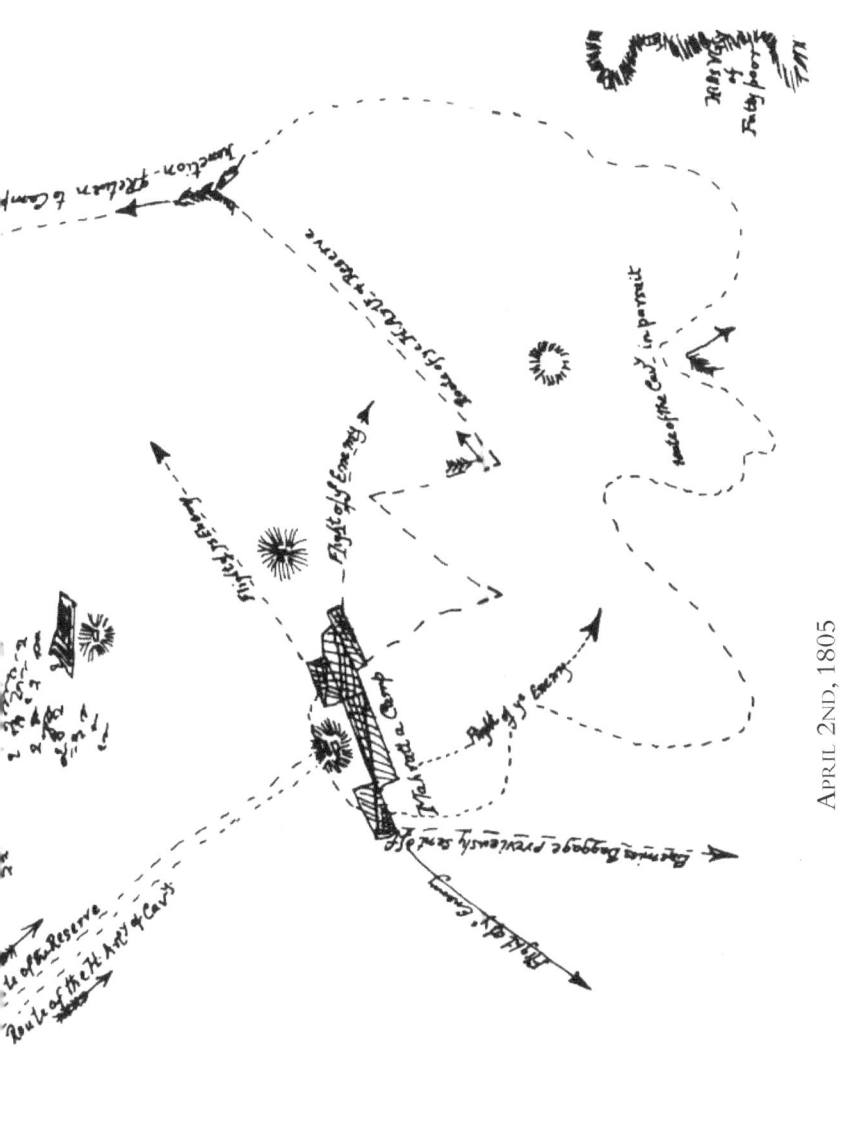

April 2nd, 1805

from every quarter and several of them paid with their lives or property[2] for their temerity. But nobody came within gunshot, after the example of the leading party, who forgetting our guns, altogether approached nearer than usual, but fled at the first discharge in every direction.

From the prudent and cautious slowness of that excellent Officer's (Lieutenant Colonel Don's) movements, we were not all in our position for the night, till long after dark, but not a bullock was lost! And we or rather Don's detachment encamped and we lay without any camp equipage, Sub dio, in the form of a square, under the hill, having all the Banjarrahs and store hackeries in the centre. Unfortunately for our part of the detachment it was the only cold night almost, that we have had for a long time, and after being frailed alive all day, we felt it bitterly. To the pleasures too of cold, we should have had the happiness of adding those of hunger and thirst, but for the kindness of a friend from Agra of Don's party, who sent us some beer and wine and but for the little remnant of meat we brought with us. So we made a snug fire of dry forage, round which we squatted and after our little repast and smoking a few churoots, to dispel the cold, we wrapped ourselves up in our cloaks, and stretched ourselves alongside the fire, having previously complied with the precept of Horace *"Dissolve frigus-Liqna super foce large reponens,"* to keep ourselves warm and sunk, pretty tired, into the arms of Murphy. (*Rod Random* - Vol. 1).

January 30th—The general belief in the morning was that in the night time, seeing how small a force they had to contend with, the enemy had sent for his guns and infantry, and we expected a serious encounter very speedily, a thing which not a man of sense, I do believe, in the army, wished for. The safety, a loss of this invaluable convoy involved the fate of the campaign

---

2. The horsemen of Indian armies, are with scarce an exception, independent soldiers, who follow perhaps a particular chief, but all find themselves, for a certain pay and chance of booty in horse, matchlock, spear, cloths and provisions. They take all risks on themselves, and commonly, their whole property is embarked in the equipment, the loss of which is nearly ruin to them. It will not therefore, be supposed, that they are always ready to risk the property by fighting and as they never drill or practised together, each acts for himself, without dependence on his neighbour!

and if we had had to draw off part of, or all our forces to fight a battle, the enemy's horse would have broke, during the combat, in upon our convoy. And while we should doubtless have captured guns and killed men, they would have gladly sacrificed those, for the more substantial advantage of compelling us to raise the siege of Bhartpoor.

We did not move off the ground, owing to carts breaking down and other accidents till 7 o'clock. There was a prodigiously thick haze, which prevented our seeing what we had to expect and which permitted some of the enemy to come down in a most daring style. We had scarce quitted the high hill, when they ascended it and by aspiring at and molesting one rear guard, who kept immense bodies of them at bay with the gallopers, killing many of them, we slowly moved on about a quarter of a mile, then halted for half an hour. Then again crawled on, again halted to keep the rear closed up and this being horribly tedious and burning work, we kept up till our return to camp, but this was the only possible mode, in which we could keep our convoy together and much of it is to the general's credit. That he so steadily and invariably kept firm to his grand purpose without yielding to any temptation to fighting and confirming himself, at the head of such an army and surrounded by myriads of teasing foes, to the rigid execution of a duty, confessedly the most fatiguing and disagreeable of any in a military life, the escorting of a large convoy.

When the haze completely cleared away, we perceived ourselves surrounded on every side, with the same bodies of horse which familiarity makes us hold cheap, but the numbers and appearance of which must seem indeed formidable to the eye of inexperience. I never saw, since I have seen a Mahratta, greater number, nor never such well dressed, well mounted men. But they wisely confined their courage to skirmishing with the flanking parties now and then, in the course of their *Bahadouring*,[3] coming near enough to attract a 6-pound shot or two from the nearest guns.

---

3. Bahadour, a Lord, a great man, acting the great man by what the natives term Karowly Kurning. Riding individually pretty near the enemy, going round in circles. Brandishing the spear, a matchlock, with threats and defiance and gross abuse vociferously shouted all the time.

As day advanced, they grew somewhat bolder, and at one time, for nearly two hours nothing was heard from front to rear (right to left) but incessant peals from guns, matchlocks and pistols. At one time thirty or forty gallantly charged with dreadful screams eight or nine skirmishers of the 8th Dragoons, who were advanced some hundred yards from the main body, but these gallant Irishmen, compelled their cowardly antagonists soon to fly, with the loss of three or four lives, while of the 8th two men were wounded slightly. As forage was so scarce in camp and we passed over a great deal of it early this morning, almost every hackery and every bullock in our immense convoy had, in addition to their own loads, a truss of straw above this. A circumstance of the danger of which we were not aware, until two rockets thrown by the enemy, came whizzing in among them, fortunately without killing any person, or what was infinitely more to be apprehended inflaming any part of the immense quantity of moving dug straw that made our square look like a walking field of grain.

Had I been commander-in-chief, I should have been inclined to order all this straw to have been thrown down and left, for as a great number of the hackeries were powder carts, if the forage on any of them had inflamed and set fire to the barrels below, what the consequences might have been no one can calculate. The enemy however, from some unaccountable reason, fired but these two, and as they had ceased, it was thought a pity to lose all this forage, accordingly it was all brought in.

From the fortunate circumstance of that great lake, or morass being impassable, I was aware, that if we kept close to it on our return, the enemy would be obliged to abandon the attack on that side, as soon as we got near it. I was therefore very glad when we came to this place, where we were enabled to gratify our wearied, hungry, thirsty horses with a draught of water. I considered us, from the moment we closed up to pass the only road through the morass as, in a manner, at home or at least in comparative safety. The enemy, about 1 or 2 p.m., seeing no hope of making any impression on our little phalanx or even of picking up a stray bullock, as soon as we neared the lake, struck off to their left, home to their camp behind Bhartpoor, to our infinite satisfaction.

It was now sunset and the convoy proceeded, though unmolested, every instant slower and slower. Don had marched from Agra on the 28th., this was now the 3rd day, that the unfortunate bullocks and cattle had been on their legs from morning till evening, without anything to eat and scarce to drink. Most of them were completely knocked up and unable to move. The general sent on to camp (about three miles off) for all the spare bullocks in camp, to replace the tired ones. And the powder-shot etc., which would have been left on the road, were picked up and brought on by the *doolies*[4] of the army. The last light of the declining day gave the old general and his army the happiness of witnessing, that every hackery, every bullock were across the morass, not a man of the enemy was near. We were now, in a manner at home. The relays of bullocks had arrived, so leaving the rear guard to see the last of the convoy safe in camp. We all came on to camp, where we arrived about an hour after dark, to our infinite joy.

Thus ended an expedition. The best conducted of the most important consequence and I will add, to the troops employed, the most troublesome and fatiguing of any that has happened since the commencement of the war. We brought into camp, without losing one article by the way, 44 days' provisions and 10,000 18-pounder shot with powder and other military stores in proportion. Had we not gone to reinforce Don, he must either have taken up a defensive position (which he meant to do) on being attacked and have endeavoured to make his situation known to us, or have marched on, with the certain loss of great part, if not all his convoy. For the numbers of enemies were such, that it would have required all his care and all his ability, to defend himself and preserve his troops alone.

January 31st—Nothing of note, occurred.

---

4. A kind of stretcher.

CHAPTER 7

February 1805

February 1st—The old story of negotiation is revived, in somewhat a different form, Runjeet Sing it seems, is tired of paying daily 25,000 rupees to allies who do nothing for it, and has, it is said, stopped payments and discarded Messrs. Holkar, Ameer Khan and Tantia, with their forces. Alleging in excuse, their having failed to cut off the convoy on the 30th., although the Mussulmans and the Hindoos in the armies of those chiefs had been previously sworn on the Koran and Ganges, to execute this scheme. To all this, it is added, that a negotiating, or rather sounding correspondence, has been opened between the fort and Ram-Narain, a Brahmin of the first quality in our camp, employed as a commissary of supplies, under Captain Morrison. This story, I do not believe, all the previous part of it, likely enough, but I do not suppose, the general would have anything to do with so underhand a business.

February 2nd—A report prevailed yesterday, that some distant firing, heard, or rather fancied to have been heard, early in the morning, was occasioned by Major General Jones and the Bombay army, having assaulted the Fort of Waer. But Waer, is not above two marches from Bhartpoor and as, on the 6th January, Jones, was at Shabadad, on the other side of the Chambal River and between Kotta and Gwalior, he cannot as yet be so near. Although he certainly is on his way here.

February 3rd—The minds of all the camp politicians, are puzzled much, at our not commencing operations yet, against Bhartpoor and the story of negotiation really gains ground. One fact I know, from my friend Lieutenant Swiney (Artillery), that an hurcarrah calling himself the Rajah's was permitted to pass into the fort yesterday, through the batteries, by order of Mr. Mercer, the agent, as he called of the Governor General. In reality, Governor General himself, of this army and at present arbiter of the fate of India in the political way, a flourish of his pen with the cabalistical words "By order of H.E. The most noble Governor General" is of more efficacy than the glittering of ten thousand swords, and he, in this army, is a living instance of the old adage verified *"Cedant Arma Togce."*[1] In short, in this army the previous system, of field deputies, that which unnerved the Dutch armies under the Duke of Marlborough and had nearly caused the ruin of the fine Bombay army in 1782, prevails here in full vigour, and all treaties and negotiations are carried on through the Civil Commander. No wonder there, on seeing a hurcarrah professedly of Runjeet Sing's, carrying a letter from Mercer the great, people should suppose something to be in the wind. But indeed, the hurcarrah himself, declared peace to be his object, which ends all questions at once.

If any decent honourable terms should be offered, we should from prudential motives accept them. But if Runjeet Sing effects to ride the high horse, on account of the repulse of the 9th and 21st of January and indeed, does not humble himself to our superiority as siege Lords, to whom he owes fealty and submissions, we should prefer enduring any hardships of climate, any losses of war to sinking in the minutest degree, in that opinion of the natives, by which alone, we may be said to rule in India.

February 4th—It is said that Holkar and Co. have shifted their quarters, from the immediate neighbourhood of the city, to about three miles beyond the right of the hills. Probably with a view of intercepting or annoying our next foraging party, as the last went out in that direction.

The active and gallant Captain Hutchinson (Artillery), Commandant of Rampoorah, has again been signalising himself by the

---

1. Let military authority yield to the civil.

capture of another fort in that neighbourhood. The enemy had cut across the causeway leading to the gateway, so that he could not get near enough to effectually blow open the door. He then tried to escalade, but his ladders were too short, and in these different attempts he lost a few men. At last, he advanced a third time and himself, accompanied by a few pioneers, while his guns and musketry kept, with the grape, the walls clear, actually is said to have cut a way up the side of the low mud wall, which with his sepoys he then mounted. A second wall was overcome in the same way and he actually, with a few companies, became master of this fort, in which were 2000 men, some of whom escaped, some were taken and many made prisoners!

An action of some importance lately took place at Kanoor a Fort to the N.W. of Delhi, in which we have a few *Nigeebs* (irregular matchlock infantry). Narain Row, a Seik or Mahratta Chief besieged it with many battalions and several guns. A Captain Harrison commanding two battalions of Tellingies (Regular Musketeer Infantry) formerly Sindhia's, heard of Narain Row's having sat down before it and of the garrison being straitened for want of provisions. Captain Harrison apprised the Commanding Officer of his intentions, and marching suddenly at night, from where he then was, arrived early next morning and engaged 11,000 with his 1100 or 1200 men. The Commandant of the garrison, at this moment sallied out in the rear, and Narain Row, beaten in every quarter quickly fled with the remains of his army. We took, on this occasion, nine guns and killed many of the enemy.

February 5th—At 12 o'clock, the horse artillery and cavalry were ordered under arms! The whole of us were bursting with conjectures about the object of this uncomfortable movement in so hot a day. Some said Ameer Khan was going off to the Dooab and we after him, an idea, of not the most pleasant sort, in such weather as this. Others said, we were going to play the fool, after all the experience we have had this campaign, by driving the enemy from their camp and of course, being harassed all the way returning to our own. A third set were bold enough to affirm, that we were going to usher into camp some of the Bhartpoor blood royal, as hostages, but their reasonings were silenced by the fort guns, which opened just then, with more than ordinary vigour. The last and most rational idea, was that General Jones's was near camp and having no regular cavalry, might be harassed much by the enemy, to prevent which we were going to escort him in. About 5. p.m. a second order arrived for us to unsaddle, but remain in our lines, ready if called on, and in this state we remained all the night.

February 6th—By an after order yesterday the army moved ground at 10 a.m. about a mile, or two round to the right and somewhat nearer the fort. We moved for security, in two lines, baggage between and encamped nearly on the ground when we skirmished with the enemy's horse on the 21st ultimo. It was, in fact, their present camp and our approach thus composed them. They tried to molest the quartermaster general's people, while marching out the ground of encampment, but they retired on the line coming up. They hovered about the camp however still, in such myriads, that we were all kept ready saddled, till 2 or 5 p.m. The commander-in-chief, going out to reconnoitre in front, was struck by a spent matchlock ball, but fortunately for this army, was not hurt much as the ball did not enter.

The cause of our shifting ground today was to get to the right of the former breach a little more, where at least as yet, there is no wet ditch, although the enemy, with such command of workmen, may in a night deepen and fill the dry one with water. Last night 150 of the European Regiment and 1st of the 2nd Native Infantry moved down after dark, and entrenched themselves in a new parallel, within 600 yards of this side of the town. Their situation has been very hot all day as the fort fires bitterly at the intruders and with our usual sagacity, we have suffered the enemy to remain in possession of a village 200 yards to the front of our right, where they have guns and musketeers who annoy us much. Ten casualties, four of them Europeans, occurred this day and one poor wretch, sitting on his hams, with his elbow across on his knees, had all four limbs broke by one shot

February 7th—The trench is deepened, and consequently safer, this day but the enemy in the village are more impudent and stronger. So much so, that an artillery officer was obliged to go down to take charge of the guns and two howitzers of the trenches, with a view to keep the enemy in order. The old trench guard of Europeans is diminished to fifty, and the new trench guard is ordered to consist of 150 Europeans and a battalion of sepoys.

February 8th—At 8 a.m. the marching orders came, with a recommendation for us to leave all baggage we could spare behind, from which we augured dire and long marches and our fears pointed to the Dooab, the "Sweet Siren Hope," deluded us that we might only be going to escort General Jones. All these visions were ended by our marching over our old camp ground, straight for Muttra, as numbers of hackeries and bullocks etc. took advantage of the convoy to Muttra, we got on terribly slow. Not an enemy was visible and we arrived at our ground, near a high village called Soone precisely at sunset, after as hot and fatiguing a march, as ever I made. Ameer Khan and Holkar, bag and baggage, are said to have crossed into the Dooab this morning, so we are to have another possible run for it.

February 9th—Halted at daylight and marched eight miles to Muttra, crossed the boat bridge, proceeded about three miles farther and halted at half-past 12 under the ruins of a commanding old mud fort, where we encamped to let the baggage, retarded in crossing, have time to come up. The name of this place was Gonsmow.

Holkar is not crossed, he remains at Bhartpoor, Ameer Khan and his horse, only 7000 or 8000 are across and said to be gone towards Hattrass!

February 10th—In consequence of information relatives to Ameer Khan's movement, we struck off near to the northward, on the road to Coel, encamped for the day at Toolseyghur, a ruined fort, three or four miles to our left of Hattrass.

Ameer Khan, it seems crossed at Mohabund, six miles below Muttra. The inhabitants resisted him and in consequence he has been plundering and burning all the villages near him. He arrived on the 8th at Juwaur, where he was encamped when he heard of our crossing the Jumnah. He instantly decamped and proceeded to Mussaoun, a large mud fort and city of Bugwaunt Sing, Rajah of Sassaney, Bidjigur etc., who rebelled against us in 1802-3, and lost his forts in consequence, but on promise of good behaviour etc. etc., was restored in part to his Zemindary and profiting by past experience, has ever since been our steady friend.

Ameer Khan wished to place his baggage etc. in Mussaoun, confident of support from Bugwaunt. To his surprise, this wish was not only refused in toto but Ameer Khan's army on nearing the fort, were fired on. He next went to Hattrass and, it is said, met with a similar refusal from the politic Diaram, in consequence of which he set of for the large and rebellious city of Coel. We passed over his encamping ground at Juwaur, which was of prodigious size indeed, and from the irregularity with which the Mahrattas usually encamped, huddling together soldiers, horses, bazaars etc. etc. leaving not an inch unoccupied. It could not have contained for short of 8000 or 9000 men.

Had Bugwaunt or Diaram, or both, heartily joined Ameer Khan, he would doubtless have made a stand, and a formidable one too, aided by their battalions, guns and horse. Especially as we, having as infantry to guard our baggage, could only have engaged him, with part of our force, but failing these Rajahs, there are no powerful friends on this side the Ganges, to whom he can look up for assistance. He is evidently afraid to cope with us single handed and therefore, if he does not chase to recross, he must run for it, and we after him. His professed aid, besides the general one of distressing our country, is to cross into Rohilkund, his native country, and that of thousands of proud, disaffected ferocious Patans, who by joining his standard may turn for a time, the whole of that fertile province into a scene of dissolution and carnage.

This object cannot be accomplished without his going above Anop-Sheher, sufficiently high, to find a ford on the Ganges and we must keep so close on his heels, as to catch him in crossing, or at least by following him close up through Rohilkund, deter the Rohillas from joining him. In short, if we do not contrive to catch him in three or four days, he may lead us a dance of twice as many months, all down the other side of the Ganges. If he goes too far down he never can recross and unless he beats us, which God forbid, he is caught in a trap. So deserted and drained of troops is the whole of the tract in question that he can meet with no opposition. Our offensive armies have required almost every soldier we have and thus he may harass us, till the dreadful and fast approaching hot season kills or disables all our Europeans.

February 11th—Marched to Allyghur, where we found, encamped under the walls, Colonel Grueber and his detachment. In all twenty-six companies 1st Sepoys and Captain Skinner's regiment of Irregular Horse, 1400 strong, with a detachment of Artillery, under Captain Best. Colonel Grueber, on the approach of Ameer Khan, was compelled to raise the siege of Kamoona, a Fort of the notorious rebel Doondee Khan and the same, which on our passing by it in November, almost bullied us and made the commander-in-chief, from a praiseworthy prudence, withdraw his flanking parties from near the walls, that no outrage might be committed by the garrison which would place him in the disagreeable dilemma, of either taking no revenge for an insult offend a British grand army, or wasting before an inconsiderable place, the time then so preciously occupied by pursuing Holkar.

About two and a half miles before we arrived at Allyghur, we passed close by the large and populous city of Coel, and through the once famous cantonments of Sindhia's Regular Infantry under Generals Du Boigne and Perron. The situation and appearance of Coel is picturesque and grand. The central part is built on a considerable eminence, crowned with a magnificent mosque of five domes, gilt at top, and which we saw from a considerable distance on passing the other side, on our route down the Dooab in November.

The cantonments, formerly the station of nine battalions of sepoys with the European officer's bungalows, are almost entirely in ruins. Genera Du Boigne and General Perron's houses, being now occupied by the civil magistrates of our Government, are in good repair. From Coel to Allyghur, all is classic ground. We passed over the field of action of the 29th August 1803, when first the hostile armies met, and encamped almost on the very spot, famous for the most desperate exertion of intrepidity perhaps ever known, the blowing open the gates and assaulting the Fort of Allyghur. The strongest place in Hindoostan, defended by a ditch of wonderful depth, by four gateways, the roads leading to each of these successively flanked with outworks of great strength and height and to crown all, resisted by the bravest garrisons we have yet met with in these wars. The height of the body of the place, especially of the numerous round bastions, is astonishingly great and a fausse-bray surrounds the whole. All is of mud and we have rendered it impregnable by a native power by adding to it, the only strength it wanted, that of good drawbridges erected lately in a masterly style by Captain Best.

It was most unfortunate for us, that Grueber was obliged to raise the siege at this time, for the breach was really made and all in readiness for a storm. But his detachment is an acquisition of the last importance to us, as it leaves us the fewer new, of making a push without fear of our baggage.

Ameer Khan did not come to Coel, he passed near it and is gone to Kamoona, then it is said, being joined by all the forces of Doondee Khan, and Naiar Ally, he means to make a stand.

February 12th—At 1 a.m. The native artillery and cavalry, received orders to get instantly ready to march, leaving the infantry with the baggage, to follow at daybreak. At 2 o'clock we started, with the professed intention of Furruckabadian Ameer Khan and Co. at Kamoona, supposed to be only thirteen miles off. Though our march of yesterday was so fatiguing and long, (we did not encamp till 3 p.m.), we most willingly set off in hopes of terminating by a successful enterprise, this dreadfully annoying warfare. But we were cruelly disappointed, and so we shall again and ever be, until the intelligence department is conducted on a more liberal scale, and confided to more intelligent heads, than those of Major General Smith's staff, all of whom are ill qualified indeed, from want of local knowledge and experience of the necessary kind, as well as insufficient acquaintance with language for so important a post to a pursuing army, as the conduct of the guides and spy department.

As to the Commanding Officer, himself fresh from England

and the guards, his head filled with ideas of continental warfare only and altogether ignorant of the very different situation he is placed in, in India, from what he was accustomed to in civilized Europe. Nothing of this kind can be expected from him and he is said, from violence of temper joined to those causes, to have quarrelled with Major Campwell and Captain Bradford, of the grain and supply department, the only officers of the General Staff with us, who from long experience in India, and of Indian war, are qualified to give good advice.

On arriving at the banks of the Kaulee Nuddy, near Kamoona, not a trace of an enemy was visible, they having decamped in the night, on hearing of our being so near. Some of their followers, to the number of about 200, were followed and cut up by Captain Skinner's Irregular Horse, who afterwards swept from under the very walls of Kamoona, which fired great guns and matchlocks incessantly, some hundred bullocks and sheep belonging to Doondee Khan's people.

Our attempting to pursue the main body would have been folly, as they comparatively fresh, to people who had marched forty miles within the last 24 hours, could never have been overtaken. We therefore dismounted to wait for the infantry and baggage, and wasted a day, as miserably and wretchedly as ever I did in my life and more so, than I wish ever again to do. For, as no guides were sent to Colonel Grueber to direct him to the place where we were, he kept going on, in hopes of coming up with us, till he got six miles beyond Kamoona, on the Anop-Sheher road, meanwhile, as a report was current of Holkar's having crossed into the Dooab and having been yesterday, eight koss from Coel, we began at 4 p.m. to wonder at the baggage not appearing and to be alarmed for it's safety.

Messengers were now sent in all directions, while we mounted and began to retrace our steps. When one of them, having overtaken Grueber, and informed him, where we were, he and the baggage returned to Bunnuahah, on the N. Bank of the Nuddy, about a mile from where we then were and we, retracing our steps, crossed the Kaulee Nuddy and joining our baggage, pitched our confused camp about sunset, after a truly diabolical day's work of it.

February 13th—Marched to Soukein, N by W of Anop-Sheher about four miles. The infantry and Skinner's Horse, came up in the rear with the baggage, which did not come to the ground till near 4 p.m., having been retarded for an hour on the road, by a transaction which would scarce merit recording, had it not been for the melancholy circumstances of its costing us the life of a young Officer and very fine lad, Lieut Abeline, 2nd of the 1st Native Infantry. The whole of the towns, and even petty villages of this barbarous country, are either surrounded by mud walls, or have adjacent to them small gurries, or little forts of mud, into which the wretched inhabitants retire with their little movables and cattle, on the approach of any armed force whether friendly or hostile, for in either case, they are equally plundered. The British armies indeed, do not often act so, on the contrary, it is daily proclaimed in our camps, that all plunderers will be hanged instantly, but the numerous hordes of camp followers and servants that follow in the train of all Indian armies take care, after the troops have passed, to make ample amends to the wretched villagers, for our neglect of the established customs of this barbarous world.

Colonel Grueber and the infantry in passing a small village today, which belonged to Doondee Khan, found the gurry occupied by armed men. Grueber inconsiderately enough, considering the insignificance of the place, which was one of the smallest of small gurries, not fifty yards square, sent Captain Skinner to demand its surrender. The garrison, in number seven Rajpoots, offered to comply, if they might march out with their arms and go where they would, to which Skinner, like a prudent man, agreed, and pledged his word for their terms. Two of them descended to accompany him to Colonel Grueber, for a confirmation of this capitulation, he refused this by the advice of some of his more foolish officers, in spite of the remonstrances of Captain Skinner, who, having served ten or twelve years, in Perron's army among these men, knew their manners and conduct better than Colonel Grueber could do and assured him, that these Rajpoots would fight till death, if these honourable terms were refused. Colonel Grueber however, persisted and Captain Skinner, having pledged his honour, caused them to return into their fort safe. Colonel Grueber ordered a grenadier company, and 6-pounder under Captain Best, to force the gates. It was blown open.

The sepoys entered and after an obstinate resistance from these seven Rajpoots, who fought with the fury of tigers at bay the enemy were all killed and the possession of this pitiful mud house, into which we did not leave even a corporal's guard for garrison, and the name of which was not of importance even to be known, cost in one Lieutenant wounded (since dead), five sepoys killed, and seven or eight wounded! Nay the poor young officer's relations, will not even have the satisfaction of knowing that he was honourably killed, doing his duty, for the happy Government, under which we served never suffers an officer's death to be published in the newspapers as it happened, unless the siege or battle, in which it may have happened, should be thought fit to detail in the Government Gazette. And as we are supposed never to suffer defeats and our administration too popular ever to be disturbed by rebellions, very few accounts of the former, and none of the latter, find their way into the Calcutta Papers.

Ameer Khan came near the city of Anop-Sheher[2] in the fort, of which, we have a garrison of one company of sepoys, under a Lieutenant Lewis (2nd Native Infantry), stationed there to cross over, and forward supplies of grain from Rohilkund. Ameer Khan was not favourably received, so did not come very near the city but struck off due North, along the banks of the Ganges, certainly intending to cross over into Rohilkund. He expects to find a ford at Poot-ghaut (poot—ford or pass) whither he is gone today. In consequence of his movement, we did not go near enough Anop-Sheher to see the city, which I much wished to do, from its size and importance it having been formerly the frontier town to the northward of the Vizier's possessions in the Dooab, ceded to us in 1801, and having been a station for two battalions of sepoys and a detachment of artillery.

---

2. Anop-Sheher, Anop-city, Sheher being Persian for a city. What Anop or rather Anoop means, I can't discover, probably it is the name of some clarissimo Moosulmaun who built the town.

February 14th—To Pulwur, on the banks of the Ganges, our camp lay on a fine plain of prodigious extent, into which we descended from dry, barren high lands, which being terminated towards the plain by high precipitous banks, intercepted with deep gullies, seem to indicate that the river once flowed under these heights, and has now gradually retired, leaving the plain, once its bed, to become the fertile set of rich cultivation. Indeed from its low and level appearance, as well as the richness of its vegetation, contrasted with the rest of the surrounding country, I suppose that it is either annually overflowed in the rainy season by the river or is at least rendered a complete marsh. We saw for the first time since we were at Futtyghur, the Ganges, not far from which we encamped.

This marching is really scarce bearable and we have staring in the face, the certainty that every day, as the season advances, must be yet more insupportable than that which preceded it, this aggravates our fatigue, the former. Besides, I do not really see when this is to end. It is clear that our former success with Holkar, has only had the effect of making other invaders more cautious how we shall surprise them and not of terrifying them from the attempt. Indeed, when I reflect on the great advantages they have over us, in this flying, predatory warfare, I am only surprised they ever attempt any other.

Their towns, their guns, we always take, their battalions we destroy but their cavalry we can make nothing of. So long as they do not allow us to take them by surprise, which they can always prevent with common vigilance, we suffer from the inclemency of a climate which is natural to them, to protect ourselves, in fact, to enable us to exist in it, we are obliged to encumber ourselves with baggage, which they dream not of and in consequence, our motions are slower than theirs. They obtain by terror and plundering all they immediately want, subsistence for themselves and their cattle, we have but our way of distressing them, which is by following them so close, as to keep the disaffected (nine-tenths of our subjects) from daring to join them and to give courage to our friends to resist them.

By continuing this conduct for a considerable time, the inhabitants and country will get tired of them, and they of it. Although procuring a subsistence for the time, goes a great way with them, yet sooner or later, they must and will have pay to recompense them for the harassed life they lead, to subsist their distant families and to replace their clothes which must wear out, their arms, their horses which die of fatigue, all are killed.

If they have a potent and rich friend in the country, who will supply them with money, they will stay in till doomsday, many such they have in Rohilkund, but if we keep close at their heels and they keep running away from us, who will supply them with cash, to incur our wrath and get nothing by it? How far we are at present in a condition to do this is, I am sorry to say very questionable at best.

Colonel Grueber and the infantry, with 400 of Skinner's Horse, are left behind at Anop-Sheher, for what possible reason no one, not in the secret, can divine, our baggage if we overtake the enemy this instant must have a guard, or fall into the hands of the enemy. This weakens our small army, that disgraces it, besides ruining the whole of the indigent officers of low rank, whose whole little capital is vested in their camp equipage, which if lost, or taken, contrary to the more liberal custom of the King's service, is not replaced to them, even in part by Government. If some infantry is necessary to be left at or near Anop-Sheher, surely out of twenty-six companies, a battalion or even the six Sebundy companies might have been retained, now, we are positively tied by the leg from all exertion. And if Ameer Khan only left a few hundred Pindaries to annoy our line of march, he might, with the main body, go unmolested, when he would, unless our commander put into practice a humane idea, which he is said seriously to entertain and which even his local ignorance cannot excuse, that of burning the baggage!

Ameer Khan is coasting the Ganges in quest of a ford meaning to cross into Rohilkund. The sanguine gentry in camp assert there is no fort until we come to Hurdwar (Lat 30°). The natives say there are several. If the former are right, we must attempt to catch him before he gets there and by Colonel Burn's aid prevent him from joining the millions of rapacious Seiks, always ready to side with a plundering adventurer. If he should however cross, we have nothing for it, but to keep as near as we can and even then, our utmost exertions may be unable to keep him from forming in army of 20,000 Rohillas and, as we have not a single sepoy in that extensive province, he may compel us to remain inactive with our 1800 men, until a reinforcement of many battalions, arrive from the grand army and enable us for the 3rd time, to crush the Rohillas, and retake that country.

In the meanwhile, the deadly hot winds are coming on, a season when Europeans, even in cantonments, are not exposed to the climate, die, as we last campaign experienced, twenty or thirty in a day! I positively sicken to think of Ameer Khan's crossing. Our Governor, trembling for fear of being called to an account for his profession in domestic government and his ambitious temerity in entering into this ruinous war, whilst he cheated his employers into a belief that all was peace, has by a ten times more scandalous economy, in not raising forces to carry on the war, risked, at this instant, the richest flower in the East India Company's Indian territories, the fertile province of Rohilkund, termed the garden of Hindoostan.

Every sepoy we have is drawn off the armies, not a man remains to defend even our cantonments and magazines, except a few raw recruits raising now that it is too late at Cawnpore and Futtyghur, so that while Ameer Khan overruns Rohilkund unopposed, if Holkar, like a wise general, should cross into the Dooab, whilst our forces are employed before Bhartpoor, he may traverse it from Allahabad to Hurdwar, plundering and burning wherever he goes, and thus cut off all hopes of revenue from those rich district, for this year at least. I daily tremble to hear of his being across. I only am astonished at his delay. If Bhartpoor speedily falls then the face of things would be materially altered. The Rajah will always be glad to have peace, and I will venture to say, that this time it will be joyfully granted by us, whether it is or not, I trust the old general will instantly cross the Jumnah with great part of his army leaving to General Jones and the Bombay army, to follow up Holkar or pursue the Bhartpoor war. This will enable us to defend our own country, to expel its invaders, without some such step is taken.

God knows when this real Mahratta war will be finished. Ameer Khan, a Rohilla by birth, left his native province after the battle of Rampore in 1794, which reduced that province forever, as we hoped, under the Vizier's authority, in quest of employment as a private soldier, with many others of his compatriots. By dint of his valour and activity, in these few years, he has risen to be a great commander and prince. He is said to be almost worshipped by the Rohillas, for his valour and good fortune. His family and connections anxiously wait it is said, to join his standard when erected in Rohilkund, and many thousand idle, discontented men, reduced by the success of our arms to subjection and servitude, and who hate their victors and burn for independence, will flock to his standard.

The Rohilla Patans have ever been rebellious and turbulent. They are naturally furious and brave and by profession soldiers. The occupations of agriculture and commerce they disdain and leave to the inhabitants, the Hindoos from whom, on the irruption of their tribe into Hindoostan, they conquered this province, or live idle and sulky at home. In 1774 and 1794 their spirit broke into open rebellion, both times, by the aid of his allies, the British, the Nawaub Vizier was enabled to bring them back to obedience. What formidable foes they are, let Sir Robert Abercrombie tell, one wing of whose fine army even in the successful battle of Rampore, was cut to pieces. Ever since then, they have been pretty quiet. Almost all those who had horses left the country to take service as soldiers elsewhere. Those who had no such means remained, as I have described, in the great towers and cities, and will no doubt be ready to join their favourite hero and country man in any attempt.

Our only way is therefore to keep close up and if there are few horsemen in the province to join him. The footmen will not risk perhaps, joining an army altogether of horse, without infantry and guns and which, if pressed hard by us, will abandon them to be cut up by us. Bhartpoor was battered in breach on the 10th and the storm expected to take place in three or four days. If we could but now hear of this so much to be wished event, Ameer Khan might be afraid to cross and all yet be well.

February 15th—Marched to Gur-Muctessar. We then learned that Ameer Khan passed it at 12 midday, on the 14th, and crossed the river at Commendnagur Ford, to which we instantly proceeded. At Gur-Muctessar, Ameer Khan tried to plunder the town, but was intimidated by the commanding appearance of the brick fort, which however, could not have defended so large a place as this seems to be. The *Dewan*, or native officer, of our Government came out to meet the general and told him all these particulars. Gur-Muctessar is built on the junction of the high and low ground. The fort, which is very old, being on the highest part, The appearance of the town, fort and neighbouring gardens is pretty picturesque.

The deed is done and we must now make the best of it! Ameer Khan expected to find the river fordable at Gur-Muctessar, and sounded it for that purpose, but finding it impracticable, proceeded to this place instantly on hearing of our infantry having been left behind, and expecting an attack immediately. He must have crossed in a great hurry, as the numerous bodies of sheep and bullocks drowned in the attempt and some hackeries left behind, sufficiently testify. Had he gone leisurely to work, he could have easily got all over, as the water here, although the knowing ones said it was nowhere fordable, was not breast high! After our arrival at the bank, some of the villages on the Rohilkund side, were set on fire, so that his rear must have been very late in getting over. As the water would have wetted all our ammunition, we unpacked our tumbrils. and gave the dragoons and native troopers each a round to carry over. On our arrival at the other side, having dried the cartridges sufficiently, we repacked the ammunition, which thus was undamaged.

Ameer Khan marched this day to Amrooah, twenty miles off. From thence to Moraudabad, on the banks of the Ramgunga, is about thirty miles, and Rampore, the capital, to which he evidently is going, as far farther. People differ about whether the Ramgunga is fordable or not, so they did about the Ganges itself, yet have we been travelling these provinces for thirty or forty years, but it is as true as it is a severe observation, that we know far less of our own country, than of our neighbours. All our cares being about intermeddling with other peoples.

February 16th—I enjoy a halt, which gives me a few hours that I can call my own and spend in my tent, reading or writing, yet I would have given almost anything, that we had marched today and everyone in the army is of the same opinion. The reason of it, is said to be, that the cattle are too fatigued to move tomorrow. Nonsense! Did we not move seventeen days in the Dooab after Holkar? Here we have only marched eight days! Besides, I am told from good authority, that Major Campwell, the Grain and Camel Commissary, declared to the general, that the cattle were able to march. A good deal of rain fell in the night, which made the tents heavier! So did then, but nothing sufficient to retard us, if every drop of rain is to cause us a halt, Ameer Khan may go where he chooses, unmolested.

February 17th—Marched to Amrooah, on the east side of which we encamped, among beautiful and verdant groves of mangoes, bamboos, baiar[3] trees, interspersed with ruined mosques and tombs and gardens, which bespeak it's former greatness. It's population, seems immense, and for the first time in my life, I saw Rohilla town. All the inhabitants were armed with swords and shields, spear or matchlocks, and looked most indifferently on us and all our little army, which filed through the narrow streets. This manoeuvre, exhibited our numbers, to the best advantage, and was certainly politic. Ameer Khan did not get admittance into the town, but plundered the suburbs. By a precaution, very right and proper, when among the Rohillas, so fierce and treacherous, the camp and avenues leading to the city were guarded strictly all night.

February 18th—Marched to Moraudabad, which Ameer Khan left during the night. About three miles before we entered this city, we crossed the nullah and after passing through the place, crossed two channels of the Ram Gunga, which at this season is very shallow. On the side of the city, which we first approached, stood the cantonments of the Sebundy corps (Captain Cruttenden's, now in the Dooab with Colonel Grueber), the civil-

---

3. A low prickly tree, which bears at this season, a small yellow stout fruit in size, appearance and taste (when best cultivated and largest) and somewhat resembling a very small apple. It's size is about that of a green-gage plum.

ians and the officers bungalows, all of which, with the exception of the judge, Mr. Leicester's house, we found burned to the bare walls. The jail also, had shared the same fate, and the convicts and prisoners were all released by the enemy. In Mr. Leicester's house, all the gentlemen and two English ladies, repaired with two companies of Sebundies. The house, by surely some second light, had been surrounded by it's possessor, with a tolerably thick bastioned mud wall and ditch, and had three bad, small country guns mounted on it.

The enemy, enraged at not getting possession of the English, who they unquestionably would have put to death, several times attacked it, but men fighting in despair, as we found to our cost at Bhartpoor, fight more than bravely. The enemy were each time repulsed, and had fifteen or sixteen killed, more enraged than ever at being baffled then by a handful of men. Ameer Khan, like a fool, threw away in vain attempts the whole day, which we had given him the start of us by our imprudent halt on the banks of the Ganges, and which was inexcusable in him, if, as is generally said, he is going to head a political party at the Rohilla capital

Rampore, where to form his party and arrangements, time was necessary, and must have been invaluable. Moraudabad, which we, as before, filed through is a large and populous city. Ameer Khan was, as at Amrooah, shut out! This looks as if people were not so eager to join his standard, as our fears represented? He plundered all the large suburb without the walls and from one banker in particular, extorted, it is said by torture, three *lacks* of rupees.

February 19th—Intelligence arrived of the enemy's having taken the road from Rampore to Cossipore, a rich town of Hindoos, perfectly open, and very rich, at the foot of Almora hills, 40 miles off. We halted till after sunrise, for what reason God knows, unless our wise conductors did not know what route to take, and might be deliberating for three or four hours.

At last we started again, halted on the banks of a *nullah* at and then encamped, having in ten or eleven hours some ten or twelve miles. The Kemaoun or Almora hills, which have been in sight, ever since the 14th ultimo, looked truly grand but though grandest and most sublime spectacle I have ever yet seen in India, was the ancient Imaus or Indian Caucasus, a mountainous range which appeared above the Kemaoun hills. Until this day we supposed these to be the same range of mountains, but now that we were within thirty miles of the smaller mountains of Almora, we distinctly perceived the snowy and picturesque tops of the others, crowning to appearance their dark and wooded summits.

The height of the Kemaoun hills must be indeed great, to be seen from near Anop-Sheher, but what must be the size of even at this distance make the others, seem pygmies. The sunbeams, shining the snowy and uneven tops, gave them a most brilliant and charming appearance from the relief afforded to the dazzling Easterly projections, by the abrupt and dark masses of shadow in which every other part was placed. These mountains separate India from Tartary and Thibet, running along from N. W. to S. E. a prodigious distance. Whether the snow on their summits ever is completely melted, I know not, that it is there at all, in a climate when the heat of the sun is so intense from the altitude from the surface of the earth, and consequent rareness of the atmosphere and be very great. It is supposed, that in the months of April and May, the snow of these hills, beginning to melt, causes the first swelling of the Ganges, and probably it is the case as the swelling certainly commences, long before a shower of rain has fallen.

The regions of the Kemaoun hills are said to be very cold indeed from their producing firs, turpentine, hemp etc. as articles of trade. The Company, I am told, have a resident (a Mr. Gott) thereabouts, who cultivates and sends down, these naval articles to Calcutta. No country in the world can be better provided with the means of transporting them. Numberless rivers, of greater and less sizes, flow from these hills, into the Ganges, so that the whole way from the hills to Fort William, they can be transported by water carriage, at a comparatively small expense and with great rapidity.

February 20th—In consequence of some information brought during the night, leading to suspect, Ameer Khan of intentions on Barelly, we marched at 8 a.m. crossed the *nullah* in our front and then to Rampore. In crossing the river, about knee deep at this season, but of a very broad channel, one of our tumbrils and two of some other regiments, in following the track of those that preceded them, suddenly sank to the axletrees a deep quicksand. By the exertions of our Europeans at the drag ropes, with much difficulty, we got all of them out, but one horse was drowned or smothered before he could be extricated. Our camp was just on the other side of this, having the river to it's rear and the hedge of Rampore to the front and right.

In the evening, I went on horseback, to see this celebrated capital of the Rohillas and the site was altogether new. The inhabitants seem a totally distinct race from any inhabitants of India, I have ever seen. Indeed being proud of their race and their complexion, they do not much intermix any with other tribes and this same sentiment has caused them to degenerate, in character, as well as colour, from their ancestors, the Afghans, less by far, than any other of the numerous hordes of emigrants from the N. and N.W. who have at different times entered Hindoostan. They are all fair, some of a yellowish tinge with jet black beards, others of a red fair and many with brown and even red hair. They are altogether free and easy in their conversation and address to European gentlemen, and this, which in Europe we should style independence, is here called insolence. The fact is, that these people though twice subdued by our superior valour or discipline, yet recollect how hard they fought for it and indeed feel a conscious equality with us in respect to courage, which no other Indians do. When to this is added that national or religious antipathy, which most Mohammedans have for a Christian, we shall not much wonder at the freedom of their address or manners, sometimes bordering on insolence.

On the present occasion, they admitted us into their city, showed us the mosques, palaces etc. and some of the officers were conducted to the Nawaub Naziroola Khan, Regent, who embraced them and was exceedingly polite to them. I passed by his palace gate, which was on one side of a crowded oblong square bazaar. The gateway, or portico, built of brick and stucco, was much after the fashion of Moosulmaun edifices. Pierced through with numberless verandahs and pigeon-hole rooms and projecting balconies, but a terrace extending forty or fifty feet on each side of it with guards drawn up, all matchlock men, well dressed handsome Rohillas, with shield at the back, sword by their side and matchlock on the shoulder, bearing red turbans and sashes over white clean clothes, presented a coup d'œil striking and new to me.

All round the city (which has no walls), at about 100 yards distance from the houses, a thick hedge of the elegant and slender bamboo is planted as the only defence it has. Cavalry could not easily penetrate it, as the bamboos grow (like most other grapes) in thick clumps, which being planted pretty close, form a barrier, not easily penetrated and when a few men with matchlock, planted behind the clumps, could destroy great numbers of the assailants, without suffering much themselves. Guards of thirty or forty matchlock men each, were stationed in tents, all round the outside of the bound hedge, at about 300 yards distance. But the whole city, the population of which is incredibly great, seems one swarm of soldiers, not a man is unarmed and if they chose to heartily resist, no invader unprovided with numerous artillery, could even take Rampore.

In the evening, the Regent, attended by eight state elephants and numbers of horse and foot, paid a visit of ceremony to Major General Smith, who went out to meet him in front of camp. Afterwards they adjourned to the general's tent and in an hour, the Regent returned to the city. We were all pretty alert during the night, lest the known duplicity and treachery of these people, should instigate them to attack our camps during the night, they did not however. We get considerable supplies of grain out of this place, to obtain which, was, I fancy, the principal reason of our coming here, as our store in camp was nearly out.

Ameer Khan, was approaching Rampore, in confidence of being well received but a message he received from the Regent, intimating the kind of reception he would meet with, made him turn off to the northward, to Kossipoor.

If he expected to become the head of a rebellious party (as was said to be his hope) and to be joined by the Rohillas en masse he has certainly failed completely. It was said that the

Rohillas wished to destroy Naziroolla Khan, the Regent and to dethrone Ahmed Alli, the young Nabob, who certainly was forced on them by the victory in 1794 by us.

After the treaty of Loll-Dong in 1773-4, which reduced Fyzoolla Khan to his allegiance to our ally, the Vizier of Oude, as a simple *Jaghirdar*,[4] of a territory yielding fourteen lacks of rupees annually, Fyzoolla Khan retired to his dominions, and employed his remaining days, entirely in peaceful occupations, especially in improving his country, which soon came to produce twenty-eight lacks. On his death in 1794, his eldest son Mahommed Alli, succeeded him and he, at the instigation of his next brother, Gholaum Mahommed, was deposed and murdered. The Vizier of Oude refused to grant the murderer investiture, as rather the English refuse to allow him to do so. As Gholaum Mahommed was of a popular and winning demeanour, and excelled in the warlike exercises, and was very popular among the Rohillas who did not besides much relish subjection to the Vizier of Oude, and had not stomached their defeat by us, ten years before. They were however beat, driven to the hills, obliged to give up their treasure. Gholaum Mahommed was taken prisoner and at last a treaty with the principal chieftain was concluded, which placed the infant son, of the murdered Nabob, on the throne, where he now sits.

It was said that the Rohillas, feeling themselves getting strong again and seizing the favourable moment, of our being engaged in a foreign war, and having left Rohilkund defenceless, meant to throw off our yoke and our protege sovereign, and to place some other in his situation, and that the military character of Ameer Khan, pointed him out as a fit instrument in the revolution, perhaps to become it's head. Either our apprehensions, regarding this conspiracy, were groundless or what is not improbable, on our rapid pursuit of Ameer Khan, made a wide alteration in the state of things, and gave Ameer Khan the air of a retreater and a fugitive, instead of a brave hero fit to head the

---

4. Holder of a small territory by military tenure, harassing and stipulated tribute or quit rent. *Jaghirdars* enjoy all rights of sovereignty, the *Jaghire* reverts however, to the Lord Paramount on the death of the holder, whose heir is commonly obliged to pay a considerable fine, to procure his investiture as successor.

armies of his country. Certain however it is, that the Regent's party seems at present the strongest, though, whether that may not in some measure be influenced by our army being so close at his heels, I will not pretend to say.

February 21st—Ameer Khan is said to be menacing Barelly and we are moving sufficiently far, to keep between him and that place. Our march of this day, was through the heart of the *Jaghire*, the only part of Rohilkund, not our own, all the rest, of which Barelly is the capital, having made part of the cession in 1801. At Rampore, which is the capital of the *Jaghire*, there is a neat country without the bound hedge, in which is the tomb of Fyzoolah Khan. A mere piece of shell work, enclosing a sarcophagus. This country, from having been merely desolated by war and ruin, was by the careful and excellent administration of Fyzoolah Khan, especially near the close of his reign, converted into one of the most productive a rich provinces of India.

The adjacent mountains affording a constant supply of water, so absolutely necessary in the wheat and barley crops, that come to maturity in April and March. Small canals of four feet broad and three or four feet deep, are dry in all dimensions, intersecting the country in all directions and affording regular and plentiful means of irrigation. The excellent effects of which are visible in the richness and abundance of the crops, which far exceed anything of the kind I have seen. The soil in the Dooab is, I fancy, as good, if not better, but the same advantages of water do not exist and watering is performed by drawing up water from wells, the digging and working of which, render agriculture of course more expensive to the labourer, and therefore, less productive to the landholder.

The *nullah*, or rivulets, that everywhere intersect this country leave beautiful and spacious meadows of green grass, covering the ground which their channels, so spacious in the raining months occupy at that season, but now leave entirely, or nearly dry. Verdure, except in the wet season, and for a month or two immediately following, is never seen in India in general and this circumstance, contribute greatly to the excessive heat. But in all Rohilkund, though nowhere so much do as in the *Jaghire*, the surface of the earth, is covered with grasses of different texture and the whole face of the country being also studded with plantations, the appearance of the surrounding scene, is everywhere refreshing beautiful.

February 23rd—A party of Skinner's horse, went off early to Barelly, only twenty miles distant, to bring in a supply of grain, much wanted in camp. Ameer Khan is among the hills, to the northward, plundering and it is said, recruiting. He sent, to my certain knowledge, a message to Captain Skinner, intimating a kind of wish, to accommodate disputes, by negotiation instead of fighting and a mode, that at this season, cannot be more desired by him, than by us, if it can honourably be done! Of this, however, I doubt. Terms granted to an invader, without a previous defeat, must every carry with them the appearance of being bullied on the part of the invaders. The general however, has sent in return a message, implying that any terms wished for by Ameer Khan, must be put in writing, when they shall be forwarded to the commander-in-chief.

February 24th—Halted again, ostensibly on account of the Barelly convoy, but I fancy really because to move is of no manner of us. Ameer Khan remains quiet under the hills and we have now a position, nearly centrical for defending Rampore, Barelly, Chandoussy and Moraudabad, the safety of all which we are much interested in, of the two first, on account of their magnitude and importance, of the two last, on account of our cantonments and civil stations there. The destroying or burning of which would be disgraceful to us and hurtful to the individual British who have property there. Although this consideration is more one of humanity than of necessary political importance. If then, it is necessary for us to cover and protect these places, we have done well in halting at once.

To assail and defend, to protect and to pursue are impossible, when there are no garrisons of any kind, when the invaders have such an extensive and fertile country to range in, and where the pursuers cannot keep close to the heels of the retreating army, for want of any infantry to guard their baggage, in the event of their making a long and forced march. The country besides, where Ameer Khan now is, gives him two advantages: In the first place, he can retire if missed, among the hills and second if we succeed in bringing him to an engagement, the nature of the country, intersected with deep water courses, natural and artificial, while it presents no obstacle to his irregular light troops, destroys to us that confidence of victory, which we repose, in our regular, unbroken charge and our horse artillery. I do think, that until we can bring into the field eight or ten battalions of infantry, we shall be able to effect nothing.

Had we this force, we could in the first instance, disencumber ourselves of all protecting cares, by throwing small but competent garrisons into the important places, or forming in central positions, small armies, ready to move down in a body to the defence of any place menaced. While the remaining battalion moving along with us, or the whole of our united force, being formed into two light armies, we might be able to act in conjunction and with effect against the enemy, and even cut off from him at possibility of retreat. In short, until the fall of Bhartpoor, things will probably remain much in status quo.

Ameer Khan, as well as half India, is most likely only waiting for the event of that siege, to determine whether war or retreat is to be object. The period is one truly eventful, Sindhia, Amboogee, the Rohillas, the Seiks, the Begum and the Berar Rajah. All those nations of India that have hitherto detested each other, but whom our infamous policy has contrived to unite in the common bond of greater hatred to us, anxiously watch that event, waiting but for the auspicious moment, when our good fortune shall by an act of inconstancy, give them hope, that she has forsaken our standard, to pour in on us their myriads of horse, plundering and devastating our provinces and ruining our resources of men and money.

There is not, in all united India, an army of regular infantry and artillery to be found to cope with us. We have annihilated the one, captured the other, but this war has shown all the East that their true strength lies in a different species of force in a different mode of fighting. Nor will they fail to profit by the example, if they are possessed, of the common powers of comparing and observing.

February 25th—We encamped at Kauttar. The road for the first six or seven miles was, like that of our two last marches, but latterly the cultivation got to be less plentiful and luxuriant, and the country more open. Captain Martin, General Smith's Brigade Major, informed us on the line of march this morning, that he had received a letter from the native, who conducts the dawk of the grand army, with the news of Bhartpoor's having been taken on the 20th, notwithstanding the questionable shape of their intelligence. It was a fact too much desired and too movable on the whole, for us not to grasp at it with joy. Everyone believed it and we congratulated each other on the good news, which afforded so speedy a prospect of peace and of a termination of our almost insupportable fatigues. We have raised to this immoderate pitch of hope and joy, only to experience a tenfold bitter and cruel disappointment in intelligence arrived in camp, with the Burrelly convoy, which was exactly the reverse of the former. It's shape too, admitted of our doubting it, as it came in a private letter from Futtyghur. Like the drowning, we caught at straw to save us from sinking, and even when Captain Martin confessed that his letter, so far from announcing success, as he had formerly declared, was of the precise same terror as the Futtyghur one. People in general, could not believe that an officer and a gentleman, would even have told a deliberate falsehood for any end whatever, even the assigned one, of keeping up our spirits!

February 26th—The whole of this day we spent in the most wretched state of uneasiness and suspense that men possibly could be in. Not alas! that we have now any doubt of our having suffered a third repulse at Bhartpoor. Dreadful as the blow is in itself, and in probable consequence to the politics of India, no one now affects to doubt it, it is but too certain from the conquering testimony of the Burrelly, and the danger from his letters, and the information obtained at Rampore. Our greatest unhappiness is that we are ignorant of the circumstances attending this calamity, of it's extent, it's causes and I may say above all of the names, or numbers of the brave men who must have perished. Everyone who has a friend with the grand army trembles

RAMPOORA, 1805

Mountains —
retreat of the Enemy - & Baggage

a
aBalger

N
W—+—E
S

first seen

retreat of the remaining &

Great

charge on the ab 2 9° & 27th. by & Horse

Nallah

1st C. and 2d G. Stoops

charge of the 2 Squad 5th

6th D

for his fate! How often do I thank God, that my poor and dear young brother is not there! Yet I have friends, and dear friends, who at this moment may be no more.

The Regent at Rampore, or one of his principal ministers, came out to visit General Smith. He brings with him intelligence, said to be brought from Bhartpoor by his *hurkarrahs*, that we were repulsed on the 20th, but on the 22nd took the city and fort, with great slaughter. This is believed in camp by the numerous factions of the sanguine. The more sensible party of the croakers (of whom at present I am an unworthy member) disbelieve it altogether.

February 27th—We have been repulsed a fourth time, from Bhartpoor! The details of the affair of the 20th and of this horrible, and petrifying disaster on the 21st reached us together. My excellent friend Lieutenant Swiney, wounded himself badly, on the first storm (20th) has nevertheless sent me an able and faithful report of that one and the chief particulars of the last (the 21st). I have also learned from the other member of our dear triumvirate, my dear and young friend Lieutenant Pollock (Artillery), who has escaped, thank heaven, unhurt. His is not near so particular as Swiney's. It was written, while his affectionate heart was full of grief, for the wound of Swiney, and the death of a fine young man, our companion and brother Officer, Lieutenant Gowing of the Artillery, who was shot on the 21st. Such particular, as I know, or can learn in a day or two, I shall then relate, one thing, as allowed on all hands though shocking and disgraceful and calamitous.

I may now mention, that the cowardice of the Europeans, chiefly, the famed 76th, the victors at Allyghur, Delhi, and Lasswarree was the sole obstacle to success, the door was open, they would not enter! Ten thousand repulses, would be in comparison to this afflicting piece of intelligence men trifle, but that now for the first time, since we have established ourselves by valour and discipline alone in India for fifty years, to think that our countrymen, whose very name and appearance, used to strike a panic in Hindoostan, hang back and are afraid, is more than scandalous or disgraceful, it is alarming! It threatens the very existence of

British India! Another reflection that suggests itself to me, I now mention, as it is a certain and immutable truth. It struck me on the 9th and 21st January and I may say, in sorrow I speak it, that I am a true prophet. But it required not second sight, to be convinced, that men fighting in despair, whose prayers for peace and pardon are haughtily rejected, whose utter destruction is vowed, whose humiliations we spurned in the proud hour of victory, in the haughty confidence of success, become so ordinary opponents. Such have we made the Jats, by our insolent treatment of their *Vakeel*, after the fall of Deeg and even posterior to our first repulse and such enemies have we found them! How much altered, is now the state of affairs! That conduct, which success alone could have vindicated in the eyes of the worldly minded, our disgrace and defeats, will cause to be traced with every appellation of reproach and abuses, which no one can, in convenience, deny to be merited!

Had the commander-in-chief taken Bhartpoor with honour, the Governor General would have heaped on his behaviour in refusing peace, every praise, as it is, he will do exactly the opposite, and will, I doubt not, throw on the general's shoulders, however unjustly, the whole of the responsibility of this now odious transaction. The expense, injustice and duplicity, which have distinguished the origin and conduct of their war, on the part of our Government, might have passed unnoticed, had we brilliantly succeeded, as matters now stand, the ambitious Lord Wellesley will have enough of responsibility on these scores already and from his conduct in every similar instance that I have known, he will allow the general the honour of bearing the whole blame of this transaction, or in homely English, make a scapegoat of him, though doubtless he acted on the spirit of Lord Wellesley's instructions.

February 28th—The English are equally credulous here, as in the Haymarket Theatre, when they went to see the bottle conjurer, people here, incredible dieter, flatter themselves still, that on the 22nd ultimo Bhartpoor was taken!

CHAPTER 8

March 1805

STORM OF BHARTPOOR

March 1st—On the 17th or 18th, the besieged made a sally on our advanced trenches, and destroyed the materials for a 6-pounders battery, about to be erected close to the breach. On the 20th, the breach being perfectly practicable, at 5 a.m. all the European flank companies of the Bengal army and 300 battalion men, with the 12th, 9th, and 15th Sepoy Battalions, moved down to the trenches. And most fortunate it was that they did, for at sunrise, a general sally from the gates and breach was made by the enemy, in prodigious numbers, though repulsed with loss in the former sally, yet no doubt their success, in destroying our fascines, made them assured of destroying us entirely with their immense numbers. Had the usual trench guards only been down, all our guns, batteries, tools and men, would have inevitably become their prey.

They attacked the old trenches, the new ones and the right works all at once. After a dreadful and obstinate combat, they were repulsed with great slaughter. They returned to the charge and did all but succeed. Even a third time, with renewed vigour they tried and on being a third time compelled to fly, gave it up. Our loss was prodigious, two officers and thirty-six Europeans killed, all others in proportion but theirs, from the fire of our batteries with grape was infinitely greater. At half-past three, the storming party, under the command of Lieutenant Colonel Don, was to move out of the advance sap and on their clearing it, two, 6-pounders, under Lieutenant Swiney, were to move out of the battery to their support. A column to the right, under Colonel Taylor of the Bombay army, consisting of 300 Europeans and two battalions sepoys (Bombay) were to proceed to a gate, which they were to blow open and a third column, in the centre, consisting of 300 (Bombay) Europeans and the 1st of the 8th Bengal Sepoys, was to advance to the village on the right front of our works, where the enemy with guns and infantry were posted, and after dislodging them, they were to try and enter with the fugitives. This column was to move out first, and the noise of it's firing, to be the signal for Don's advance.

At half past three, the centre column accordingly moved out, quickly drove the enemy from their guns, but the Bhartpoorians, sensible of the danger, shut their gates on pursuers and pursued, most of four battalions of the enemy, in the village, were cut to pieces, and eleven guns brought into camp. Colonel Don would now have advanced but to the utter astonishment and despair of every officer present, the Europeans, (chiefly the 76th) refused to stir out of the sap, not a man would move. Colonel Don ran about like a distracted person, tried by every possible means to rouse them, but all would not do. As a last attempt, and more in the hope of stimulating the cowardly Europeans than with any hope of succeeding, the gallant colonel ran to the battery and called on the glorious 12th Regiment Native Infantry to follow him.

This distinguished corps, to the eternal disgrace of the Europeans name, in an instant obeyed their gallant and well known Commander[1] and accompanied by Lieutenant Swiney and his guns, they moved up to the fort, with the regularity of a parade. And instead of going to the breach, when the enemy were springing mines, they edged off to one of the collateral bastions, where no one supposed it possible to climb up and to the astonishment of everyone, clambered up within a few feet of the top, where they stuck like bees and when the brave Lieutenant's

---

1. Lieutenant Colonel Don, is Brigadier Commanding the Reserve, the elite of the army, consisting of the well known Flankers 22nd Foot and the three Ragged Battalions as they are called, from their appearance after Monson's return. The 1st and 2nd Battalions, 12th and 2nd Battalions 21st Native Infantry.

Grant and Fagon, planted the colours, from the censor on the dastardly Europeans, must be expected five men of the 22nd Flankers, all that, I understand, remained fit for duty out of forty, who went down in the morning. The brunt of the sally had fallen on them and they had suffered cruelly.

One of these fine fellows sprung in at an embrasure but the gun in it, at that unlucky moment, went off and blew him[2] into the air. About thirty Europeans, ashamed to see the sepoys alone advancing, had followed the 12th, but this accident so disturbed them that they turned away and run off! The enemy, confused, yet desperately bold, sprung three mines, one in each gorge of the adjacent bastions, and one in the breach. Had the scoundrelly Europeans, who unmoved stood in the trenches, seeing the officers and sepoys unable to get up and overpowered by numbers, gone to the breach now, success had been ours, almost without resistance, as the explosion of the mine cleared it for a time of the Jats and proved that there could be no more mines, but they saw all the slaughter and distress without stirring.

The 12th at last were called off, after losing about one half of their men and then the storm ended. The Europeans were to have advanced, each with a fascine, which having thrown into the ditch, he was to stand to the right or left and keep up a brisk fire on any enemy who might appear in the breach, or on the dismantled ramparts. The ditch, especially after the explosion of the mine, was nothing at all, and had they possessed but common courage, Bhartpoor had now been ours.

Colonel Taylor and his column, after wandering about for an hour among the jungles, in quest of a gate, from bad information or treacherous guides, were led in front of a face of the fort, which cannonaded them severely, and after sustaining great loss, they were obliged to return to camp.

On the 21st, the batteries played on the bastion, which the 12th had ascended, supposing that a few shots would make it

---

2. The Flank Companies of H.M. 22nd Foot left Calcutta and arrived at the grand army in February 1804, 202 strong. Sickness, but more the sword, for they have headed every storm, has annihilated them nearly and all the officers, have been killed or wounded.

more than sufficiently practicable. The enemy had already almost built up the breach, which somehow, unaccountably, did not seem to be the object of our next attack, Although the great practicability of it the preceding day and the explosion of the only mine the enemy had, then should have convinced us that it was the best place to assault. Major Menzies, A.D.C. to the commander-in-chief, a gallant but hot-headed soldier, reported to the general that the place could easily be taken. The general went to the 76th parade, reproached them for cowardice and reminded them of their former exploits.

They replied that headed by their former own Colonel (Monson) and not obliged to march through the sap but at once out on the plain, they would take it, scandalous and undisciplined like, as it was, for soldiers to make their own terms for fighting or doing their duty. Yet so urgent was the present case, that the general accepted their offer, Colonel Monson was ordered to head a fresh storming party, composed of all the Europeans of both armies and the flower of the sepoys. The party, marched by the general, cheered him as he wished them success and were determined to conquer or die, the latter fate befell the greater part of this column. Stimulated by the shameful remembrance of their former conduct, they are said to have displayed a valour and steadiness, almost supernatural. But all would not do and the remains returned to camp, to mourn a fourth repulse. That such efforts as they made should have not been attended with success, seems unaccountable, precipitation here, as frequently before, was our ruin.

Major Menzies was the cause of an attack, made with the inconsiderate haste of passionate revenge, instead of the deliberation of real bravery. The few shot fired at the bastion had rendered it little better than it was on the 20th. It was accessible only by clambering, or scaling and those who attempted both, were deliberately destroyed by the desperate Jats, as they ascended, were pushed off with spears or cut down at the top of the wall. Grenades, stink-pots, earthen globular vessels filled with powder, burning wood, cotton and oil, were thrown on the assailants, who though four different times they planted the colours near the top of the wall, were never able to muster near them above five or six men at a time. Parties, likewise attempted the breach, but the vigilant enemy had built it up, all except a narrow hole, into which three men at a time could enter. The same means of defence, aided by whole forests of spears which filled up the entrance, compelled the assailants to give away these also. Major Menzies, in despair at this scene of butchery without hope of success, into which his rash advice, had brought so many brave men, threw away his scabbard and rushed on destruction.

All agree, that on both sides the most prodigious acts of valour were shown and so might be expected, when combatants meet. On one side stimulated by shame and revenge, on the other by every motive, dear to men, and with the fury of despair. Their wives, children, name, tribe, and property all at stake. May it teach our pride an awful lesson, and it will be a useful one, sixty-three officers and above 2000 rank and file, European and native, were killed and wounded on these two melancholy occasions, a quantity of blood for the wanton shedding of which, an awful responsibility lays somewhere or other.

March 2nd—We passed through the remains of Rampoora, to all appearance once a great city, though now almost in ruins. The inhabitants, who were very numerous had all been plundered the day before, by the enemy, who were at Afzulghur, eight koss off, It was shortly after midday, horses from continued marching were fagged and some knocked up, we descried Afzulghur, and on the immense plain that extended from that place down to the groves at the foot of the Almora hills, the enemy drawn up to receive us. A long line of dust extending to our right, along the bottom of the hills, indicated that their baggage was gone off in that direction south eastward, we had our left in front at the time, I think that we ought to have brought our right in front and moved down, between the enemy and his baggage, keeping our front to the enemy, by which we should have effected the double advantage, of cutting him off from his baggage, and of driving him, if successful, to the north westward. Whereas we moved down, left in front and drove him to the south eastward.

The enemy's position was a good one. Both his flanks were secured by *nullahs* with little water, but steep bands. His front was covered by a small hollow water course. The ground was either barren hard soil, with long jungle grass tufts, hard and irregular or when cultivated, was intersected by deep ditches and canals for watering. Circumstances favourable in the highest degree, to irregular skirmishing fighters and diametrically the reverse to us, who being always so greatly outnumbered, are forced to keep comparatively close order and trust to concentrated fire power in our artillery, and to unbroken, rapid charges of cavalry.

As we neared the enemy, we perceived to our astonishment, a body of infantry drawn up in their front and centre, but a good deal to the left of our line of march, with numerous white triangular standards and on their right and left flanks of their foot and at about 100 yards distance, were drawn up two large masses of cavalry. The whole plain in the rear of their infantry was covered with the same swarms of scampering horse, that we have so often seen before. As we continued advancing, a third compact body of horse, moved up from their rear and fetched a circuit round our right flank at a considerable distance, but received several shots right in the centre of it, from the galloper with the advance guard, though without much quickening it's pace. It's aim, object, was our rear, into which it got. Troop of the 29th Dragoons was sent out to reconnoitre those horse but was surrounded and harassed by a prodigious number, and with the loss of five men wounded, effected it's return to the line.

This body of the enemy, afterwards dispersed among the bearers and followers in our rear, whom it cut up and plundered, without interruption from us, who were warmly and desperately engaged at the time and were, withal, so prodigiously outnumbered, that wherever we went, we were surrounded on all sides.

As we now closely approached the enemy, who stood firm, on their ground, Captain Philpot, acting Field Officer of the day, being in column, heading with his advance guard, having received no instructions, went to General Smith, and asked him if he should form and charge, or might form line at all events. He received an ill-natured reprimand and was told that he "should receive orders soon enough." At last the enemy's infantry wheeled obliquely to their left and began advancing intolerably regular echelons upon us, up to this moment no disposition had been ordered by the general. In short, nothing was thought of, nothing ready, and these footmen were allowed to advance, till having come opposite our guns, they suddenly wheeled up and ran forward shouting sword in hand.

The brave artillery battery opened, the first round or two appeared to have great effect but the Rohillas, who were now quite close, planted their standards and squatted down for an instant, flat on their bellies in the long grass, or in the little water course, so that we fancied they were destroyed and the 27th Dragoons moved out to charge. The enemy were so close, and the 27th so entangled among our guns and other corps, that before they had time to form in good order, or get out of a trot, far less into the three quarter speed that charge requires to be effectual, they were among the enemy.

At this unfortunate instant, the general himself, it is said, called out to the regiment to halt, as if thinking them too near and ill-prepared he wanted them to retire and charge closely from a greater distance! Some of the 27th heard this word of command, some did not, some pulled up their horses accordingly, others neither did not nor with such bits as we use, could they.

The Rohilla Infantry now rose up sword in hand among the 27th who were all in disorder and to regain their ranks and reform, were obliged to retreat in much disorder, followed up by the enemy's infantry and by their cavalry of the left wing, even to the very guns, which could not fire without destroying our own people.

As the general himself, who was with the advance guard (which had moved to the right flank but was still in column left in front!) had been completely taken by surprise, all was confusion, when the gallant and steady 8th Dragoons in the second line were ordered by their Brigadier Vandeleur to throw out two squadrons to support the 1st line. The whole regiment could scarce be kept from following but they were restrained and in three minutes after these Royal Irish set up a howl and dashed in among the foremost of the enemy, disordered as these were, by their own impetuous advance, not a man was to be seen, all were killed or fled. A danger even more imminent, at the very critical moment of this right and centre attack, threatened the left flank, which was protected by the Irregular Horse, men, who it was thought never could be depended on, and who, if beaten had here no second line to protect or support them.

The large body of horse to the right flank of the enemy's infantry consisted of Meer Khan's bodyguard, and his select Patans, 700 or 800 in number, and as we afterwards learned, it was commanded by that chief in person and was to be the principal point for him, the left guns, whose weakness he saw, were to be attacked in front by the infantry and in flank by the cavalry. So great was the confusion in the centre and on the right at this time and so much was every one taken up with his own more immediate share in the mêlée that few observed the danger from this flank attack, or witnessed the good conduct of him who saved the guns and perhaps the army, Captain James, Skinner.

I saw the enemy moving down on my left. I told the next gun to me, to keep a look out on them, all my attention being taken up by the 27th retiring, and the infantry rushing in on our guns in front. The cavalry came on at a gallop, two guns of the 27th at this time, moved down to the front of my left, and prevented my own gun from seeing the enemy. My left guns had just time to give them our round of grape, which did great execution, and made part of the enemy waver. The main body however, galloped down shouting and brandishing their spears. Destruction seemed altogether inevitable, an order came to limber up and retire.

I gave up all for lost, mounted my horse and drew my sword, with the resolution, of course, to sell my life as dearly as I could, and while with greater indifference than I could have even supposed possible, I expected the worst, to my surprise and delight, I saw Skinner's Horse trot up in column right in front, wheel up into line enpotence to ours and meet the enemy's charge coolly and rapidly. A volley of our matchlocks, from their Skinner's line at the moment of wheeling up, staggered the enemy. Skinners dashed in among them. They turned and fled in disorder, pursued at speed. The *nullah* on the right of the enemy's original position, which was in the rear, as they retreated from our left, so that it stopped their progress. They dashed down the steep banks into its slimy bed and Skinner's brave fellows, precipitated themselves after them.

Many were killed and wounded, many horses taken. Skinner's men were called in now, the whole of our forces moved on about one and a half miles, as quickly as the exhausted horses could go, and in good order, formed in two columns of brigade, right and left in front. One on each side of the gun, which were in line, the enemy retiring in good order also before us, but never suffering us to near them.

As experience has taught us, how vain pursuit of these horse enemies, is we content ourselves with giving them a few rounds of shots, with some apparent effect and they made off. We halted for an hour and fearful of the baggage being attacked, returned to Sheercotty about sunset. This affair, or victory as it pleases us and the Governor General to proclaim it, was attended on our part, with the slender loss of a few troops, Europeans and native killed. The enemy lost many standards, most of their small but gallant body of infantry were killed, forty or fifty horse men killed, many doubtless wounded, and twenty or thirty horses taken. None of great value and richly adorned.

"All is well that ends well"! These few words give my real opinion of the business. The Rohilla Foot soldiers, the known of old and by fatal experience to this army, by their enthusiastic bravery and skill in the use of the sword and target in 1794, they nearly destroyed a wind of our army after routing our cavalry, by being allowed unaccountably to rush on unbroken, too near the line before the action commenced. But, Sir R. Abercrombie, had at least formed his own disposition for battle. We, many in camp say, we should have pursued the enemy close, but the guns certainly could not have gone farther, their loss, was not to be risked.

Whether our jaded force of 2000 regular and irregular cavalry could have done much, without their assistance, against a multitude of swarming, active and comparatively fresh horse, admits of doubt, or more than doubt. As the enemy had not gone off in the direction of our baggage but followed the track of their own, I think we ought unquestionably to have sent for ours and pitched our camp on the field of battle, which is a point of some importance in the eyes of the natives, a regiment or two might have been sent to protect it back, as the distance was but a few miles.

March 3rd—A *Ressaldar* (commander of 4000 horse) of the enemy, wounded in three places, was brought in today. Surgeons were ordered to attend him, and every attention to be paid him by Skinners, in whose charge he is. He says, that Ameer Khan was a coward, that after leading the bodyguard or Khas Russalah of select Patans, up to the charge on our left flank and guns, he fled at the first round of the grape, and left them to go on. Two of the standards taken, belonged, he says, to the bodyguard. The battle was occasioned by the mutual reproaches of Ameer Khan and his chiefs, on the subject of their constantly flying before us.

The baggage etc. was sent off at daybreak and they resolved to try their fortune. The infantry, only 300 in number, all choice men enlisted at Rampore and the towns in Rohilkund, on terms of five rupees monthly and free plunder, were tired of marching they said, but would stop and fight with all their hearts, how well they performed their promise, we can testify. Their plan was to storm our guns, in which they were to be supported by Ameer Khan and his best Horse. A *lack* of rupees was to be their reward, if successful. All the troops engaged, were sworn on the Koran to conquer or die. The infantry alone, performed their promise in toto.

Commander was not making game of us, but I rather fancy that this is to pass for a glorious victory, and it is supposed a royal salute will be fired at Fort William on the occasion. Necessary perhaps, to keep up the spirits of the Calcutta Folks, after the dreadful tidings from the grand army at Bhartpoor.

Indents for supplies of ammunition, were sent to the magazines of Allyghur and Futtyghur, for in all Rohilkund and the Upper Dooab, there is not a single depôt! If the enemy but knew this, and would by harassing us frequently, cause us to expend the little we have, he would do a most politic thing!

March 5th—Ameer Khan seems to intend a new trip downwards, and downwards must we follow him. It was his intention to have recrossed, it is said, on the 1st, but (in my opinion very injudiciously) Colonel Burn, with his three battalions and Irregular Horse, was ordered from Sahawrunpoor to stop the ghauts (fords), which prevented the enemy from moving across. From what we hear the enemy were much dispirited and confused by the affair (or as from this circumstance we may now term it), the victory of the 2nd inst. He marched, without halting, to Moraudabad, where he arrived at 12 next day, in a confused and struggling manner, *"tant meiun!"* say I. He is now said, to be gone in the direction of Sumbul, where his family reside. He received an invitation, we understand, from the Regent and people of Rampore, in consequence of the Bhartpoor failures, to return but the rough handling his infantry met with at Afzulghur, may alter the opinions of those time serving Rohillas.

I mentioned soon after our marching from Cawnpore, in my journal, volume first page, my opinion, that the rashness of —— who commands the —— would one day cause the destruction of his officers and men, if not the capture of his guns. I pointed out the danger, inutility, impropriety of his opinion, about going close up to infantry, before he opened his fire. I also frequently hinted as much to himself and his prudence hitherto, in opposition to what I feared, and prophesied he would do, made me hope that he had thought better of the subject and meant to behave with caution, instead of risking his guns and men, to no purpose.

Judge, reader, of my surprise when I learned from his own mouth, that it was, by our imprudent general, left to himself when he would choose to begin the action by opening his guns and that the enemy's being suffered to approach so near us, was entirely his doing. His excuse, or rather reason, for having so nearly caused all his men to be killed on the 3rd ultimo was to show general, who never had seen our corps in action, how brave we were! This surely requires no comments and I have only to look forward, to the destruction of this valuable part of our army, when next Ameer Khan chooses to favour us with another engagement!

March 7th—So admirably are things managed by our Generalissimo and so accurate is our information, and knowledge of the country, that at starting, the general could not inform the quartermaster general where we were to go! And when determined on going towards Shahabad, of which name there are many towns in Rohilkund and Oude, he did not know which of them was the place in question, nor when that was settled, whether to recross the Yawaufdar or not, an hour and a half, was lost in adjusting these preliminaries.

Ameer Khan was at Chandoussy yesterday. He there received a lack and a half of rupees from the citizen, to spare the town, but he burned the cantonments, and the bungalows and property of the unfortunate officers of the 6th Cavalry, who will not receive one louis of reimbursement from our liberal Government. Ameer Khan detached late on the 6th, some thousand men, to intercept Lieutenant R. Skinner, who, in a shameful or inconsiderate manner, was detached yesterday morning with 400 of his brother's horse, to Allyghur by the route of Anop-Shehar, where he is to cross in boats. Ameer Khan was much nearer Anop-Shehar than we, and if he got early intelligence of young Skinner's movements, which doubtless he did, this unfortunate party will probably be cut off.

By accounts from Bhartpoor, of the 2nd we learn that on the 22nd the batteries and trenches were abandoned and instantly burnt by the exulting Jats. On the 24th, the army shifted ground about six miles by a circuitous route, round to the extremity of the marsh, three miles from the avenue of trees and four miles from the fort. The cattle had previously been five days without forage, many were dead and many died on the marsh and left their loads, public and private to the enemy. Battering guns etc. had been sent for to Futtyghur and Allyghur, shot and grain, from Agra, Deeg and Muttra. Materials for new work were preparing and miners hired, yet many people thought all these seeming preparations for the siege, only a feint, to save appearances and cause Runjeet Sing to offer terms.

Lieutenant Colonel Hammond (2nd), Major Radcliffe (12th), Captain Morton (86th), Lieutenants Moore and Hamilton (European Regiment) were dead of their wounds. Captain Morton shot himself in despair of recovery and excess of pain. Many more officers and men, were expected to die, from the same melancholy cause as these gentlemen. All the grand army is drooping!

March 8th—Captain Skinner received information this morning, that Ameer Khan with his whole army, had moved down to Sumbul, the native place of Ameer Khan, and where 5000 men, whom he detached yesterday, had surrounded young Lieutenant Skinner and his 400 Horse. Captain Skinner begged the general to move to his brother's relief, as he would certainly be destroyed if he did not, but our considerate commander, having no doubt politically good reasons for his inhuman conduct, smiled at Captain Skinner's anxiety, and marched nineteen miles, in the exactly opposite direction, *viz.* the Barelly road! So that if young Skinner trusts to relief from us, he is deceived, as we are now forty miles distant.

March 9th—General Smith at last seems to think that he may as well save young Skinner as not, so after having gone nineteen miles in the opposite direction, he has now returned towards Sumbul. But, instead of making the twenty-two koss at one march, or of making the greater part of it at least, during the night, he goes deliberately on, thus fagging out, his already exhausted men and horses, by describing on useless circumpeadions, while the enemy is quietly laying by. Captain Skinner is scarcely in doubt, as to the fate of his brother. He had, when surrounded on the night of the 6th, occupied an old garden, walled and a ruinous *serai* near Sumbul, he had at that time, but one day's provision, and his men must be firmer than irregular troops can be expected to be if they can starve themselves, see their women, children and their horses die of hunger and not surrender on any terms.

Captain Skinner says he is not afraid that Ameer Khan will maltreat his brother if he surrenders but as the young man is full of courage, he dreads that he and thirty or forty faithful adherents, may in despair, make a desperate sally and be destroyed. The acquisition of 400 horses alone, would be a prize indeed to Ameer

Khan, and he says that if General Smith does not succour this unfortunate party, whom he sent into the very mouth of destruction, many of his regiment will desert him, for ever. Since Colonel Monson sacrificed the brave Lucan and his Irregulars, to cover his retreat through Mokundra Pass, the Hindoostanee Horse, have always been fearful of experiencing similar treatment.

March 10th—News arrived last night from young Skinner, informing us of the enemy, after attempting four times to storm his position, without success and with the loss of eight or nine killed and fifty wounded, having raised the siege last night on our approach and moved off towards Amrooah. Pray heaven he may cross the Ganges!

Skinner came into camp today about 2 p.m. Horsemen, though deserted by every hope of relief, stood by him like heroes. They knew not of our approach till the enemy were moving off and though stormed by Ameer Khan's Horse and Foot and all the male inhabitants of Sumbul, they repulsed their repeated attack, with the utmost firmness and escaped at last. No thanks to General Smith! His ball ammunition was expended and he cut the shoes of his horse into iron slugs for his matchlocks! He and his party do indeed deserve every recompense for their constancy and courage, but even thanks from our gallant old general he probably will never get, as it is not probable General Smith will be very ample in his details of an affair evidently caused by his own mismanagement

March 11th—We have now been in pursuit of this enemy, through our own valuable provinces of the Dooab and Rohilkund, for a month and three days and we seem about as near the accomplishment of our object as when we set out. We have marched to and fro, about 700 miles after him, and what have we done towards expelling or destroying him? What shall we ever be able to do? Every day's march must weaken us and consequently strengthen him. Half of our horses are already totally, or nearly, unserviceable and everyday, in the dreadful weather, must diminish the effective number of our men, not so our enemy. He, a freebooter and invader, subsists his horses and men sumptuously wherever he goes. We cannot plunder our own people. We are foreigners in India and to us the heat of the sun and winds is deadly. He and his people are natives of the country and it is surely a fair presumption, that nature created them capable of enduring the climate in which she placed them. He has nothing but defeat or disgrace to fear, he relinquishes his scheme, at least as well off, as when he invaded us. We have every thing to lose, territory, riches, dominion, our lives and that reputation, by the opinion of which alone, we exist in India. The comparison is an afflicting, but a true one.

A flying report pervaded camp, of Colonel Burn having crossed the Ganges and defeated Meer Khan.

March 12th—Colonel Burn, was to remain on the Dooab side of the river, but being in want of cash to pay to his detachment many month's arrears, he sent off Captain Murray, with 600 Irregular Hindoostanee Horse, and some 200 match-lockers, to Moradabad for treasure. four days ago (8th), at Amrooah, Captain Murray fell in with Ameer Khan's whole force, on their march from Sumbul. Murray took post in a village, he was there blockaded by the enemy for two days, in which time Ameer Khan, at the head of his dismounted Rohillas, stormed three different times and was repulsed always with loss. Murray having sent intelligence of his situation to Colonel Burn, that gallant old officer not wishing to abandon to their fate his detachments, instantly crossed the river, and made on the 10th (the same day) a forced march with his battalion of sixteen *koss*.

He arrived just at sunset and so prompt and rapid, were this old boy's movements, that Ameer Khan had not an idea of his movement, until the dust of his approach betrayed it. The cowardly enemy, instantaneously retreated, as soon as they could saddle their horses. Murray sallied out of his village and he and the battalions fell on the more tardy and the baggage. 400 or 500 men were killed on the spot and much baggage and plunder horses, camels, etc., etc. taken. The people of Amrooah behaved very well in this affair, for they shut out and refused supplies to Ameer Khan, whilst they granted them to us, their liege Lord. Not so the people of Sumbul, all of whom, even to the women, children, dotards, and priests, assisted Ameer Khan against young Skinner. One of these, Chief Muftis, was shot through the temple, as he knelt praying for Ameer Khan's success, as Sumbul is in our territories and has been, so not by conquest, but cession, for some years.

A terrible example, similar to that of Shamley in November, should have been made of the town and inhabitants. If we treat our rebels with lenity in time of actual invasion and when actually armed against us, adieu to all government. I should have before said that though no mention officially, (i.e. written in the orderly book) was made of young Skinner and his corps, for reasons that are perhaps not difficult to guess, yet the major general was graciously pleased to express his obligations in person to Skinner and his chieftains.

March 13th—Gioja! The enemy crossed yesterday evening, at the ghaut at Commendnagur, the same that we crossed at, on the 15th February, and because to push him at this critical moment, would be unquestionably politic and right *ergo*, we this day halted!

The general has severely reprimanded Colonel Burn for crossing! Like the sailor of Admiral Watson's ship, who single handed took Budge Budge Fort, Colonel Burn should reply, that he "will be d—d if ever he beats another enemy for us, or drives one out of our country for us, when we can do neither ourselves." For such is pretty nearly the case, not we certainly, but old Burn's detachment, drove Ameer Khan out of Rohilkund and there needs not, I think, any very extraordinary penetration to discover the causes of our commander's wrath.

I wonder if, in his official letters to the commander-in-chief, he will take to himself the credit of expelling Ameer Khan. Burn could not do less than go to the rescue of a detachment of his army, although our system seems to be different. But he is blamed for sending this detachment to Moradabad and thereby being obliged to cross himself to it's support. Now, before we are too apt to blame him, we should recollect: first, that his detachment a great part of which is Irregular Horse, are many months in arrears and if Irregulars are not regularly paid, they make it an invariable rule, to desert. Besides, second, Colonel Burn commands an army, independent of General Smith. His is the Delhi detachment for the protection of the northern parts of the Delhi Subahship and under the order of our resident (Lieutenant Colonel Ochterlony) at that court. It is surely therefore allowable, even though residents did send Burn to co-operate with us, that some discretionary power may be exerted by the commander of such an army. Be all this how it may, the good, Colonel Burn has done the Government, in expelling the invading Seiks from the north Dooab twice in two successive years. In the gallant defences of Delhi-Shamley and on many former occasions, was never greater than the good he has done at this critical conjuncture of affairs, in frightening away so formidable an enemy as Ameer Khan. Next to General Lake (old Cogie as Burn is nicknamed) is, I truly think, the most useful military man in the country.

March 15th—Ameer Khan is said to be gone off to Hawpur. It is conjectured that he is going towards Delhi, either to return via trans Jumniana to Bhartpoor or, what is more probable to join 6000 Seiks, who taking advantage of Colonel Burn's absence, have made an irruption into the country near Delhi, which they are plundering. Some fancy Ameer Khan will re-cross again into Rohilkund, were plunder his sole object, or were his army entirely composed of Pindaries, perhaps he might, but from the letters he wrote to the Rohilla chiefs, I am inclined to think he, and his Patan followers, aimed at something higher, at dominion. In this however, he has certainly failed and the general firmness and loyalty of the inhabitants, has been really as great as unexpected. Whether this be owing to the presence of our army, I know not, probably in a great measure it has and at all events, I should long to see the experiment of their affections, made without an army of our's in Rohilkund.

It is to be hoped, that Lord Wellesley will, when he receives the returns of the diminished revenues of this year, seriously reflect how near he was losing altogether, this fertile country, from his scandalous want of management alone. In having so few sepoys, as to be unable to leave a single garrison in this valuable country, and that to his good genius, a good fortune alone, and not to the powers of his army, or Government, he is indebted for being able to call Rohilkund yet his own.

March 17th—Marched to Jehangeerabad, a very large town surrounded with an irregular, and a very strong mud wall with round bastions. The *Zemindar*, or, as he styles himself Rajah, is brother to the Rajah of Anop-Shehar and has been long a rebel to us.

On this occasion, intimidated probably by the sight of so large a force, he was very civil, and being sick himself, or pretending to be so (a thing usual when these people are afraid of trusting themselves in the hands of a powerful chief), his brother came to wait on the general and our Captain Skinner, who knew him of old, when this country belonged to the Mahrattas. Ameer Khan with his Patans (6000), is we hear, waiting for us at Kamoona-Doondee Khan's Fort and one march from this.

I do not believe it, because I suspect Ameer Khan can have no wiser to fight us now, because Doondee Khan instead of assisting him, wishes to be pardoned by our Government. This man, though a rebel, and in arms, is not so very guilty, as the term rebel in Europe, would lead readers in that country, and who had never been in India, to imagine. Under all the native government, the allegiance of the great land holders, was of a feudal kind and though they contributed regularly their quota of rent, yet the entire military and civil jurisdiction within their *Zemindary* remained to them. To defend this imperialism in *imperia* would be folly. The feudal system, though at the time a great benefit, as being the first stage of improvement from downright barbarism, is universally reprobated, as pregnant with every political evil, yet a similar Government prevailed in India and the privileges of these military landholders, were by long descriptions, rights in their eyes.

Our first step on gaining possession of a tract of territory in India, is to annihilate every right of government or jurisdiction exercised by the petty Rajahs and *Zemindars*. The change is too violent to be acceptable, the governed, as I observed of the Hattrass people in November, are equally aversed to it as the governors, and these Rajahs are never surrendered; without a violent struggle. Such were the causes of the mud fort campaign in 1802-3, when we obtained from Saadut Ally, the sovereignty of Sassney, Bidjigur, etc. Their fall, made many of the remaining zemindars quietly give up their forts, or at least in part demolish them. Doondee Khan was one of these. It is a great error of our Government, when their new authority is not supported by the confidence or attachment of the subjects, but by the strong arm of power alone. To send up to govern their turbulent requisitions, crowds of civilians, judges, collectors, etc. etc., most of them young men from Calcutta and all of them totally unacquainted with the temper and manners of the Hindoostannies, known only to the officers, who have all served many years, in this constant theatre of war for years.

These civilians in time of foreign war too, are unsupported by any military force, yet this impotence, seems but to increase their imprudence. The elder civilians seem to fancy themselves among the timid and peaceable inhabitants of Bengal or Bihar, and treat these half subdued naughty new subjects, with all the rigour of the British customs. The younger civilians, are generally under the absolute authority of some black Bengally *sarkar*,[3] raised to the high office of *Dewan*[4] and this upstart Jack in office, takes every opportunity of insulting the natives of high birth and large property, under the shadow of the collector's name, until by repeated aggravated tyranny, they are driven into rebellion. Such, it is well known, was the origin of the present rebellions that at present convulse the whole Dooab. Mr Russel (collector of Allyghur) *Dewan*, in open court, threatened to beat with his shoe, Doondee Khan. At this greatest of all possible affronts from such a low scoundrel, Doondee Khan retired to his fort, saying that if he lost his "honour, he might as well fight for it, or lose his life too."

Repenting now of his conduct, and seeing that in the end, he will certainly be subdued, he has behaved with the greatest civility

---

3. Money lending men of business or writers and accountants, a set of Calcutta sharks, who feed on the necessities of the young writers on the arrival, by administering to the necessities and pleasures, and thus get them deeply in debt and then of actually by threatening with a jail, procure the highest appointments and do, unpunished, the most oppressive acts to the nation and iniquitous to Government. For which, if discovered, the unfortunate collector or judge is responsible, and suffers.
4. Deputy Minister.

to people of ours whom he took prisoners and wrote repeatedly to Captain Skinner, to try and procure his pardon, in the event of which, he would demolish his fort, pay his arrears of tribute, and two tenths more on produce, than was customary with other land holders, would keep the whole Dooab between Anop-Shehar and Muttra, clear of all depredations from other chiefs and would give his son a hostage for the performance of those conditions. One would suppose, that at this critical juncture nothing short of downright insanity, could make us reject such an offer, yet we have with our usual ruinous blind pride, refused them!

March 18th—Marched to the W. bank of the Kolly Nuddy, which we crossed about two miles from Kamoona. We remained all day, waiting for our baggage, though our out-flankers passed under the very nose of one of Doondee Khan's Forts, the garrison did not fire on them, nor did they molest any of our baggage.

Ameer Khan, on hearing of our approach, left and made but one march to Juwaru, twelve miles from Muttra. On his arrival here, he sent to Doondee Khan, for the loan of a lakh of rupees. Doondee Khan promised fare but sent it not and when Ameer Khan again sent, Doondee Khan replied that the English were so near, he feared the lakh of rupees would be taken by them, a hint which Ameer Khan evinced that he perfectly understood, by decamping instantly.

March 19th—Marched to the south of Allyghur. I went over the whole of this extraordinary fortress and was so much struck with the wonderful strength of it's only entrance, that I can scarcely believe it possible that it was taken, sure I am that a very few men, now we have made bridges on the ditch, could defend it against any assault. I do think that extremest necessity alone, could vindicate an attempt to take such a place by storm. The capture of this place, may be almost set to have decided the war, and when one thinks of the repeated failures of our troops to take Bhartpoor, it is really incredible, that the very same man should have been able to take this. The ditch is very deep, wet and in some places, a perfect lake. It has an inner citadel all round to go to decay, an immensely high wall with round

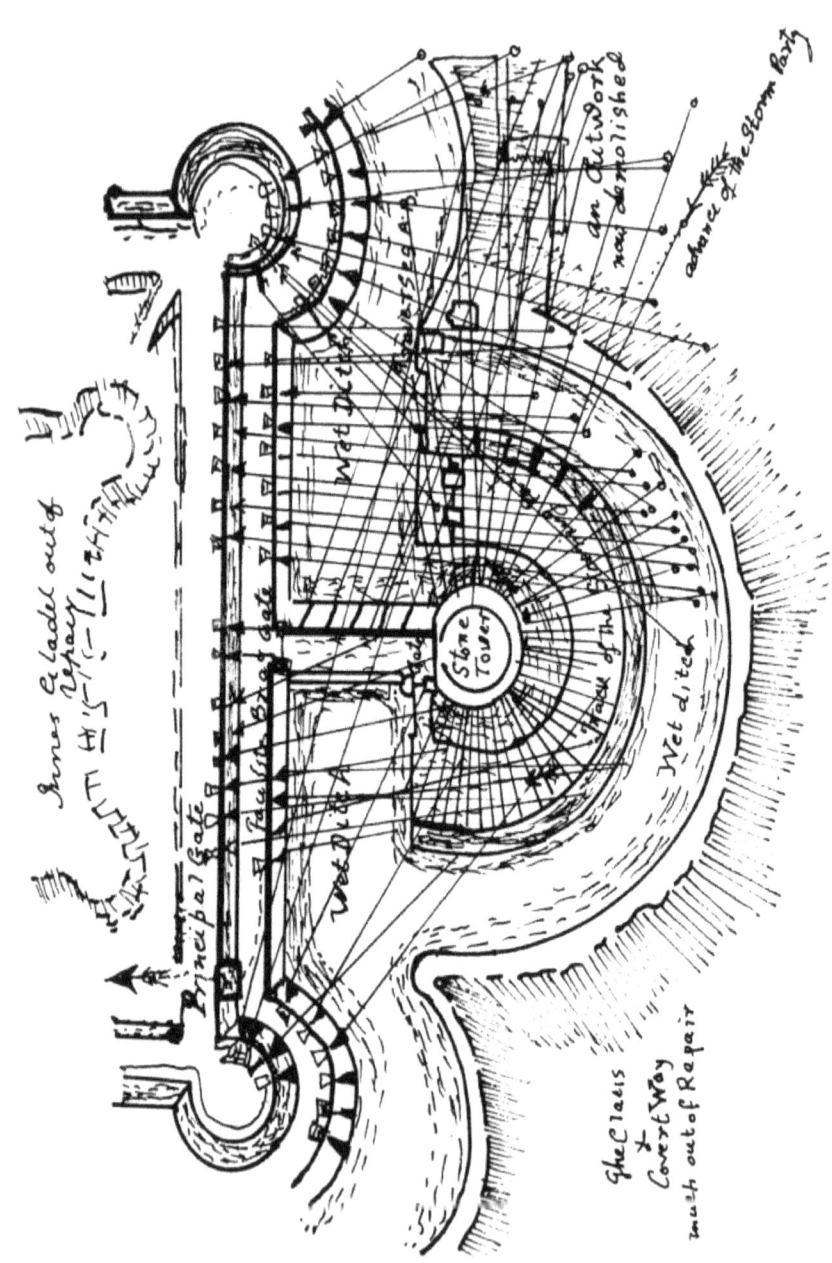

THE WORKS AT ALLYGHUR FORT

towers, fausse bray and a semi-circular ravelin and ditch, with a stone round-tower redoubt and ditch in it's centre, round the bottom of which the road winds. Four gateways (successfully blown open by us) defend this long road, everywhere seen by canon and musketry.

March 21st—We received orders to return to the grand army. It is certainly foolish in the extreme, carrying a sickly and knocked up cavalry as we are, to the grand army, where the cattle, public and private, are daily dying of positive hunger. The advantage to be derived, by our presence, is very small and by no means balances the risk of our being altogether knocked up and rendered unfit for any service.

March 24th—We have now been trotting almost incessantly about, for forty-five days, and have undergone more continued heat and fatigue than I fancy troops ever before did. The trip down the Dooab was a comparative party of pleasure to this. The season was cooler, and grew daily more so. We were under an old chief, who liked us, whom we liked, whose temper and manners, tho sometimes bathes crusty, were in general affable and kind. Who finished the expedition with eclat, with honour to himself and credit to us, because he was eagerly bent on accomplishing his end, as speedily as possible and because we knew he would not give his men or horses, one hour's unnecessary trouble and therefore every man worked with spirit. To make a long comparison between the two commanders would be an easy matter, but as the comparisons would be pursued only by the readers of these memoires, I may save myself the trouble. The account I have given of our expedition, is of itself, a sufficient condemnation of General Smith, and, I understand, our old chief, who well knows what his Horse Artillery and Cavalry can do when led as they ought to be, is so, fully convinced of general bad conduct, that he says he will take care and shall not again command "his Cavalry".

That General Smith has neither the temper nor manners, of a gentleman is unfortunate, but this circumstance would only make him a disagreeable person to command. In judging of his military character, as a general, those adventitious circumstances must be overlooked. Although they can not be forgiven. But there are several gross errors in the conduct of our expedition, which effectually stamp General Smith's character, with the marks of obstinacy or ignorance. It is a matter of indifference which may be the cause. The effect is too obvious. In the first place our not marching on the night of the 9th February from Muttra to attack the enemy, then within five *koss*. Secondly, our shameful burgled business, when we did march to surprise the enemy at Kamoona on the 12th February. Thirdly, our halting at the Rohilkund side of Commendnagur Ghaut, after crossing the Ganges, a measure astonishing to everyone, without any possible cause and which left the civilians at Moraudabad, and the cities of Moraudabad, Amrooah, nay Rampore and Barelly and all Rohilkund, to the mercy of the enemy. Unless (as actually happened) they could defend themselves. Fourthly, the action of Afzulghur, of which the name need only be mentioned, to recall to the reader how nearly the whole cavalry and horse artillery were being cut off by the precipitation and mismanagement of our commander. Fifthly, our marching to the southward, and leaving poor young Skinner surrounded by a prodigiously superior force, to his fate, and sixthly, the never to be forgotten harassing march from Allyghur to Juwaur, after the enemy had left the country.

With regard to the good we have done by our pursuit, that is I think incalculable in it's advantages, but of it, no part is owing to General Smith. The presence, or vicinity of an army, will always have the same effect in keeping down the disaffected or wavering, and encouraging the loyal, whoever be the commander. But we had several circumstances greatly in our favour. The Government of the *Jaghire* was from interest, friendly to us, and the chiefs of Barelly, and our more immediate part of Rohilkund, were kept firm in their attachment, in a great measure by the influence of the excellent Mr Seton, Chief Judge of the province. A man of conciliatory measures, of high abilities and elegant accomplishments and actually beloved by these ferocious people.

March 25th—Certain it is that a correspondence of some kind or other has of late been going on between us and Runjeet Sing. If negotiations are not going on, we are surely unpardonable. Besides, what intricacy, what scope for diplomatic shuffling can there be, in the peace with a person, whom we consider as a vassal in rebellion, of whose strong holds and territory we have in part, already made ourselves masters. When two parties equal in power, equal in the advantages they have gained during war, meet to treat for peace. The status *ante bellum* is commonly the basis of negotiation. But when, as with us, the advantage has been entirely on one side—the utipossidetis the status quo is, with every right, insisted on by the superior. Runjeet has lost Deeg and its appending territory, his advantages over us are merely negative, he has defended Bhartpoor with success, but can this give him a right to the status *ante*?

It is said, that the once proud, but now humbled Marquis, makes no difficulty, that he will be contented with Runjeet's discarding Holkar and Ameer Khan and giving security, either by delivery, of his strongholds for good behaviour till the war is done, when all (Deeg included) will be restored. The commander-in-chief. on the other hand it is said, insists on Runjeet paying the expenses of the war, in addition to the above, and here, it is reported the difficulty lays. In truth, I fear the old general would rather fight than make peace. The political interests of British India are matters of no moment to a bird of passage as he is, who means to go home as soon as he can, and he no doubt feels deeply, the wound which his military name has received by the siege of this place.

I myself believe Runjeet wants to gain time till the hot winds, with all their fury set in, a season which he well knows to be fatal to us. Sindhia, too, is advancing towards us, with rapid strides, ostensibly against Amboojee—but it is suspected really against us. If his 180 guns, eighteen battalions and 30000 horses should find us, still before this place, we should certainly find ourselves in an awkward predicament to say the best of it. The style, used by Runjeet, in his addresses for peace, are humble in the highest degree, he calls himself the "Company's *Zemindar*" and on the general being created Baron Lake by the King, which honours arrived during our absence in Rohilkund, the Rajah sent him complimentary letter and presents and begged to know "What was to become of his vile slave" and hoping that the general would let him keep "his house (*gur*—a house, or fort, *i.e.* Bhartpoor) and take all the rest"! To those accustomed to the tiresome hyperboles of the Eastern style, this is after all mere verbiage, nay to some it seems to be insultingly ironical in this state of affairs now. Yet were the Rajah sincere, he certainly would have altogether discarded our two enemies, Holkar and Ameer Khan, whom he still keeps (aid and fed by him) under his walls. This is, in my opinion, a damning proof of insincerity. Time will show however, and shortly too, one thing however, it is impossible not to remark viz. the difference of our style and conduct now, and on the 28th December last, when it was positive treason to suppose it possible that the high and mighty English could condescend to treat with a rebel, a traitor, *tempora mutantur entnos mutantur* etc., etc.

March 26th—Halted, I have taken some pains to collect from the intelligent friends, I have in the artillery and engineer corps, what has been the real cause of our want of success in our different attempts against Bhartpoor. In the first place, the cowardice of the Europeans, prevented our even trying to storm the breach on the 20th February.

On that day, no one disputed its practicability, on the 21st, our non-success was entirely to be attributed to our own folly in trying to do, what we know, or ought to have known was impossible, on the 21st January the great breadth and depth of the uninjured ditch, was the obstacle. And, on the 9th January, the confusion of a night assault, aggravated by the want of good management, in the part of the commander of the strong party, caused the first miscarriage, which gave fatal confidence to a desperate enemy. But the true and grand cause, in a greater of less degree of all these misfortunes, has been the want of a sufficient ordnance establishment. I mean, of an adequate field engineers establishment of European and native artificers and pioneers as well as of a sufficient siege train and of artillery officers and men. The truth is, that we have never in this country, met with such resolute opposition before and our usual mode of taking of besieging, has universally been, to erect a breach, batting instantly, for six or eight guns and having made a hole in the wall, to scramble to the assault.

Wet ditches being unusual, I may almost say unknown and equally so, had been the desperate courage, that on this occasion we have met with at Deeg, reckoned by the natives, one of the strongest forts in Hindoostan, we succeeded in our old way. And although after we had twice been repulsed from Bhartpoor, the critics in our camp blamed our commanders of artillery and engineers, for not besieging in form, they yet never dreamed of it before these disasters and now only showed their ignorance by talking of such a thing as a regular siege, against so irregular a place with the impotent force of artillery, which we had scrapped together and collected, drained from every possible place in our upper provinces.

So scandalously starved is this department in India, whilst at home and all over military Europe, it is thought worthy of having at its head, a cabinet minister, of being under the command of officers of it's own only and of being uncontrolled in it's expenditure and establishments. Well, with our formidable establishments of artillery and men, we did attempt to work up, under the walls in Europe, whilst the approaches are run up to the very ditch, the enfilading and dismantling batteries, twelve or twenty perhaps in number, cover the workers in the trenches, by totally ruining the whole place adjacent to the front attacked.

Our brave engineers and artillery men, on the contrary worked in the approaches and batteries, subject to the almost undisturbed fire of the whole place, for the few men and few guns we had, were barely sufficient, taking every man from the battalion guns, to complete the breaching battery of six or eight pieces, and two 12-pounder batteries! With such a force do we expect to take a place well defended? When in Europe forty or fifty heavy guns are required and as many howitzers and mortars to attack a place in form, shall we wonder if we fail with our establishment.

I hesitate not to say that Bhartpoor required far more guns and men to besiege it, than almost any European fortress. The curtains and the bastions though small, were twice as high, planted more closely. The circumference of the place was so vast that to enfilade the curtains of faces (the first grand rule, in besieging) was impossible, for the prolongation lines would have carried the enfilading batteries a mile or two away to the right or left.

The curtains were very short and the bastions which projected very far were united to the place, by long and comparatively low necks and thus the high bastion, formed an impenetrable traverse for two or three guns on the neck, which could only be dismounted by chance mortar-shells and were thus reserved to pour dreadful volleys of grape, at twenty yards distance, into the ditch and the breaches. Which were of necessity made in a curtain, for if they had been effected in the salient bastion, from their construction mentioned above, they could have been with ease cut off from the place, while to make a lodgement in them had been vain, as they are everywhere seen, and commanded from the town walls and towers of the citadel, yet with all these difficulties the artillery and engineers did their duty in the hottest fire and under more disadvantages than ever before perhaps were encountered.

The batteries and approaches were absolute furnaces of fire and when we consider the possible certainty, which by experience the infantry felt, that to go to the breach between the fires of the adjacent bastions, was almost certain death, shall we feel ourselves altogether justified in accusing of cowardice, those poor men who refused to walk deliberately into the fire?

So close were the bastions to one another, that it was next to impossible to see the flanks at all. In the attempt to do so the engineers carried them so close to the walls that the garrison actually pelted them with dirt and stones from above! The gallant artillery men, served during the whole siege of six weeks, without being relieved once! Did these men not do their duty? If we are ever to take Bhartpoor, we must have 800 or 1000 artillery, black or white, and a very large force of Europeans and native infantry to guard our trenches. As we find by woeful experience, that we have a fighting enemy to deal with, with a daily guard of 400 Europeans and 2000 native and the above artillery men, with a corps of 1000 pioneers and a good set of engineer, sergeants, but above all with thirty, 24- or 18-pounders as many heavy mortars, twenty howitzers, besides 12-pounders and with an abundant ammunition.

I would engage to be master of Bhartpoor in days from time of breaking ground. I would imprimis, every now and then, when the garrison annoyed me bombard them, for a few hours. I would keep up a fire of shells and grape from mortars on the ditch and works all night. I would begin by laying in ruins, two of the bastions, until, at least, I would get at the gorges and prevent anyone from living there, or on the bastions. I would then breach the curtain, having previously seen my approaches so close, as to see the bottom of the wall, and covered them by brisk and numerous fires, on all the bastions that could see my saps or batteries, and on the curtain in front. If the ditch was impassable from depth and breadth, I should be able to fill it uninjured and when I had made my breach, my stormers should have nothing to fear, but those of their opponents, who chose to meet them in the breach, with a less formidable artillery we never shall take it!

March 28th—Two new regiments of cavalry, are certainly to be immediately raised, but not a native artillery man. Although hundreds of such brave Golundauze, as we have found to fight so well against us, and with us, could in an instant be procured! Not a single additional horse artillery gun is added to the establishment. Although they had been found so eminently useful, nay necessary, this war! Is this infatuation?

March 29th—This day was distinguished by two great events, one, probably the consequence of the other. Two *vakeels*, from the fort, came during the night into our camp, where they remain and, in consequence of the Rajah and Holkar being no longer one, and the former not being likely to afford protection to the latter, at half-past two, the reserve were silently turned unsuspecting, out of their beds and formed on the cavalry parade. The old Lord accompanied us and off we set to surprise the enemy's camp.

The plan was a good one. Holkar lay behind the hills, in front of which our first Bhartpoor camp was. He was just opposite the pass. The five companies of sepoys under Captain Lawley, were to have marched inside of the hills and silently occupied the pass, but this, the best part of the plan, was not executed, for the guns of the five companies were unable to get on, from the badness of the bullocks. So when we arrived at the avenue, they were sent back with the five companies to camp.

Colonel Don and his column of infantry reached the enemy's camp about ten minutes before day. The noise of his guns, had betrayed him and while he poured in a few volleys among them, they got behind the thick four feet high walls with which the fields are intercepted, so that his balls have very little effect. The instant the colonel, ignorant of this, from the total darkness, rushed on with his bayonets, the enemy ran off.

March 30th—Halted, notwithstanding that the vakeels are actually in camp, the grand question of peace and war, we seem undecided. I should suppose that the principal points in dispute must have been pretty high settled before these people came into camp. It was reported that the Rajah's son is coming tomorrow into camp, as a hostage.

March 31st—It is truly singular, that we should still occupy ourselves, busily as ever, in daily cutting down materials for, and making up, fascines and garrisons of which we have far more than we can ever want ready. It is, they say, to keep up appearances, but the working money to the men employed thus, and which is said daily to exceed 300 rupees, must make these very expensive appearances.

I do not think that we shall besiege Bhartpoor this season, we could not afford the men and officers (to talk in the cool calculating style of political reasoning) that would fall victims to the severity of the season. A more near danger is, I fear, on the side of Sindhia. Yet, here nothing is yet certain, we know not even whether to call him friend or foe, "be his interest wicked or charitable, he comes in such a questionable shape" etc., etc., we know that we deserve to be treated as enemies by this injured prince, for Dholpoor and Gwalior, which by the treaty of peace, were to be restored to him, remain in our hands to this day, above 15 months after the treaty was concluded. It was supposed, that Umbajee or Amboojee and he were to unite against us, yet Sindhia advances hostility against Umbajee, our enemy, who flies from Narwah, to take refuge in a hill fort!

Our acting resident is said to be virtually a prisoner in Sindhia's camp, yet his hurkarrahs and dispatchers, pass and repass! Ameer Khan's battalions and guns, are in Sindhia's service, but whether as allies, or by desertion to him, does not seem to be clearly understood. In short, our confounded crooked politics, had involved us in a labyrinth of confusion, with all India. Every man, seems to have become, by our baneful contact, hostile to all his neighbours and to ourselves.

The peace with Bhartpoor, will probably cause a great alteration in the state of affairs. Sindhia probably, has collected an army, to look on and take advantage of the times to "get something" and his near approach, will I fear induce Runjeet, if insincere, to procrastinate the negotiation, in hopes of a total deliverance from our authority or influence, by Sindhia's Arms.

Chapter 9
April 1805

April 2nd—At 12 last night, we were, without any previous intimation, roused out of our beds and ordered to get ready. We did so, and in a few minutes marched off from our parade, with all the cavalry and the native infantry of the reserve, under Don, nearly in the same direction as on the 28th ultimo, to surprise the enemy again. We were pretty certain that we had a very long way to go, for all the cavalry corps, were ordered to take but one galloper and to carry with them, ready harnessed, the horses of the other gun, left behind, as spare horses would be required.

Our corps, for the same reason, took but four 6-pounders and two tumbrils. The infantry took no guns. Just at daybreak we were within half a mile of the enemy's camp. The column of cavalry (left in front) and that of infantry (right in front) marched in two parallel lines, our guns between, the cavalry formed two lines. We were ordered to join the reserve, and with it to go to left of the high village, round which the enemy lay, while the cavalry went to the right. Afterwards, the cavalry with the old general, were to pursue and we were, under Lieutenant Colonel Don, to walk over their ground, following the cavalry, to pick up stragglers, wounded and guns that might be left behind. For by some strange neglect, no guns but ours, were ordered to join the infantry, as if it were possible for artillery to follow dispersed cavalry over hedge and ditch at a gallop. This order was very good, and had the first line of cavalry been ordered to charge as soon as formed, just at break of day, our success would have been complete.

As it was, we did very well, for we annoyed and harassed our enemy and showed him that seven or eight koss, was no securer for him, than two or three. About ten minutes was lost, waiting for the formation of the 2nd line of cavalry. Day now broke pretty clear and we saw the enemy on all sides hastily mounting, drawing up or running away and all in the greatest confusion. The cavalry and our column advanced on each side of the village right in our front. The enemy never stood to us but fled in every direction.

We now thought of returning homewards to camp, from which we were distant an immense way. The mosque and tomb, at the romantic hill tower of Futtehpoor Sicri, were scarce two miles off. In passing the fort, the leading corps, (8th Dragoons) spied a body of men with matchlocks and standards, in the jungles. The whole column instantly gave chase, the 8th came up with them, killed twenty-five or thirty of them and took their standards. The rest, about seventy or eighty, threw down their arms and (in my opinion very improperly) received quarter, and were brought prisoners into camp. They were, according to their own accounts, Rohilla Infantry, coming from our own provinces, to enlist as *allygoles* in service of an enemy, the Bhartpoor Rajah. About an hour after this, as we were all looking eagerly, while passing at this novel point of view of the fort and city, thinking ourselves out of gunshot, on a sudden, a gun was fired at the column from the fort wall. In a few minutes, another shot, from the same place, and nearly as well aimed, came among us, but fortunately without killing or wounding anyone. They fired at us however, no more.

It was certainly strange, that with an accredited minister in our camp, the Rajah should commit hostilities on us. I conclude however, from their firing but twice, that they only meant to give us a caveat against coming too close. They were, perhaps, alarmed and very naturally so, at the near approach of so large a body.

April 3rd—The villages and country on the side of Bhartpoor, that was new to us, seemed to bear the marks of very recent plunder, they were totally deserted and the houses stripped, un-roofed and gutted. This probably may have been done by Holkar, in consequence of Runjeet's pacific measures with regard to us.

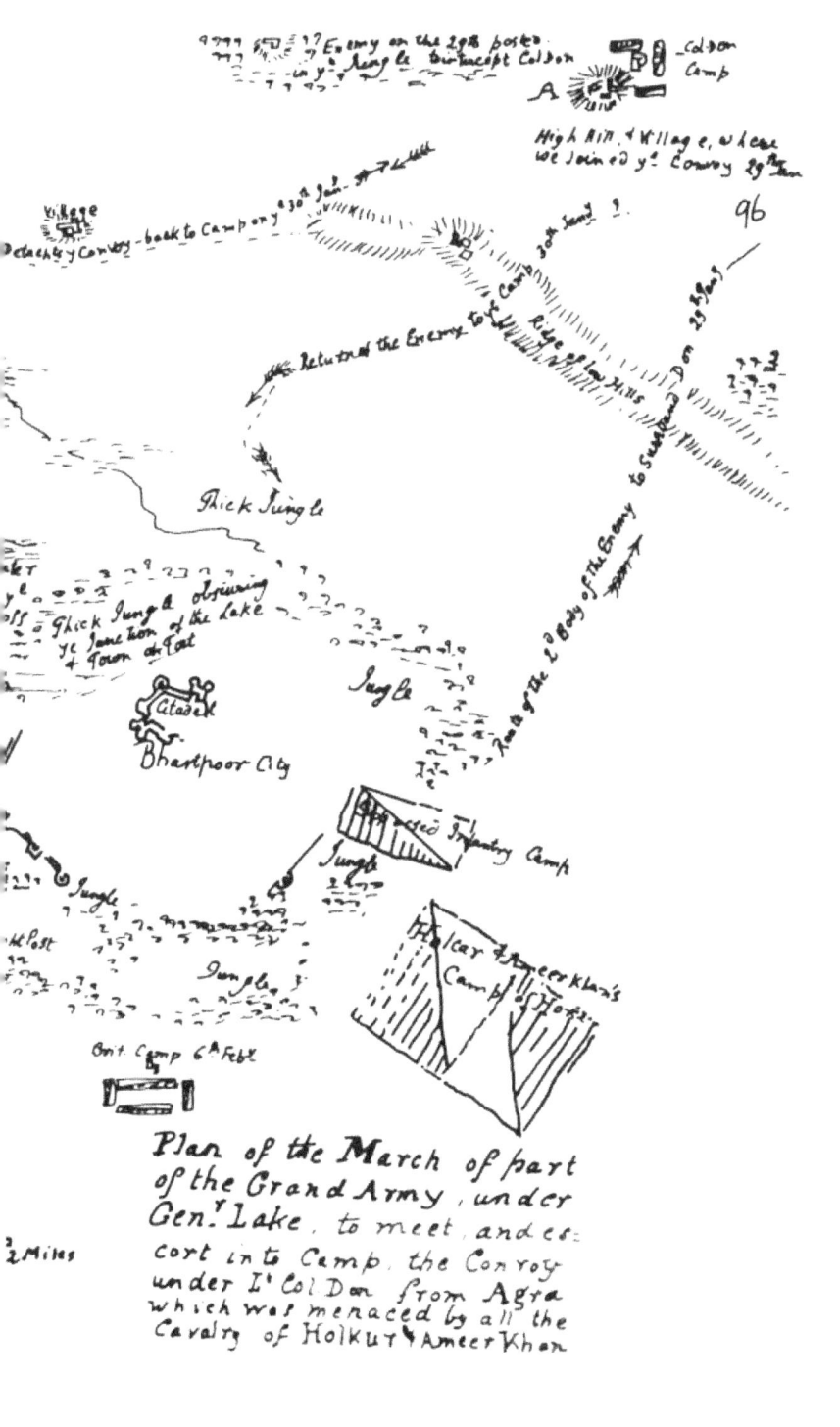

April 7th—Messengers are daily hourly passing to and from the fort. I much fear Runjeet is deceiving us, for all the natives say that Holkar is again close under the walls, if so, peace cannot be in the intentions of the Rajah. The old general himself begins to talk about a fresh siege and says that hot winds are cold, he will take the place. My European readers will think this the greatest proof of spirit and bravery etc., etc., my Indian ones, who knew how totally impossible it is without losing two-thirds of the poor Europeans to be out in trenches and batteries all day in the sun, will more properly call this conduct of our commander's selfish and obstinate. His name, till now coupled ever with conquest, has had it's lustre, if not tarnished, at least a little dimmed by his failure before Bhartpoor. The critical and mal-a-propos moment too, when he was loaded with merited honours, for his successes of last campaign. If we besiege the place, at this inclement time of the year, I say we are fighting not for ourselves, or our country, not even for the wicked ambition of our Governor but for the reputation of General His Excellency the Right Honourable Baron Lake. I will whisper another prophecy "we shall be a fifth time repulsed!"

Of what political importance is Bhartpoor? Formerly, when our enemies disputed with us the palm of superiority and were strong in every kind of force, it was of the last consequence to us, that they should not receive support, nor food, nor money from anyone. But now that these enemies are crushed and their guns taken, it signifies comparatively nothing. Who is their friend? who their foe? On the contrary it is perhaps advantageous to us, that Runjeet Sing should have such drains on him, as Holkar and Ameer Khan, for his superfluous cash, for all he bestows, while it weakens him, strengthens not them, as it must be immediately distributed in small portions among their needy rabble. Let us then leave Bhartpoor. The honour of the British name is concerned and we ought to take this pitiful place. Let us not condescend, since we have been so disgracefully baffled, to treat with one whom we call a rebel, but like the great Cornwallis at Seringapatam, let us retire towards our frontier, recruit sepoys, raise artillery men, collect a powerful train and above all give our dispirited Europeans a little breathing time to forget their defeats and miscarriages, and of the commencement of the ensuing cold season, let us return, irresistible, we should then be.

Two regiments of native cavalry are ordered to be immediately raised at Ghazipoor but not a single artillery man! These regiments are, God knows much wanted. Had they been in order to be raised last rains, when approaching war was too obvious, and our great want of cavalry, even men so, by this time they would have been almost mounted and ready on any great emergency. But it is the fate of our Government, even to do things after it is too late.

April 8th—Letters from Colonel Martindale's army, informed us, that Sindhia had been reconciled to Umbajee(Amboojee) and that they had, with their 20000 or 30000 horse, crossed the Chambal, leaving the infantry and guns, under Monsieur Jean Baptiste De La Fontaine to follow, and that Bhartpoor was their destination. They are said to give out that they come as mediators to negotiate a peace between Runjeet Sing and us. Mediators with arms in their hands are commonly very like dictators and the natives ought to know the British too well to suppose anything of that kind, will ever be permitted. The very act of entertaining Monsieur Baptiste in his service is a breach of Sindhia's treaty with us, as however we have so flagrantly broke that treaty, by keeping Gwalior and Dholpoor, I suppose we are ashamed to tax him with faithlessness. Not to mention that our hands are at present full enough.

Our spirits were raised a good deal, by learning, on the march that Major Royle, who with his own and another recruit battalion and some irregular infantry and horse, had been sent from Agra against Hemaut Dada (Holkar's adopted brother or cheela), had fallen in with that chief and utterly defeated him, taking his guns, baggage etc., etc. and killing vast number of his people. The particulars of the affair, are unknown. Hemaut was collecting the revenues, in the Dholpur and Agra districts for Holkar, Ashraff Beg, Holkar's Commandant of artillery, who with Hemaut, commanded at the siege of Delhi, and battle of Deeg, has come over to us and is now in camp.

April 10th—It is said that Ameer Khan is gone off to join Sindhia and that Holkar's Horse are gone off towards the country of our faithful ally, the Row Rajah, but that Holkar himself is at this moment actually living in Bhartpoor, in a palace belonging to Begum Sumroo! Surely Runjeet Sing is not again tempering with us? I will believe nothing of the peace they talk of so confidently, till I see it in black and white, or at least till I see Runjeet Sing's son in camp!

April 12th—The long wished for event happened this day. The son of the Rajah came into camp yesterday evening. The Honourable Lieutenant Colonel Lake and Mr Mercer, agent for the Governor General met him at our pickets, and conducted him to tents pitched for him near headquarters. In consequence of this desired event, after orders were issued for the heavy guns, under charge of Captain Paschaud and Lieutenant Frith to be sent into Agra immediately, which shows of how much importance this event was.

April 13th—The foraging party were, while on their return to camp, attacked by some thousand horse, who carried off a vast number of camels and elephants, all of which, excepting five elephants and forty camels, were recovered.

The public indignation has been greatly excited at the young Rajah's having brought into camp a guard of soldiers, dressed in the coat, belts and arms of our poor officers and Europeans. This certainly is most insulting and should not be permitted. If any of these guards, in their borrowed pleasure should be encountered by the comrades of the poor fellows whose clothes they were, the consequences might be the cause of a rupture with the Rajah, as the Europeans would most assuredly handle these fellows not a little roughly.

April 14th—Halted. The old general is exceedingly indignant at Captain Steward of the Bombay Native Infantry, who commanded the foraging party of yesterday for the loss of the cattle. A circumstance which embitters His Excellency's displeasure, is the uncertainty of who the robbers were, some say that it was Holkar and his Horse, who were leaving the town of Bhartpoor, in consequence of the peace and who on their march fell in with our forages. But many people, the natives especially, say that the act was committed by a division of Sindhia's Pindaries under his father-in-law Saroje Row, should this prove true, the honour of our name will compel us to consider it as a declaration of war, if a prompt apology and disavowal, accompanied by the restoration of the cattle, is not immediately made by Sindhia.

April 15th—Holkar has certainly gone past Biana, towards the South plundering and burning. It is said he is going to Sindhia and should sooner suspect fire and water of uniting. It is to Holkar's standing aloof from the confederacy of the Mahrattas in July 1803, after having been a principal fomenter of it, that Sindhia has to attribute his misfortunes and present reduced state. Can he coalesce with the author of his ruin?

The question of "What does Sindhia want?" is one that I find great difficulty in answering. What he did want, when our hands were full of Bhartpoor and Holkar and Meer Khan, I can easily tell and the consciences of government, must have instantly made plain to them by the treaty of peace, certain districts cis-and trans Chambal, were to be continued to Sindhia, or his vassals, as having been a long time in Sindhia's family. The districts in question, were Gwalior and Dholpur, Sindhia was by the same article of the treaty, on no pretence even to introduce troops into these districts.

Whether we justify our detention of the forts and towns of Gwalior and Dholpur, on the quibble that the forts could not be included, as no garrisons were to be admitted in the country or whether we justify this act, on the broad basis of "political expediency," I know not, but I can not doubt but that one of Sindhia's designs, to take advantage of our distracted and enfeebled state to bully us into, or forcibly procure, the restoration of his rights. But the peace with Runjeet Sing and the weakened state of Holkar and Ameer Khan's forces have made a wide difference in the politics of Hindoostan, yet Sindhia, with an immense force of horse, foot and artillery, is on the other side of the Chambal, near Dholpur, there he has remained for many days stationary. Colonel Martindals, on this side, and at a very short distance (ten or twelve koss) is watching his motions, it is reported that he wrote to the commander-in-chief, saying that he had come with an immense army to assist him against the Rajah and Holkar. It is added, that at the same time, he wrote the Runjeet Sing a letter, containing a similar offer, and that the Rajah sent his to the general at once.

This is not, I think, by any means improbable. If Sindhia thinks to do anything against the grand, Bombay and Bundelkund armies united, he will find himself miserably mistaken in his calculations. The only evil we have to apprehend, is the inclemency of the season. The hot winds, which have at last set in with great violence and the nearly vertical sun, are terrible disadvantageous to us and would cost us many a European life. Yet that we should conquer, it were folly to doubt, nor is it possible, that Sindhia himself, can offer his experience of last war, doubt it, this is almost proved by his not commencing war instantly and trying to defeat Martindale before we can relieve him. Also by our resident being still in the camp. All my reasonings are drawn from appearances and probabilities and therefore must be taken *cum grano salis*, as the truth, the mysterious truth, is known only to the happy diplomatic few!

April 16th—Halted. A report prevails that Holkar's chiefs in Guzzeraut, have raised 16000 men, with which, in his name, they are overrunning that fine province and collecting its revenues. Jone's is the Guzzeraut army and as during it's absence, that province is, according to our universal rule of practice, almost totally destitute of troops, it is said that the Bombay army will instantly return.

It is given out at headquarters that the plunderers of our foraging party, were certainly not Sindhia's, but Holkar's. A body of Sindhia's however, under Saroje Row, have appeared in the neighbourhood of war and the Rajah, who informed the general of the circumstance, added that he had ordered his *Killahdar* at that place to fire on them. In answer to a demand from His Excellency to Sindhia, what he or his people wanted in these parts, the latter is said to have apologized and said that the Pindaries, without his consent, had gone across the Chambal to plunder and that they were under no command or discipline, and that he could not restrain them.

April 17th—The poor Bombayers are quite, are desespoir, at the idea of such a long march at this dreadful season. The hardships this little corps suffered during the rains last year, has quite sickened them of the Deccan, at this season. The Bengal Company of Artillery are particularly desirous not to be again sent back, they have to a man petitioned His Excellency to this effect, saying they would prefer being shot to returning. The Bengal Golundauze and lascars declare they must desert if compelled to return. The men of the Kings Regiment (65th and 86th) are equally discontented, sergeants have been begging to be allowed to enlist as privates in the region this establishment and the officers are nearly as unwilling as the men. No one can wonder at these sentiments, who has heard the details of the famine, fatigues and sicknesses these poor fellows had to contend with and which has thinned the numbers of the Europeans, by two thirds.

April 18th—Sindhia's Pindaries, are at Kerowly in that neighbourhood, the country of a Rajah near which the grand army passed in March 1804. The Rajah was then friendly to us and as I fear is our ally, I fear, because I have always feared that our lust for alliances and influence with every snivelling Rajah, would bring us into eternal wars on their accounts. I hope it may not do so in the present case but if Sindhia's people plunder this Rajah and he is our ally, I do not see how we can avoid in honour, taking his part.

April 19th—What the terms of peace are with Runjeet Sing, seems to be known to those immediately concerned in making them alone. Various are the reports on this subject, some make the peace truly dishonourably to us. Deeg to be restored after the war, three or four *lacks* of rupees paid down, and six or seven in small annual instalments. Others, with more probability on their side, say that Deeg is not to be given up, nor it's annexed district. That the Rajah is well bound down, as to connections with other powers. That the district worth four or five *lacks*, which we gave him last year, is taken from him and that the total sum he is to pay, at various periods, amounts to forty *lacks*.

The young Rajah has visited the old Lord several times. Yesterday morning Mr Mercer and his deputy, Mr Metcalfe with Captain Wood of the engineers went to visit the Rajah in the fort. They are the first Europeans that have entered it, as yet all persons belonging to our camp, having been prohibited in General Orders from going near the place, to prevent quarrels, no doubt and to keep up an appearance of a power to permit people to go in, which in fact the general knows he does not possess.

April 20th—Halted. Sindhia has certainly united himself to Holkar and Ameer Khan, an act of itself proclaiming war, or which in days of high British *hauteur*, would have been considered as hostility and executed accordingly by immediately marching against the author of such an insult. Those proud days, however, seem to be "gone by" and our conduct at present is far more temperate. We are negotiating, sending in ultimate projects etc., etc. and in short carrying on all those tricks of diplomacy, which are in reality, only modifications of mutual fear. *Tempora mutantur nos et mutamur in mis.* Our late misfortunes, joined to the heat of the weather have cowed us nor is to be much wondered at.

April 21st—Marched. Colonel Simpson encamped within two or three miles of us and close to Futtypoor, which *en passant*, he permitted his sepoys and fellows, to plunder and burn, in just retaliation for the treachery and cruelty of it's inhabitants, to the scattered fugitive Europeans, officers, and sepoys of Colonel Monson's detachment. The 2nd of the 9th and 1st of the 14th, now with Simpson, were a part of Monson's army and from the universal indignation that prevails against the Futtehpoorians among all ranks. The sepoys would doubtless have sacrificed them all to the manes their comrades and the English officers but that suspicious and conscious of guilt, they fled on the approach of Simpson's party, and when the men entered this immense place, only a few old cripples and women remained.

April 22nd—Marched South to Kahana. The villages and neighbourhood are altogether remarkable. It is composed entirely of red stone, without cement, and by the ruins of tombs surrounding it, seems to have been once a considerable place. It is built on one of many small hills, or rather rocky, bare ridges, of diminutive size, among which our camp was pitched. These ridges are the beginning of that chain of hills which traverse the country to the S., E., and W. of Kahana and their appearance, from their absolute nakedness and sterility and from the strata of rock upon rock, all at the same angle (60°) with the earth, is uncommon.

What our intentions are, in moving forward thus towards Sindhia, no one can doubt, we are going to try if he cannot be bullied into a retreat. I hope and think, he will, for if he meant to fight, why not first attack Colonel Martindale's comparatively small array? That officer, by the junction of Major Royle's detachment, has of Regular, and Irregular fighting men, 12000, and letters from his camp laugh at the idea of an attack from Sindhia, and express every wish that they might be allowed to be attackers. Pleasing as this spirit is, yet it were certainly best to avoid fighting at this dreadful season, if it can be done with honour. The mere battle itself, is nothing, but what dread are the horrible fatigue which we, specially the cavalry and horse artillery, will have to undergo, previous to, and after the engagement. I mean that partisan work, that turning out of pickets, foraging, rescuing, pursuing, which if we found so distressing in the cool season, must now be absolutely deadly.

April 23rd—Marched to Rubass, a considerable village of red stone with an adjacent mud fort of six bastions, intolerable repair. On the west side of the village are the ruins of a once magnificent, though small hunting palace of the great Akbar. It is of red stone, the architecture is like that of all Moosulmaun palaces even to this day. A fine tank, now half choked up, is one of the appendages of this seat.

The Bhartpoor Rajah's son, who continues with us, took up his quarter here, we are still in the Bhartpoor country. This day and yesterday, our soldiers or followers, committed most scandalous disgraceful outrages, burning and plundering every village we came to, conduct which the Right Honourable the Commander-in-Chief animadverted on with great and just severity in General Orders of today. His Excellency directed that the safeguards, posted at every village we approach, shall instantly shoot any plunderer, European or native, and that anyone taken in the face, shall instantly be hanged.

This country is astonishingly full of game of every sort, hogs, deer, hares, partridges were killed in numbers on the line of march.

A letter from Colonel Wallace's army, dated 18th March, mentions that Colonel Close had passed through their camp on his way to take charge of the residency with Sindhia, vacant by Webbe's death. Where can he be? Is he afraid of going? A station of the utmost political importance as that was, during the Mahratta wars, and the period following an insecure peace, should never have been left so long in the hands of so young a hand in Indian intrigues, as the present *charge des affaires* is. Had Mr Webbe lived, Sindhia had now been our friend.

April 25th—Sindhia has not we understand, moved from his position, as was expected. He seems determined to stand, and yet shows no symptoms of hostility to Martindale, or to our resident, who is still with him. So much the contrary indeed, that a party of his horse, escorted supplies of all kinds of Mr Jenkin, from Martindale's camp. Yet, on the other hand, Holkar and Ameer Khan have joined Sindhia, or at last encamped pretty close to him, visits of compliment, etc., etc., have been exchanged. Is not fostering and cherishing our mortal enemies, tantamount to declaring war? This, even in Sindhia, who is not as many affirm, an ally of ours. By the Argaum treaty of peace, Sindhia was, if he chose to be admitted to the benefit of the alliance between the Paishwah, Nizam, and us. In the event of his acceding to which, he was to be furnished in two months with six battalions, and artillery in proportion, without any further subsidy, than the revenues of the districts ceded to us in the treaty. Now he never has had these six battalions or even one company of troops from us either, therefore, he never acceded to the alliance, or, if he did, we have neglected to perform our part of it, (the furnishing of six battalions) and consequently the fault lies with us.

DHOLPOOR FORT

A RED STONE BRIDGE

April 26th—Letters from Colonel Martindale's army are filled with strange contradictions. They do not seem even to dream of war with Sindhia. Amboojee, the execrable, crafty, treacherous, disturber of Hindoostan has certainly been seized on, and imprisoned, but whether by Sindhia or Holkar, is unknown, some accounts say the one, some the other. If by Holkar, I think it must have been by Sindhia! Permission or connivance, whoever of them has got hold of the prize, will find it a valuable one, the monster in question, has fattened by setting people by the ear, for twenty or thirty years, and is rich by the misfortunes of his neighbours, beyond belief. Greatest part of his treasures, will now fall into the hands of those needy Mahrattas. One hope we have, that the three captors, will fall out about the distribution of the valuable prize. However, Sindhia might, from policy, affect to take Holkar by the hand, at this juncture. Yet it is not to be supposed that he will even permit him to aggrandize himself at his expense. There former enmity may be shifted for a moment, but cannot be eradicated from the bosoms.

April 27th—The town of Dholpoor, lay in our front, even now of considerable extent but from the vast numbers of tombs, almost totally ruined, which are spread over the palin, interspersed with mosques, and walled gardens that were. Dholpoor must once have been a very large place. Our camp lay under a range of considerable hills, with fable summits, that stretch away to the S.W. The smallest, surmounted by a stone enclosure and faquir's house, garnished with a few trees, had a romantic appearance. From the tops of these hills the view was immense. In very clear weather, Colonel Martindale's camp was visible about eight or nine miles off and the town and Fort of Dholpoor, bordering on the prodigiously deep and extensive ravines, among which the Chambal meandered gave diversity to the tiresome, uniform flat country around.

April 28th—In the evening, I took a ride to the fort, a pitiful place, built of stone and so thin are the walls, that cannons could not be mounted, on any part of them. But from it's situation, it is indeed wonderfully strong. The gateway, or rather entrance of three gates, is constructed much as usual in Hindoostanee forts, so as to prevent an assault, by obliging the assailants to pass by winding road, under a destructive fire. But the singularly strong natural situation of this fort, is without probably, a parallel. It is built on the top of ravines, not higher than the level of the country, but of a depth and extent, and variety of figure, truly wonderful. The ravines close under the fort walls, are perhaps 150 feet deep, craggy, rugged, precipitous, impassable and the only approach of the fort, is by an artificial stone causeway. It is wonderful that during last campaign, the Mahratta garrison should have evacuated this place, even after we had once been before it, and had been unable to do anything. Our great name, occasioned by the capture of Allyghur, did that for us which our own efforts would never, I fear, have achieved.

April 29th—We were in terrible apprehensions that we were going to have a third pursuit, as the news of the day was, that Holkar and Ameer Khan had moved off towards Bundelkund, with the professed intention of ravaging Mirzapoor, Benares and all the Company's rich and peaceful open country thereabouts. The very thoughts of such a thing, a chance in this weather, was enough to make anyone go distracted, for we dread not the Mahrattas, but the sun. Jean Baptiste and the infantry and 120 guns, joined Sindhia this day, at Summulgur, forty miles from Martindale. Of these guns, thirty are said to be gallopers! I believe we shall in time teach these fellows to beat us!

The Chambal is a beautiful clear stream, running on a bed of fine gravel and winding through a set of horrible barren ravines, one of them, in front of our camp, topped by a gurry of mud and all of them inhabited by desperate tribe of robbers who like the Goojars, always assassinate. The closeness of the stream tempted almost every officer and men in camp to bathe, two European Dragoons of the 26th and 25th Regiments were unfortunately lost as the stream was deep in every few places, they were supposed to have been destroyed by alligators one of which was seen in the river.

On this subject, I forgot to mention that a day or two ago, one of the 75th Europeans shot himself, saying that there was no end of broiling and fighting in India, that he should never again see his home, and that it was better to die at once, than by inches!

Chapter 10
May 1805

May 4th—Halted. Sindhia is certainly gone off post-haste to Kotta, and with him Holkar, Ameer Khan, and the prisoner Amboojee. It is said that Amboojee is to get from Kotta, sixty *lacks* of rupees, which Sindhia, Holkar and Ameer Khan are to divide. Amboojee, at the breaking out of last war, seeing how matters were going against the Mahrattas, made separate terms for himself with us, of which Gwalior and Gohud were the price. Previous to this, and with a view of being prepared for the wars, he sent a great deal of his treasure to the Kotta Rajah, who was out of the way of the theatre of war, to keep for him. This is common enough among the native powers but it is as usual for the keeper of the money, to keep it to himself, as to restore it when demanded. This however, the Kotta Rajah will be deterred from doing, by the great force of Sindhia. Baptiste and the 150 guns would be too strong for so weak a place as Kotta.

We can only hope that the three spoilers may quarrel about the prey among themselves. Report says, after the division they are to separate, their purposes are unknown, but I heard from good authority, that a letter had been intercepted from a Sardar of Sindhia's saying that their plan was to temporize till the rains, and then to attack at once Delhi and the lower Dooab. This may prevent our cantoning, but if we station strong parties at Delhi, Hardwar, Pulwul, Muttra, Deeg, Agra, Etawah, Kalpee and Mirzapoor, what have we to fear during the rains? The rivers are, at that season, a sufficient protection against invasion. Besides, except in the case of a very strong temptation to plunder with certainty of victory, as last year was the case, when Holkar pursued Monson, I do not believe that the Mahratta Horse or Foot, will willingly undergo without tents, or protection from wet or sun, the fatigues of a second campaign in the rains.

May 5th—Halted. A letter from an artillery man at Rampoorah mentions that some infantry and sixteen guns of Holkar's are thereabouts retaking all the little forts that Captain Hutchinson took, intending to lay siege to the crazy walls of Rampoorah itself. The letter added that could they easily sally out and take these guns, but that the 2nd of the 8th Native Infantry were disaffected and almost mutinous could not be depended on nor is it any wonder that unfortunate garrison has been nearly a year shut up in that fort, almost starved and twelve months in arrears:- without hopes of relief or pay!

Mr Jenkins, the acting resident, is said still to be with Sindhia, perhaps *nolens-volens*, Lieutenant Colonel Malcolm, just arrived at Calcutta, it is said coming up by dawk instantly, to take charge of the residency. I wish it may be so as in the tottering state of Sindhia's affections towards us, we much want an able minister at his court but whether, he will accept, or our Government condescend to lend a resident after Sindhia's connecting himself with our enemy, and having menaced us as he did, is to me very doubtful.

May 11th—Halted. Pinching poverty makes rapid strides among the officers of this army, on the 15th inst. six months will be due to the officers. The men, having at different periods had small sums advanced to them, are not quite so ill off. To our great relief we hear that a battalion from Lieutenant Colonel Richardson's detachment at Buldee is soon to bring out from Agra four or five *lacks* of rupees, which will give us a month's pay.

May 13th—The anxiety felt by every one in this camp is truly incredible to anyone who has not been grilling in a campaign in India for eight or nine months. Every flying report, about the destination of the army is ducked in with thirsty avidity, however questionable it's shape, and it is really no small amusement, to write down the reports of the day and after some time, when this event in question has happened or is decided to look back on the weakness and folly of many things which were seriously believed for their day and were attempted to be reasoned on, and demonstrated with sapient plausibility.

This said today, that the reason we do not move, is that the political importance of such a measure as cantoning the Europeans at this juncture is too great for the commander-in-chief to do it without the sanction of the government. On the 30th (the epoch of Sindhia's flight and our crossing) the general is said to have written to the Governor General informing him of this event and recommending the Europeans to go into cantonments.

It is said Holkar is gone towards Joudpoor and Ajmeer, where his family and remaining possessions are. That Ameer Khan has taken leave of Sindhia, previous to setting out for Khoosalghur, where he means to erect a principality, in which he may probably meet with a little opposition from a certain General Jones. Sindhia himself has written, apologizing to the commander-in-chief, for not sooner answering his letter, but the political contents of this important epistle are of course unknown.

If Holkar is gone to Joudpoor, which is S.W. of Delhi, we shall probably reinforce both that garrison and Burn's Seik army. Holkar and Ameer Khan have, it seems, still left some of that remaining artillery, which the public despatches mention to have been so often taken, but both these gentlemen are certainly broken powers from whom we have nought to dread.

May 17th—Halted. This morning the 2nd Battalion 25th Regiment, with a valuable convoy of cash (six lacks) marched into camp and in the General Order of the day, to our inexpressible joy, two months pay was ordered to be issued.

May 21st—Halted. The quartermasters of the different corps of native cavalry and infantry, were this day ordered to repair to Muttra and Agra. There to erect, as expeditiously as possible, temporary stables and barracks for the respective corps. This at last, does look like breaking up and as no European quartermasters go, it is supposed the European troops will retire to cantonments.

It is confidently reported that these temporary cantonments

are ordered to be ready for the reception of troops by the 20th June and that we who go to Cawnpore are to leave this to go backwards as soon as the intended resident with Sindhia, Lieutenant Colonel Malcolm, arrives in camp and as soon as General Jones shall have arrived at Toonk or Rampoorah where he is to spend the rains. The long looked for, much desired return to cantonments is probably not very far off.

May 22nd—The whole of the Gohud territory, on the frontiers of which we are now encamped, is studded with forts of all sizes. For numbers of years this fruitful country has been in anarchy and confusion from the eternal change of masters, in consequence of which every petty *zemindar* has erected a fort, at first, probably from the necessity of having some place wherein to deposit the grain and property of the *ryots* from the depredations of perpetual enemies. In process of time however these forts have been found of use in enabling the refractory owner, to withhold his lawful tribute, from a nominal prince, too weak to compel him to obedience.

Now, every pitiful hamlet, every collection of three or four mud hovels, has it's gurry of dimensions and strength, suited to the number of inhabitants. The smallest and weakest of these, are likely to give much trouble to besieges, as their height is very great and their ditch deep and wide. Many of them have no access but by ladders and in most the gate is but large enough to admit a man and situated at the bottom of the ditch, inaccessible to a gun. Every one of those *ghurries* may stand a siege. The Rajah has never been able to collect a rupee without it.

This climate during the rains, is almost pestilential and cost us many men and officers last year. Upon this dangerous and blackguard services, and at this dreadful season, this unfortunate detachment is now going. No motives of glory or honour to stimulate them, and with the certainty that if they are killed, as many of them must inevitably be, their relatives will not even have the satisfaction of knowing that they were killed in the discharge of their duty. It being an invariable, as it is an atrocious and unprincipled maxim, of Lord Wellesley's, never to suffer any officer's name to be put in the newspaper as "killed," unless His

Excellency chooses to avow the cause in which they fell. During the destructive war in the Northern Circars and that in the Dooab, in 1802-3, when so many officers fell, they were all put down in the newspapers as "dead in the upper provinces" "died to the Southward etc. etc." Is not this an encouraging Government to serve under?

May 30th—Our fate is at last decided. We are all to remain on this side of Jumnah! Although, after two such severe and long campaigns and after having now been almost nine months under canvas, we all, as is most natural, are most desirous again to see our homes. Yet the thinking part of the army, cannot but agree to the propriety of this measure which may, eventually, accelerate the desired event of going into quarters, and that too, for years of peace, instead of two or three precarious, and joyless months of tumult and alarm.

Sindhia is playing a singular game, he seems cautiously to avoid any act of positive hostility to us, for as uncivilized nations have not the refined notions of politics, and the law of nations, his civilities (for they are nothing more) to Holkar cannot be called an open act of hostility. Our minister is still in his camp. He seems at present to be altogether engrossed in squeezing money out of Amboojee. Yet if we left the *Cis*-Jumna country, as we did last year, destitute of troops, by sending the corps into rain cantonments in the Dooab, I have little doubt, but that Sindhia now wavering, perhaps would be tempted to join with Holkar and Ameer Khan, in a grand attack on General Jones and on this part of the country, in hopes of destroying Jone's army, and doing great damage to us, before they could be stopped, before we were able to get ready our army to oppose them. If this had not been their hope, and intention, why did they decline the offer made, of giving them battle with half our army, when we crossed the Chambal, just a month ago. If they had conceived their force, a match for ours at any time. then was the moment. when four European regiments and ten native corps, were behind at Dholpoor, when the weather at so dreadful season, though innoxious to them was deadly to us. Lastly when we were covered with recent humiliation and shame, our names, clipped of its ancient charm! They however declined it, they now find our whole force, European and native ready to repel aggression, as soon as the rainy weather is over. They well know we are doubly strong, from the ensuing mildness of the season, will they fight us in the cold weather, who dared not in the hot? More, the battles of Delhi and Assaye, and indeed the beginning of that memorable campaign may show them how we can fight, if obliged, even in the rains.

What are they to do? Sindhia will be tired of his new friends, tired of having no prospect of success. His army will be tired of serving without pay, and more money will not be procurable. He will look in dreadful anticipation, to the cold season's approach, which will bring with it, Colonel Wallace from the South and General Lake from the North, leaving him only the dreadful alternative of choosing by whom he will be destroyed. He will be glad to make peace and will think himself but too happy, if in his present intoxication, he shall not have committed any act of violence to us, that shall preclude him from our forgiveness!

Chapter 11
June 1805

June 1st—Marched to Sooroo. Here the commander-in-chief, with part of the army, encamped. The other part, among which we were, marched about two miles farther.

About a mile to the southward of the commander-in-chief's encampment, we passed the dry bed of the nullah. Alongside of which, and not across, for a course of ages have altered the channel, stands a large fine bridge of red stones, consisting of many pointed arches, intolerable preservation. In the centre, are four octagonal pavilions with domes and at the four wall-ends, as many of those kind of pillars, of irregular shape used by the Mogul Emperors to mark the *kosses*.

The appearance of this bridge was venerable and fine. Although it was as to sculpture, and other decorations, commonly so profusely lavished by Indian architects, deficient entirely. The stucco however, which once probably covered the stone is quite gone, and it is therefore impossible to be certain of this. At the northern extremity of the bridge, stands a fine serai, seemingly more modern than the bridge, and of very considerable extent, containing a gaudy large mosque, with white and red striped dome, and gilt top ornaments.

The *serai*, now contains a miserable enough village, which has been built then for the sake of protecting walls, but the north and south gateways, which are perfectly entire, and new-like (of red stone) are curiously carved and adorned with cupolas and pavilions in abundance. It must once have ascertained, like the bridge, to some considerable sized city or town, of which many vestiges yet remain, in tombs and houses, now quite dilapidated. Indeed the whole of this road (the Dholpoor one) ought to abound in large and magnificent ruins of cities, serais, etc., for this the great East road from Hindoostan to the Deccan, so much frequented by travellers of all ranks, in the more early and splendid days of the Mogul Empire, and mentioned, as Dholpoor is, by the account of judicious tavernier, above a century ago.

June 2nd—Lieutenant Colonel Malcolm proceeds with His Excellency the General in Chief to Muttra, to be ready when wanted, in his diplomatic capacity. He certainly could not, after Sindhia's equivocal conduct, go to his court, without some kind of invitation, for fear of compromising the honour of the British name. Letters from Mr Jenkins, the acting resident in Sindhia's camp have, it is said, been received with the account of a fracas, between Sindhia and Holkar. The cause, was one that we expected would cause a disagreement between them, sooner or later, the division of Amboojee spoils. Amboojee was carried off, on our crossing the Chambal, to Kotta, where he kept his cash by Sindhia and Holkar. Bappoo Sindhia, of celebrated duplicity, was his guarantee for payment and had the care of his person receiving the rupees, however, Bapoojee paid it all, or chiefly, into Sindhia's treasury, to the great wrath of Holkar.

A consequent coolness has taken place, some say that in mutual fear and wrath the chiefs parted, Sindhia going to Ougein, and Holkar to Ajmeer. They add that Holkar carried Bapoojee and Amboojee off with him, and actually burnt old Amboojee's hands in the fire, to extort more money but without success. It is impossible to pity this wretched vulture, for he has fattened and lived a long life of inequity, by setting all the powers round him by the ears and then falling on them when weakened. Whatever truth there may be in these quarrels, the report of them is worthy of belief, for it is good probable in the highest degree, whatever the degree of the animosity it is for us, cold allies are almost as bad as avowed enemies and all these circumstances render it more and more probable that we shall soon have peace.

June 3rd—The little Lord, who had so long embroiled India, is going at last to England, he gives out that it is in disgust, but it is, I am told, *nolens-volens*, and high time it is, it should be so. Everything has been disregarded by him, the interests of his immediate employers, of the British nation, every tie of honour, religion, of nature, to serve one single object, with this man, his ambition, his personal ambition. He has, forsooth, wished that succeeding ages, should point to the map and say, this tract and this were added to the British Empire during the administration of Lord Wellesley! And he cannot, that those who are no politicians shall object, "But this cost his employers so many millions of debt!" "This, some thousands of British lives," "That was gained, at the expense of the national plighted faith, by the blackest ingratitude, and infraction of existing treaties," "that by every insidious art of treachery and corruption!" "To gain this, we set father against son, brother against brother." His Lordship leaves such considerations to be bugbear to the honest minds of simple men! He has had his conduct approved by the parliament of his country! True, some may insinuate that the minister of the day was his Lordship's personal friend and head of his political party and that venal majorities do exist!

The fault of this, however lays not with his Lordship and he is now going home, with an imperial fortune to set control at defiance, entrenched as he will be, behind the splendour of rank. The power of a predominant political party and the impenetrable bulwark of gold! He will set an edifying example, no doubt, to the lower ranks of people in England of fearing God and honouring the King. His attendance at Church, will perhaps be as regular as that at Court for his Lordship is a great enemy of freedom of thought, as well as of deed and is vastly religious. He could not bear the wickedness of horse racing or play-acting at Calcutta! Yet the delicate stomach of his Lordship, could digest and was indeed, at the very instant engaged in deeds which though no sins in his Lordship's political opinion, were enough to make unsophisticated humanity shudder! Oh how my whole soul revolts at such consummate, each execrable, monstrous hypocrisy!

The general estimation in which his Lordship is held in India must not be appreciated from the miserable and fulsome addresses that will be presented to this man on his leaving Calcutta. Whenever the free British inhabitants of Calcutta, are allowed to assemble together for this purpose, the addresses on the profound peace during last campaign, ought to have surfeited even the digestive powers of Lord Wellesley and at all events have taught the world to know the value of such addresses. But the joy that sparkles in the eyes of every plain, independent man when he hears or communicates the glad tidings of this man's intended departure cannot be mistaken! It comes direct from the heart and is met with on the countenance of almost the whole army, whose situation, makes them more immediately out of influence in this country, then the only other description of men, the civilians who depend on government for almost existence and can be deprived of their situations at pleasure. His ungrateful and systematic attempts, to depress the army, to whom (unwilling instruments in his political schemes) he owes the salvation of the country. His steady and un-awaiting exertions directly and indirectly, to curtail the miserable pittance for the sake of which a man sacrifices the twenty-five best years of his life, can never be remembered without curses. It is possible, it is probable, that his successor may be as bad, but in change of men we naturally look forward with hopes to change of measure.

This blessed event will probable hasten the desired period of the destructive war and give us, to recruit (as we much want) our men and resources, some years of peace. I judge not, I depend not on his Lordship's pity for the state of the country, for the bankrupt state of his too confiding employers. I rely, and with reason, on his fears. He has carried deceit and duplicity, rather too far and he would fear to trust himself at home, were he to abandon the state vessel, after he has brought her into such terrible shoals and breakers. If a peace can be made, I think therefore that he will make one before he goes, by way of a set off against all his sins, may it be so!

June 4th—Marched to Secundra, where we encamped in part of Akbar's tomb. In England, people would stare at the idea of a mausoleum large enough to contain so many people, but no one who has not seen a large tomb in India, can conceive the building at all. It is surrounded by a large garden in general, sometimes bounded by a vaulted rampant like a *serai*, sometimes by a plain wall. There are frequently four large gateways (containing many apartments, above and round the mere gateway), one on each face of the square enclosure.

The building itself, in the centre, is generally octagonal, on a square platform of vaults, very large and about twenty feet high. The centre room, containing the sarcophagus, is founded at the top, but by the dome round it however, by as much as the octagonal, exceeds in diameter, the spherical part of the plan, are small rooms, in which are usually deposited the bodies of relatives or children of the builder, or person to whom the mausoleum was erected. The chaste Taj is built in this simple style, as to plan, the more vicious and gaudy tomb of Akbar in many particulars does not agree with this description, especially in the superstructure on the platform, which is almost shapeless, from the multitudes of coloured pavilions, of windows, doors, etc. etc.

On the day following this, I obtained leave as the campaign was closed and the rains setting in, to go off for one month to see my brother who had arrived at Futtyghur. I started by myself on the 6th from Akbar's tomb and on the 7th commenced my journey on horseback to Futtyghur, which I reached on the 13th. I remained at Futtyghur till the beginning of July, when my brother's regiment being ordered to Muttra to replace the 12th, I returned to Agra, and found that my corps had sometime previous to my return, moved from Secundra, down to the delightful gardens of the Taj.

Soon after my return (on the 21st July), I was ordered down to Calcutta, for which place I set out from Agra, on the 23rd August. I have therefore here, closed my journal of the campaign. I have, in reading over this journal, scrupulously avoided any erasures, or alternations in the text, from a superstitious kind of feeling which tells me that my dear parents will have more real pleasure in reading my thoughts however inaccurate, or loosely expressed, than they would in hearing a regular digested history.

The thoughts and expressions contained in this journal, are

an exact picture of the writer's mind and of his heart. I have presumed to criticise the opinions or acts of others without sample. It was because at the time, I really thought them deserving of censor, but I am happy to say, that at this distance of time, regarding my own journal with impartiality as it were, it were the work of another. I cannot find anything in it that has the appearance of rancour or malignity and I am surprised to observe, how generally my opinion, as were recorded have been borne up by after facts. I fear sometimes, lest my parents should throw aside my work as being uninteresting, from the oldness of its date. Yet I feel that they will not, both because it is, as above said, a faithful transcript of myself and because I find, when I myself read it over, an interest, stronger than I can express, and which (owing to a thousand rural and pleasing associations which the sight of every letter, and page excites) makes it an effort, a filial effort, to part with it.

I have erased a few names and particular words which might in these days of intercepted correspondence, create me not a little trouble. As it is, I can not hope to escape appearing in print if my journal is taken but I have concealed my name, and such points as might more easily show who was the author.

ALSO FROM LEONAUR
AVAILABLE IN SOFTCOVER OR HARDCOVER WITH DUST JACKET

A JOURNAL OF THE SECOND SIKH WAR by *Daniel A. Sandford*—The Experiences of an Ensign of the 2nd Bengal European Regiment During the Campaign in the Punjab, India, 1848-49.

LAKE'S CAMPAIGNS IN INDIA by *Hugh Pearse*—The Second Anglo Maratha War, 1803-1807. Often neglected by historians and students alike, Lake's Indian campaign was fought against a resourceful and ruthless enemy-almost always superior in numbers to his own forces.

BRITAIN IN AFGHANISTAN 1: THE FIRST AFGHAN WAR 1839-42 by *Archibald Forbes*—Following over a century of the gradual assumption of sovereignty of the Indian Sub-Continent, the British Empire, in the form of the Honourable East India Company, supported by troops of the new Queen Victoria's army, found itself inevitably at the natural boundaries that surround Afghanistan. There it set in motion a series of disastrous events-the first of which was to march into the country at all.

BRITAIN IN AFGHANISTAN 2: THE SECOND AFGHAN WAR 1878-80 by *Archibald Forbes*—This the history of the Second Afghan War-another episode of British military history typified by savagery, massacre, siege and battles.

UP AMONG THE PANDIES by *Vivian Dering Majendie*—An outstanding account of the campaign for the fall of Lucknow. *This is a vital book of war as fought by the British Army of the mid-nineteenth century, but in truth it is also an essential book of war that will enthral military historians and general readers alike.*

BLOW THE BUGLE, DRAW THE SWORD by *W. H. G. Kingston*—The Wars, Campaigns, Regiments and Soldiers of the British & Indian Armies During the Victorian Era, 1839-1898.

INDIAN MUTINY 150th ANNIVERSARY: A LEONAUR ORIGINAL

MUTINY: 1857 by *James Humphries*—It is now 150 years since the 'Indian Mutiny' burst like an engulfing flame on the British soldiers, their families and the civilians of the Empire in North East India. The Bengal Native army arose in violent rebellion, and the once peaceful countryside became a battleground as Native sepoys and elements of the Indian population massacred their British masters and defeated them in open battle. As the tide turned, a vengeful army of British and loyal Indian troops repressed the insurgency with a savagery that knew no mercy. It was a time of fear and slaughter. James Humphries has drawn together the voices of those dreadful days for this commemorative book.

AVAILABLE ONLINE AT
www.leonaur.com
AND OTHER GOOD BOOK STORES

ALSO FROM LEONAUR
AVAILABLE IN SOFTCOVER OR HARDCOVER WITH DUST JACKET

WAR BEYOND THE DRAGON PAGODA by *J. J. Snodgrass*—A Personal Narrative of the First Anglo-Burmese War 1824 - 1826.

ALL FOR A SHILLING A DAY by *Donald F. Featherstone*—The story of H.M. 16th, the Queen's Lancers During the first Sikh War 1845-1846.

AT THEM WITH THE BAYONET by *Donald F. Featherstone*—The first Anglo-Sikh War 1845-1846.

A LEONAUR ORIGINAL

THE HERO OF ALIWAL by *James Humphries*—The days when young Harry Smith wore the green jacket of the 95th-Wellington's famous riflemen-campaigning in Spain against Napoleon's French with his beautiful young bride Juana have long gone. Now, Sir Harry Smith is in his fifties approaching the end of a long career. His position in the Cape colony ends with an appointment as Deputy Adjutant-General to the army in India. There he joins the staff of Sir Hugh Gough to experience an Indian battlefield in the Gwalior War of 1843 as the power of the Marathas is finally crushed. Smith has little time for his superior's 'bull at a gate' style of battlefield tactics, but independent command is denied him. Little does he realise that the greatest opportunity of his military life is close at hand.

THE GURKHA WAR by *H. T. Prinsep*—The Anglo-Nepalese Conflict in North East India 1814-1816.

SOUND ADVANCE! by *Joseph Anderson*—Experiences of an officer of HM 50th regiment in Australia, Burma & the Gwalior war.

THE CAMPAIGN OF THE INDUS by *Thomas Holdsworth*—Experiences of a British Officer of the 2nd (Queen's Royal) Regiment in the Campaign to Place Shah Shuja on the Throne of Afghanistan 1838 - 1840.

WITH THE MADRAS EUROPEAN REGIMENT IN BURMA by *John Butler*—The Experiences of an Officer of the Honourable East India Company's Army During the First Anglo-Burmese War 1824 - 1826.

BESIEGED IN LUCKNOW by *Martin Richard Gubbins*—The Experiences of the Defender of 'Gubbins Post' before & during the sige of the residency at Lucknow, Indian Mutiny, 1857.

THE STORY OF THE GUIDES by *G.J. Younghusband*—The Exploits of the famous Indian Army Regiment from the northwest frontier 1847 - 1900.

AVAILABLE ONLINE AT
www.leonaur.com
AND OTHER GOOD BOOK STORES

ALSO FROM LEONAUR
AVAILABLE IN SOFTCOVER OR HARDCOVER WITH DUST JACKET

SEPOYS, SIEGE & STORM by *Charles John Griffiths*—The Experiences of a young officer of H.M.'s 61st Regiment at Ferozepore, Delhi ridge and at the fall of Delhi during the Indian mutiny 1857.

THE RECOLLECTIONS OF SKINNER OF SKINNER'S HORSE by *James Skinner*—James Skinner and his 'Yellow Boys' Irregular cavalry in the wars of India between the British, Mahratta, Rajput, Mogul, Sikh & Pindarree Forces.

A CAVALRY OFFICER DURING THE SEPOY REVOLT by *A. R. D. Mackenzie*—Experiences with the 3rd Bengal Light Cavalry, the Guides and Sikh Irregular Cavalry from the outbreak to Delhi and Lucknow.

A NORFOLK SOLDIER IN THE FIRST SIKH WAR by *J. W. Baldwin*—Experiences of a private of H.M. 9th Regiment of Foot in the battles for the Punjab, India 1845-6.

TOMMY ATKINS' WAR STORIES Fourteen first hand accounts from the ranks of the British Army during Queen Victoria's Empire Original & True Battle Stories Recollections of the Indian Mutiny With the 49th in the Crimea With the Guards in Egypt The Charge of the Six Hundred With Wolseley in Ashanti Alma, Inkermann and Magdala With the Gunners at Tel-el-Kebir Russian Guns and Indian Rebels Rough Work in the Crimea In the Maori Rising Facing the Zulus From Sebastopol to Lucknow Sent to Save Gordon On the March to Chitral Tommy by Rudyard Kipling.

THE KHAKEE RESSALAH by *Robert Henry Wallace Dunlop*—Service & adventure with the Meerut volunteer horse during the Indian mutiny 1857-1858.

AVAILABLE ONLINE AT
www.leonaur.com
AND OTHER GOOD BOOK STORES

www.ingramcontent.com/pod-product-compliance
Lightning Source LLC
Chambersburg PA
CBHW031624160426
43196CB00006B/263